RUBY BY EXAMPLE

RUBY BY EXAMPLE

Concepts and Code

by Kevin C. Baird

NO STARCH
PRESS

San Francisco

Printed on recycled paper in the United States of America

11 10 09 08 07   1 2 3 4 5 6 7 8 9

ISBN-10: 1-59327-148-4
ISBN-13: 978-1-59327-148-0

Publisher: William Pollock
Production Editor: Elizabeth Campbell
Cover and Interior Design: Octopod Studios
Developmental Editor: Tyler Ortman
Technical Reviewer: Pat Eyler
Copyeditor: Megan Dunchak
Compositors: Christina Samuell and Riley Hoffman
Proofreader: Publication Services, Inc.
Indexer: Nancy Guenther

For information on book distributors or translations, please contact No Starch Press, Inc. directly:

No Starch Press, Inc.
555 De Haro Street, Suite 250, San Francisco, CA 94107
phone: 415.863.9900; fax: 415.863.9950; info@nostarch.com; www.nostarch.com

Library of Congress Cataloging-in-Publication Data

```
Baird, Kevin C.
  Ruby by example : concepts and code / Kevin C. Baird.
      p. cm.
  Includes index.
  ISBN-13: 978-1-59327-148-0
  ISBN-10: 1-59327-148-4
 1. Object-oriented programming (Computer science)  2. Ruby (Computer program language)  I. Title.
QA76.64.B27 2007
005.1'17--dc22
                                            2007018653
```

This book is dedicated to my parents, who bought
the first computer I ever programmed.

BRIEF CONTENTS

CONTENTS IN DETAIL

3
PROGRAMMER UTILITIES   33

4
TEXT MANIPULATION   51

6

FUNCTIONALISM WITH BLOCKS AND PROCS   99

7

USING, OPTIMIZING, AND TESTING FUNCTIONAL
TECHNIQUES   121

8
HTML AND XML TOOLS   141

9

MORE COMPLEX UTILITIES AND TRICKS, PART I   161

10

MORE COMPLEX UTILITIES AND TRICKS, PART II   185

APPENDIX
HOW DOES RUBY COMPARE TO OTHER LANGUAGES?   261

INDEX   267

ACKNOWLEDGMENTS

The most fervent thanks are due to my wife, Jennifer Cornish, who put up with my focusing too much on this book while she was finishing up her doctoral dissertation.

Thanks to Jon Phillips, Michael Ivancic, Aubrey Keus, and Scott Bliss for helpful comments. Jon Phillips in particular gave very useful technical advice in the early stages of writing, and I think of him as the unofficial early tech reviewer. Thanks are obviously also due to the official tech reviewer Pat Eyler, whose influence made this is a much better book than it would otherwise have been.

Thanks as well to professors Richard Dawkins of Oxford University and Brendan McKay of the Australian National University for their cooperation in my referencing their work.

Finally, thanks to everyone at No Starch Press and to Matz for creating Ruby in the first place.

INTRODUCTION: WHAT IS RUBY?

Ruby is "a dynamic, open source programming language with a focus on simplicity and productivity. It has an elegant syntax that is natural to read and easy to write."[1] It was released in 1995 by Yukihiro "Matz" Matsumoto. It is often described as either a very high-level language or a scripting language, depending on whom you ask. As such, it doesn't require a programmer to specify the details of how the computer implements your decisions. Like other high-level languages, Ruby is often used in text-processing applications, including an increasing number of web applications. I hope that once you've become more acquainted with the language, you'll agree that it does a good job of getting out of your way and simply letting you get some work done.

Ruby has a very interesting pedigree. Matz himself has said that the two most influential languages on Ruby's design were Common Lisp and Smalltalk—they were so influential, in fact, that he has jokingly referred to Ruby as *MatzLisp*. On the other hand, some Ruby aficionados stress Ruby's

---

[1] According to http://ruby-lang.org.

similarities with Smalltalk and Perl, as did David Heinemeier Hansson, creator of Rails, in a June 2006 *Linux Journal* interview. Hansson also describes Ruby as "a language for writing beautiful code that makes programmers happy." I couldn't agree more.[2]

NOTE *If you're interested in learning more about Ruby's heritage, see the appendix for a comparison of Ruby to other languages.*

Acquiring and Configuring Ruby

But enough with the history—let's set these questions aside and actually get Ruby installed. It's flexible, expressive, and released under a free software/open source license. (The license is available online at http://www.ruby-lang.org/en/about/license.txt.)

On a Unix or Unix-like System

Users of Unix-like operating systems such as Mac OS X, the BSDs, and GNU/Linux variants have it easy. Many of these systems either come with Ruby pre-installed or make it available as a very convenient package.

If Ruby came pre-installed on your computer, it will probably include the Interactive Ruby Shell (irb) that we'll use in the next chapter. If you've installed Ruby with a package manager, irb may come in a separate package, possibly with a specific version number as a part of the package name.

If your package manager does not include Ruby or if you'd like to use a more up-to-date version than what your package manager offers, you can simply browse to http://www.ruby-lang.org and click the Download Ruby link. Download the current stable release (1.8.4 at the time of this writing), which is a .tar.gz file. Then type the following commands as the superuser, also called root. (I'll assume you're using version 1.8.4, although it will probably be a later version when you download Ruby.)

```
cp ruby-1.8.4.tar.gz /usr/local/src/
cd /usr/local/src
tar -xzf ruby-1.8.4.tar.gz
cd ruby-1.8.4
```

Then follow the instructions in the README file. The usual set of commands for installation is as follows.

```
./configure
make
make install
```

---

[2] For more on Ruby's ancestry, refer to the Ruby-Talk archives (http://blade.nagaokaut.ac .jp/cgi-bin/scat.rb/ruby/ruby-talk/179642) and O'Reilly's interview with Matz (http:// www.linuxdevcenter.com/pub/a/linux/2001/11/29/ruby.html).

You should now have a working version of Ruby. You can test this by executing this command:

```
ruby --version
```

If it reports ruby 1.8.4 (2005-12-24) [i486-linux] or whichever version you downloaded and your system, everything worked.[3]

On a Windows System

If you use a Windows system, a One-Click Ruby Installer is available at http://rubyinstaller.rubyforge.org/wiki/wiki.pl. Simply follow the instructions there to download Ruby for your system. It's a comprehensive package—check the site for the most up-to-date list of its contents. At the time of this writing, it included the base language with various popular extensions, including SciTE (a syntax-highlighting text editor), FreeRIDE (a Ruby development environment), a help file containing Dave Thomas' book *Programming Ruby* (also called The Pickaxe), and the RubyGems package installer. It also comes with irb, which we'll explore in Chapter 1.

Motivations for the Book

This book tries to be both useful in the immediate term and informative in the long term. These goals have a profound impact on how the book is organized.

It's also meant to be accessible to neophytes, but it focuses on programming paradigms and their impact on both language design and language use—topics common to academic programming books. These days, you can use any popular language for most tasks, but that doesn't mean that solving a given problem will be equally painless in every language. No language exists in a vacuum, and a discussion of a language like Ruby should acknowledge the decisions that went into its design. You'll find that it's a very flexible language that lets you combine different approaches in powerful ways. Biologists recognize hybrid vigor; so did Matz when he created Ruby.

NOTE *When I mention programming paradigms, I'm referring to three main types: imperative, object-oriented, and functional. Broadly speaking,* imperative *languages tell computers* Do this, then do that, then do this next thing. Object-oriented *languages* define objects *(types of things) that know how to* perform methods *(specific actions).* Functional *languages treat programming problems like mathematical relationships. Ruby is flexible, meaning that you can program in any of these styles; however, it is primarily object oriented, with some strong functional influence. This book focuses slightly more on the functional aspects of Ruby than some other books.*

---

[3] Ruby, like most open source languages, is under constant development. The code in this book uses Ruby version 1.8.4, which was the stable release at the time I wrote the scripts in this book. Ruby version 1.8.6 was released slightly before this book came out.

Conventions

This book uses several conventions to distinguish among different types of information. When you encounter a new term for the first time, it will be shown in *italics*. Since this is a programming book, you'll often see small `code samples` in `code font`, as well. Code listings will be indicated like this:

```
puts "Hi, I'm code!"
```

Summary of Chapters

Here's a bit about what you'll find inside the chapters:

Chapter 1: Interactive Ruby and the Ruby Environment
This chapter describes Interactive Ruby (irb), and also introduces some key Ruby concepts.

Chapter 2: Amusements and Simple Utilities
This chapter has our first stand-alone programs (or scripts) that continue introducing key Ruby concepts while accomplishing simple tasks.

Chapter 3: Programmer Utilities
This chapter contains tools that are useful for developers in the form of library files intended to be used by other programs.

Chapter 4: Text Manipulation
This chapter focuses on processing text.

Chapter 5: Number Utilities
This chapter focuses on primarily numeric data, including pure math and moving into recursion.

Chapter 6: Functionalism with Blocks and Procs
This chapter puts a heavy emphasis on functional programming, hinted at in earlier chapters.

Chapter 7: Using, Optimizing, and Testing Functional Techniques
This chapter details testing, profiling, and optimizing your programs.

Chapter 8: HTML and XML Tools
This chapter has a subset of text processing specifically meant for markup, like HTML and XML.

Chapters 9 and 10: More Complex Utilities and Tricks, Parts I and II
These chapters both expand the scale of our programs using techniques introduced earlier in the book to tackle larger problems.

Chapter 11: CGI and the Web
This chapter talks about the Common Gateway Interface (CGI) and how to embed Ruby code in web documents.

Chapter 12: RubyGems and Rails Preparation

This chapter shows you how to use RubyGems, Ruby's package manager, and uses that system to install Rails, Ruby's main web development framework.

Chapter 13: A Simple Rails Project

This chapter contains a sample Rails application, using it to discuss key design issues useful for any Rails developer.

Now let's dive in and start using Ruby for some interesting tasks. But before we start creating separate program files, we'll explore how Ruby works with the Interactive Ruby environment.

1

INTERACTIVE RUBY AND THE RUBY ENVIRONMENT

In Ruby, as in most programming languages, we'll generally store programs in external files and execute them at once, as a unit. However, Ruby also gives you the option of typing the lines of a program one at a time and seeing the results as you go along, using Interactive Ruby (irb); irb is a shell, similar to bash in a Unix or Unix-like system or the command prompt in Windows. Using irb will give you a good idea of how Ruby processes information, and it should also help you gain an understanding of Ruby's basics before you ever even write a program.

Who should read this chapter? If you've already used Ruby and also already know the meaning of the terms *expression*, *irb*, *flow control*, *variable*, *function*, *method*, and *constant*, you can probably just skim this chapter. (If you encounter anything unfamiliar later, you can always come back.) If you've never programmed before, you should read this chapter carefully. If you've already used a language with an interactive environment, like Lisp or Python, you can probably just look at the irb sessions to see how Ruby differs from the language you already know—it's likely that it does in some key ways.

The irb program is an example of a *read-eval-print-loop (REPL)* environment. This is an idea that comes from Ruby's ancestor Lisp. It means just what the name says: It *reads* a line, *evaluates* that line, *prints* the results of the evaluation, and *loops*, waiting to read another line. The shell gives you immediate feedback for every line you enter, which is an ideal way to learn the syntax of a language.

Starting irb

Starting irb is very straightforward. On a Unix or Unix-like machine (such as GNU/Linux or Mac OS X), you can just type **irb** at the shell prompt. This should give you the following result:

```
$ irb
irb(main):001:0>
```

On a Windows machine, you'll choose **Start ▸ Run**, type **irb**, then click **OK**. You can also run the command **irb** directly from the command line.

Using irb

Now that you've started it, irb is waiting for you to type your first line. *Lines* consist of one or more expressions.

Expressions

As far as Ruby is concerned, an *expression* is just a bit of code that has a value. In fine computer programming tradition, let's see how irb reacts to the expression "Hello, world!"

```
irb(main):001:0> "Hello, world!"
=> "Hello, world!"
```

NOTE   *This listing shows the line you need to type as well as how irb responds. Note also that irb shows you line numbers at the beginning of each line. I will occasionally refer to these numbers, as well.*

What has happened here? You typed "Hello, world!", and irb happily spat it right back at you. The interesting part of this is what isn't explicit. The expression you entered has a value in Ruby, and therefore in irb. "Hello, world!" is a *String*, which is a sequence of characters, usually enclosed with either single or double quotation marks. Let's prove it.

Everything Is an Object

In Ruby, like its ancestor Smalltalk, everything is an *object*, which is just an instance of a class. "Hello, world!" happens to an instance of the class String.

Let's verify that in irb:

```
irb(main):002:0> "Hello, world!".class
=> String
```

Objects have *methods* (called on an object as some_object.some_method), which are just actions an object can perform. The method called class simply reports which class something belongs to; in other words, the type of thing that it is. Since "Hello, world!" is a String, that's exactly what the class method reports when called on "Hello, world!". There are other types of objects besides Strings, of course.

NOTE *This book assumes that you are familiar with object orientation. If you're not, here's a crash description. An* object *is a thing. It could be any type of thing. Every object is an instance of a class; for example, the objects* Glasgow, Cairo, *and* Buffalo *would all be instances of the class* City. *The objects are distinct from each other, but they are the same type of thing.* Monty Python *and* The Kids in the Hall *would both be instances of the class* Comedy Troupe, *and so on. In Ruby, you will traditionally name instances with all lowercase letters and use underscores in the place of spaces; you will name classes with CamelCase. In actual Ruby code, the class* ComedyTroupe *would have instances (objects) called* monty_python *and* kids_in_the_hall.

Integers, Fixnums, and Bignums

One other type of object (or class) is *Integer*, which is any number that is divisible by one. These should be familiar to you: 0, 1, -5, 27, and so on. Let's enter an Integer in irb.

```
irb(main):003:0> 100
=> 100
```

NOTE *If you call the method* class *on an Integer, it will report either* Fixnum *or* Bignum, *not* Integer. *This stems from how Ruby stores numbers internally. Computers can operate faster if they don't waste space, so they have to worry about how much space numbers take up. However, computers also need to be able to handle very large numbers. Therefore, they compromise and store small numbers so that they take up little space, but they also store very large numbers, which inevitably take up more space. Sophisticated high-level languages like Ruby translate between these different types of numbers automatically, so you can just deal with numbers without worrying about these specific details. Isn't that handy? For example,* 100.class *returns* Fixnum, *and* (100 ** 100).class *returns* Bignum. *That's because 100 is small enough to fit in a Fixnum, but the value of* (100 ** 100) *will only fit in a Bignum—it's too big for a Fixnum.*

We see that the number 100 has the value of 100 in irb, as you might expect. But we want to be able to do more than just see what we've typed, so let's do something with our number 100. Let's add it to 100.

```
irb(main):004:0> 100 + 100
=> 200
```

You can see that irb has added these numbers correctly, and it shows you the result. In Ruby, 100 + 100 is an expression, just as "Hello, world!" and 100 by itself are expressions. The value of 100 + 100 is, naturally, 200. Numbers have a method called +, which is how they add themselves to other numbers. That's precisely what we've done here.

Addition, Concatenation, and Exceptions

The + sign can do more than just add numbers. Let's add two other expressions:

```
irb(main):005:0> "Hello, " + "world!"
=> "Hello, world!"
```

By adding the String "Hello, " to the String "world!", we've created the new longer String "Hello, world!". Strings don't perform addition, exactly. They use the + sign to do an operation called *concatenation*, which is just tacking one thing onto the end of another. In Ruby, the + sign means *Do whatever addition-like operations make the most sense for this class of object*. This allows you to just use the + sign and assume that Integers will add themselves in a reasonable "numbery" way, Strings will add themselves in a reasonable "stringy" way, and so on.

What happens when we try to add two different types of objects? Let's find out in irb.

```
irb(main):006:0> "Hello, world!" + 100
TypeError: failed to convert Fixnum into String
        from (irb):6:in '+'
        from (irb):6
```

That expression didn't work out as well as the others. TypeError is an example of what Ruby (and many other languages) call an *exception*, which is a notice from a programming language that there has been an error. Our TypeError means that Ruby wasn't happy that we asked to add a String to a number.[1] Strings know how to add themselves to each other, as do numbers—but they can't cross types. When adding, we want both operands to be the same type.

Casting

The solution to this problem is an operation called *casting*, which is the conversion of something from one type to another. Let's see an example of casting in irb:

```
irb(main):007:0> "Hello, world!" + 100.to_s
=> "Hello, world!100"
```

---

[1] Specifically a Fixnum, in our case.

We call the method to_s on 100 before trying to add it to "Hello, world!". This method stands for *to String*—as you may have guessed, it converts the object it is called upon into a String. By the time we need to add these two operands together, they are both Strings, and Ruby dutifully concatenates them.[2] Let's verify that 100.to_s is a String:

```
irb(main):008:0> 100.to_s
=> "100"
```

So it is. But what happens when we want to convert something into an Integer? Is there a to_i method that we could call on the String "100"? Let's find out.

NOTE *Casting is common in strongly-typed languages, like Ruby. It's less common in weakly-typed languages, although it still can come up. Both approaches have their proponents.*

```
irb(main):009:0> "100".to_i
=> 100
```

We can, indeed. So we now know how to convert both Strings and Integers into each other, via either the to_s or to_i methods. It would be nice if we could see a list of all the methods we could call on a given object. We can do that too, with an aptly named method: methods. Let's call it on the Integer 100:

```
irb(main):010:0> 100.methods
=> ["<=", "to_f", "abs", "-", "upto", "succ", "|", "/", "type", "times", "%",
"-@", "&", "~", "<", "**", "zero?", "^", "<=>", "to_s", "step", "[]", ">",
"==", "modulo", "next", "id2name", "size", "<<", "*", "downto", ">>", ">=",
"divmod", "+", "floor", "to_int", "to_i", "chr", "truncate", "round", "ceil",
"integer?", "prec_f", "prec_i", "prec", "coerce", "nonzero?", "+@", "remainder",
"eql?", "===", "clone", "between?", "is_a?", "equal?", "singleton_methods",
"freeze", "instance_of?", "send", "methods", "tainted?", "id",
"instance_variables", "extend", "dup", "protected_methods", "=~", "frozen?",
"kind_of?", "respond_to?", "class", "nil?", "instance_eval", "public_methods",
"__send__", "untaint", "__id__", "inspect", "display", "taint", "method",
"private_methods", "hash", "to_a"]
```

You can see that both + and to_s are in the list of method names.[3]

Arrays

Notice how the output of methods is enclosed with square brackets ([]). These brackets indicate that the enclosed items are the members of an *Array*, which is a list of objects. Arrays are just another class in Ruby, like String or Integer, and (unlike some other languages) there is no requirement for all members of a given Array to be instances of the same class.

---

[2] Technically, instead of casting, we've created an entirely new object that happens to be the String equivalent of 100.

[3] By the way, you can chain methods together, such as 100.methods.sort. If you try that in irb, you'll get the same list of methods as you'd get with 100.methods, but in alphabetical order.

An easy way to convert a single item into an Array is to wrap it in brackets, like so:

```
irb(main):011:0> [100].class
=> Array
```

Arrays also know how to add themselves, as shown:

```
irb(main):012:0> [100] + ["Hello, world!"]
=> [100, "Hello, world!"]
```

The result is just an another Array, comprised of all the elements of the added Arrays.

Booleans

Along with String, Integer, and Array, Ruby also has a class called Boolean. Strings are sequences of characters, Integers are any numbers divisible by 1, and Arrays are lists of members. *Boolean* values can only be true or false. Booleans have many uses, but they are most commonly used in evaluations that determine whether to perform one action or an alternative. Such operations are called *flow control*.

NOTE *Booleans are named after the mathematician George Boole, who did much of the early work of formalizing them.*

Flow Control

One of the most commonly used flow control operations is if. It evaluates the expression that follows it as either true or false. Let's demonstrate some flow control with if:

```
irb(main):013:0> 100 if true
=> 100
```

We just asked whether or not the expression 100 if true is true. Since the expression true evaluates to a true value, we do get the value 100. What happens when the expression evaluated by if isn't true?

```
irb(main):014:0> 100 if false
=> nil
```

This is something new. The expression false is not true, so we don't get the expression 100. In fact, we get no expression at all—irb tells us it has no value to report. Ruby has a specific value that stands for the absence of a value (or an otherwise meaningless value), which is nil.

The value could be absent for several reasons. It could be an inexpressible concept, or it could refer to missing data, which is what happened in our example. We never told irb what to report when the evaluated expression was false, so the value is missing. Any value that might need to be represented as *n/a* is a good candidate for a nil value. This situation comes up often when you are interacting with a database. Not all languages have a nil; some have it, but assume that it must be an error. Ruby is completely comfortable with nil values being used where appropriate.

The nil value is distinct from all other values. However, when we force Ruby to evaluate nil as a Boolean, it evaluates to false, as shown:

```
irb(main):015:0> "It's true!" if nil
=> nil
```

The only values that evaluate to false Booleans are nil and false. In many other languages 0 or "" (a String with zero characters) will also evaluate to false, but this is not so in Ruby. Everything other than nil or false evaluates to true when forced into a Boolean.

NOTE   *We have to explicitly cast Strings and Integers into each other with the to_s and to_i methods, but notice that we don't need to do this for Boolean values. Boolean casting is implicit when you use if. If you were to do explicit casting into a Boolean, you might expect a method similar to to_s and to_i, called to_b. There is no such method in Ruby yet, but we'll write our own in Chapter 3.*

Let's say we want a certain value if an evaluated expression is true (as we've done with if already), but that we also want some non-nil value when the evaluated expression is false. How do we do that? Here's an example in irb:

```
irb(main):016:0> if true
irb(main):017:1> 100
irb(main):018:1> else
irb(main):019:1* 50
irb(main):020:1> end
=> 100
```

That's our first multi-line expression in irb. It should be fairly straightforward, returning 100, because true evaluates to true. Let's try again, with a few differences:

```
irb(main):021:0> if false
irb(main):022:1> 100
irb(main):023:1> else
irb(main):024:1* 50
irb(main):025:1> end
=> 50
```

This time, since false evaluates as not true, the value of the multi-line expression is the value from the else, which is 50. This format is a bit wordier than the previous tests that just used if. We also need the end keyword to tell irb when we're done with the expression we started with if. If we wanted to do tests like these multi-line expressions often, retyping slight variations of the same basic idea over and over could become tedious. That's where methods come into play.

Notice that irb gives you some useful information in its prompt. The prompt often ends with a > symbol, which is usually preceded by a number. That number is how many levels deep you are, meaning the number of end statements you'll need to get back to the top level. You'll also notice that sometimes instead of ending with a > symbol, the prompt will end with an asterisk (*). This means that irb only has an incomplete statement and is waiting for that statement to be completed. Very useful.

Methods

We touched on methods earlier, but we'll discuss them in more detail now. A *method* is just a bit of code that is attached to an object; it takes one or more input values and returns something as a result.[4] We call the inputs to a method the *arguments* or *parameters*, and we call the resulting value the *return value*. We define methods in Ruby with the keyword def:

```
irb(main):026:0> def first_if_true(first, second, to_be_tested)
irb(main):027:1> if to_be_tested
irb(main):028:2> first
irb(main):029:2> else
irb(main):030:2* second
irb(main):031:2> end
irb(main):032:1> end
=> nil
```

We just defined a method called first_if_true, which takes three arguments (which it calls first, second, and to_be_tested, respectively) and returns either the value of first or second, based on whether or not to_be_tested evaluates to true. We've now defined our earlier multi-line tests as something abstract that can be re-used with different values. Let's try it out.

NOTE *Notice that the name of first_if_true tells you what it will do. This is a good habit to get into. Method names should tell you what they do. Clear, intuitive method names are an important part of good documentation. The same advice holds for variables, described later. By that criterion, result (as seen later) is not a very good name. It's okay for a simple example that merely introduces the concept of assigning into a variable, but it's unsuitably vague for real production code.*

Remember that first_if_true tests the third value and then returns either the first value or the second value.

```
irb(main):033:0> first_if_true(1, 2, true)
=> 1
irb(main):034:0> first_if_true(1, 2, false)
=> 2
irb(main):035:0> first_if_true(1, 2, nil)
=> 2
irb(main):036:0> first_if_true(nil, "Hello, world!", true)
=> nil
```

---

[4] Ruby is object oriented, so it uses the term *method*. Languages with less of an object-oriented focus will call methods *functions*. A *method* is simply a function that is attached to an object.

```
irb(main):037:0> first_if_true(nil, "Hello, world!", false)
=> "Hello, world!"
```

Feel free to try out the first_if_true method in irb with different arguments, either now or later. It should give you a good idea of how Ruby processes expressions.

NOTE   *While methods return values when they are used, the simple act of defining a method returns nil, as you can see.*

Variables

What would happen if you wanted to use the output of one method as an input to another method? One of the most convenient ways to do so is with *variables.* Similar to algebra or physics, we just decide to refer to some value by name, like *m* for some specific mass or *v* for some specific velocity. We assign a value into a variable with a single = sign, as shown:

```
irb(main):038:0> result = first_if_true(nil, "Hello, world!", false)
=> "Hello, world!"
irb(main):039:0> result
=> "Hello, world!"
```

We assigned the value of first_if_true(nil, "Hello, world!", false) (which happens to be "Hello, world!") into a variable called result. We now have the value "Hello, world!" stored under the name result, which still evaluates as you'd expect it to, as you can see at line 39. We can now use result like we would any other value:

```
irb(main):040:0> first_if_true(result, 1, true)
=> "Hello, world!"
irb(main):041:0> first_if_true(result, 1, result)
=> "Hello, world!"
```

Notice how we can pass result through first_if_true and also evaluate it (as to_be_tested) for Boolean value. We can use it as a part of a larger expression, too:

```
irb(main):042:0> first_if_true( result, 1, (not result) )
=> 1
```

In the example on line 42, we've reversed the Boolean value of result with the keyword not before we pass it into first_if_true. We don't make any changes to result on line 42. We just create a new expression with (not result) that happens to evaluate to whatever the Boolean opposite of result is. The result itself stays unchanged.

NOTE   *I've added some spaces just to make it easier to read which parentheses enclose the arguments to the method and which enclose the (not result) expression. Ruby and irb don't care about whitespace very much.*

Constants

Sometimes we want to refer to a value by name, but we don't need to change it. In fact, sometimes we intend not to change it. Good examples from physics are the speed of light or the acceleration due to Earth's gravity—they don't change. In Ruby, we can define such values as *constants*, which must start with a capital letter. (By tradition, they are often entirely uppercase.) Let's define a constant and then use it:

```
irb(main):043:0> HUNDRED = 100
=> 100
irb(main):044:0> first_if_true( HUNDRED.to_s + ' is true', false, HUNDRED )
=> "100 is true"
```

We see that we can assign into a constant just like we did into a variable. We can then use that constant by name, as an expression or within a larger expression, as desired.

Using the Ruby Interpreter and Environment

If you come from a Unix background, you're probably already familiar with the concept of command-line options and environment variables. If you're not familiar with these terms, they're just ways for the computer to keep track of external data, usually configuration options. Ruby uses *command-line options* and *environment variables* to keep track of things like how paranoid or lax it should be in relation to security or how verbose to be about warnings. We've already seen an example of this in the instructions for installing Ruby from a source download, when we executed this command:

```
ruby --version
```

As you'd expect, that just asks Ruby to report its version. You can find out the various command-line options that Ruby understands by executing this command:

```
ruby -h
```

Environment variables can store these command-line options as defaults; they can also store other information not specific to Ruby that Ruby may still find necessary to perform certain tasks. Users of Unix-like systems store their files inside what's called a *HOME* directory, which keeps their data out of the way of other users. The My Documents folder in Windows is similar. Another important environment variable is ARGV, which is an Array that keeps track of all of the arguments passed to Ruby. When you execute an external Ruby program, as you often will by using the syntax below, the program's name will be found in ARGV.

```
ruby some_external_program.rb
```

Let's move on to some specific example programs. We'll be dealing with many of the topics we've only touched on in this chapter in greater detail appropriate to each example.

2

AMUSEMENTS AND SIMPLE UTILITIES

From the previous chapter, you should
now be relatively comfortable with irb and
how Ruby deals with various expressions. Now
we'll try some Ruby programs that are stored in separate files and executed outside of irb. You can download
all of these programs at http://www.nostarch.com/
ruby.htm.

We'll run our programs with the ruby command, so when we want to run
a script called check_payday.rb, we'll type ruby check_payday.rb either at the
shell in a Unix-like system or at the command prompt in Windows. We'll also
generally use the -w option, which means *turn warnings on*, making our example
above become ruby -w check_payday.rb. It's just a safer way to operate, and it
is especially useful when learning a new language. We'll also occasionally
see Ruby Documentation (RDoc), which allows us to put relatively complex
comments directly into our source code. We'll discuss that in relation to the
99bottles.rb example, where we first use it.

#1 Is It Payday? (check_payday.rb)

This script is a simple utility that I use to remind myself when a payday is approaching. It is very much in the quick-and-dirty style, and intentionally so.

The Code

```
❶ #!/usr/bin/env ruby
❷ # check_payday.rb

❸ DAYS_IN_PAY_PERIOD  = 14
   SECONDS_IN_A_DAY    = 60 * 60 * 24

❹ matching_date = Time.local(0, 0, 0, 22, 9, 2006, 5, 265, true, "EDT")
❺ current_date = Time.new()

   difference_in_seconds = (current_date - matching_date)
❻ difference_in_days    = (difference_in_seconds / SECONDS_IN_A_DAY).to_i
❼ days_to_wait          = (
     DAYS_IN_PAY_PERIOD - difference_in_days
   ) % DAYS_IN_A_PAY_PERIOD

   if (days_to_wait.zero?)
❽   puts 'Payday today.'
   else
     print 'Payday in ' + days_to_wait.to_s + ' day'
     puts days_to_wait == 1 ? '.' : 's.'
   end
```

CONSTANTS — lines ❸

Variables — lines ❹, ❺

How It Works

Line ❶ is a hint to the computer that this program is in Ruby. The line at ❷ is a comment meant for human readers that tells the name of the program. In Ruby, comments start with the # character and last until the end of the line.

Defining Constants

We define two constants at ❸. While constants only need to *start* with a capital letter, I like to use all caps to make them stand out. (This is a common convention in many languages and a good habit to get into.)

The names of the constants DAYS_IN_PAY_PERIOD and SECONDS_IN_A_DAY should give you a good sense of what they mean—specifically, the number of days in a pay period and the number of seconds in a day. I get paid every two weeks, which is the same as every 14 days.

The definition for SECONDS_IN_A_DAY uses multiplication (60 * 60 * 24), which is acceptable Ruby syntax, as you know from your experiments in irb. Representing these specific numbers as the result of multiplication instead of as one big final result is also more human readable, because a person reading this code will see and understand the relationship among 60 seconds in a minute, 60 minutes in an hour, and 24 hours in a day.

Why bother to define constants with more characters than the values they hold? While it doesn't make a huge difference in this program, it's a good habit to get into for larger programs.

NOTE *Constants are a very good idea. They allow you to avoid one of the sins of programming called* magic numbers, *which are examples of one of two programming sins: a literal value used repeatedly, or a literal value whose use is not obvious, even if it's only used once. Defining such a value once with a meaningful name makes your code more readable to both other programmers and yourself, after you've forgotten everything about your program. Again, constants are a very good idea.*

Defining Variables

Having defined our constants, we define a variable at ❹ called `matching_date` using Ruby's built-in `Time.local` method. This method takes 10 items as arguments, in order: seconds, minutes, hours, day of the month, month, year, day of the week, day number within the year (1 through 366), whether the date is within daylight saving time, and a three-letter code for the time zone. The values used here are for September 22, 2006, which is a day that happened to be a payday for me. The day number within a year has a maximum of 366 instead of 365, because leap years have 366 days.

At ❺, we get the `current_date` using Ruby's built-in `Time.new` method, and then subtract `matching_date` from it to get the difference, in seconds. Because we are much more interested in the difference in days rather than the difference in seconds, we divide the `difference_in_seconds` by the number of `SECONDS_IN_A_DAY` to get the difference in days, and then we round down by converting that result into an Integer with the `to_i` method. That gives us a useful value for our `difference_in_days` variable.

The `difference_in_days` variable tells us the number of days since the last payday. However, because we really want our cash, we are more interested in how long we have to wait until the next payday. To find out, at ❻ we subtract the number of days since our last payday (the `difference_in_days` variable) from the number of `DAYS_IN_A_PAY_PERIOD` to get a new variable at ❼ called `days_to_wait`.

If `days_to_wait` has a value of zero, today must be payday, so at ❽ we output that information using Ruby's built-in method `puts`. The `puts` method, which stands for *put string*, prints its String argument (`'Payday today.'`, in our script) followed by an automatic carriage return, also called a *newline*. If `days_to_wait` is not zero, we use `puts` again to tell how many days we have to wait for payday, and as a convenience, we add the letter *s* to the word day if the number of days is plural.

NOTE *We call both `print` and `puts` without parentheses enclosing the argument(s). This is perfectly legal, unless there would be some ambiguity about either the boundaries of an expression or the specific arguments to a method.*

That's the whole program. There are more elegant ways to accomplish some of the tasks that this program does, but it introduces some new concepts, such as Constants, the `puts` method, and Dates. You can run it yourself and compare what it outputs to what your own actual pay schedule is, altering the `matching_day` variable accordingly.

NOTE *Readers familiar with crontab may find it interesting that I run this on my machine with the following crontab entry: ruby ~/scripts/check_payday.rb | mutt -s "payday" kbaird.*

The Results

Your result should be a message along the lines of *Payday in 10 days*, depending on the day you run the program.

#2 Random Signature Generator (random_sig.rb and random_sig-windows.rb)

The next script generates dynamic content for email signatures, adding standard information, like a name and email address, to a random quotation drawn from a known file. The Unix and Windows versions need to be slightly different, so they have been separated into two distinct files. I'll talk about the Unix version first, but will include the source code for both files. In this example, we'll also see how Ruby handles complex assignments. That's a lot of information to cover.

The Code

Environment Variables; The File Object

The split Method

```
#!/usr/bin/env ruby
# random_sig.rb

❶ filename = ARGV[0] || (ENV['HOME'] + '/scripts/sig_quotes.txt')
❷ quotation_file = File.new(filename, 'r')
  file_lines = quotation_file.readlines()
❸ quotation_file.close()
❹ quotations    = file_lines.to_s.split("\n\n")
❺ random_index  = rand(quotations.size)
❻ quotation     = quotations[random_index]
  sig_file_name = ENV['HOME'] + '/.signature'
❼ signature_file = File.new(sig_file_name, 'w')
❽ signature_file.puts 'Kevin Baird | kcbaird@world.oberlin.edu | http://
  kevinbaird.net/'
  signature_file.puts quotation
  signature_file.close()
```

How It Works

At ❶, we assign a value to a variable called `filename`, but the value that goes into it is somewhat more complex than a single straightforward number or String. `ARGV` is an example of an environment variable. Environment variables are described in Chapter 1. For historical reasons, `ARGV` stands for *Argument Vector* and is an Array of the command-line arguments to any program when it is run.

That's not the whole line, though. Just as the equals sign is an operator that puts a value into something, the double-bar (||) is an operator that means *or*. Let's use irb to see how it works.

|| **operator**

```
irb(main):001:0> 0 || false
=> 0
irb(main):002:0> false || 0
=> 0
irb(main):003:0> nil || true
=> true
irb(main):004:0> nil || false
-> false
irb(main):005:0> false || nil
=> nil
```

An expression with the || operator evaluates whatever is to the left of it. If it is true, the whole expression has that value, whatever possible true value it happens to be. If the left side is false, the whole expression has the value on the right of the ||, whatever that value is—true, false, nil, whatever. Missing arguments are nil, and nil evaluates to false when tested by ||. The elements of ARGV start counting with zero, just like all Arrays in Ruby (and many other languages). Our filename variable is either the first argument to this program, or if there is no argument, it's set to all of that business within the parentheses: (ENV['HOME'] + '/scripts/sig_quotes.txt').

NOTE *Windows users will need to use (ENV['HOMEDRIVE'] + ENV['HOMEPATH']) instead of ENV['HOME']. We'll talk more about that in the Windows version of the script.*

ENV is an environment variable, as the abbreviation suggests, and the parentheses indicate expression boundaries, just as in a math expression, like (5 + 2) * 2 = 14. ENV['HOME'] is simply a way for you to get to the directory that belongs to a specific user. For my username, *kbaird*, this would be something like /home/kbaird, or /Users/kbaird under Mac OS X. The home directory is analogous to the My Documents folder in Windows.

ENV['HOME'] is a String, and in our expression, we add it to the String '/scripts/sig_quotes.txt'. All this means is that our filename has a default value of sig_quotes.txt, within the scripts directory, within the user's home directory. Now we know the name of the file to read quotations from, so let's use it.

Ruby creates new external File objects with File.new(), which takes two arguments: the name of the file and the manner in which you want to use that file. In this case, we want to read from the file, so at ❷ we give it a second argument of 'r', which naturally stands for *read*. We call this file quotations_file and read its lines into a variable called file_lines. Since we're now done with the file, we can close it, which we do at ❸.

The new variable file_lines is an Array with each line of the quotations file as a single element. What do we do when we want longer quotations? We've taken care of that at ❹ by combining those lines into a String with our old friend the to_s method, and turning it back into an Array with a method called split, which takes a breakpoint argument to break a String into chunks. Let's see it in action.

```
irb(main):001:0> 'break at each space'.split(' ')
=> ["break", "at", "each", "space"]
irb(main):002:0> 'abacab'.split('a')
=> ["", "b", "c", "b"]
```

In our program, we're breaking on a double line break, which is represented in Ruby, as in many other languages, with \n\n. We now have a variable called quotations, which is an Array, each member of which is a quotation from our external file.

We want to choose a random quotation, and elements of Arrays are conveniently stored with indices, so a very appropriate way to choose a random element from an Array is to generate a random number within the range of the Array's indices, and then read the element out of the Array at that index. That's precisely what we do at ❺ with the rand method, into which we pass the size of the quotations Array. We place the specific quotation chosen into a variable at ❻ with the apt name quotation.

Now that we have a quotation, what can we do with it? We want to write it out to our signature file. We usually print things with puts, which we used in "#1 Is It Payday? (check_payday.rb)" on page 14. Let's try it out in a new irb session.

```
irb(main):001:0> puts 'Hello, World!'
Hello, World!
=> nil
```

You'll notice that puts outputs whatever argument you give it, but the value it *returns* is nil. It's important to keep that distinction in mind. If you use puts on a file, it will print its argument to that file instead of printing to the screen. We already know that we can read from external files with a second argument of 'r'. Similarly, we can write to an external file with a second argument of 'w', which is the way we open signature_file at ❼. Let's take a look at the way puts behaves in irb.

some_file.**puts**

```
irb(main):002:0> t = File.new(ENV['HOME'] + '/test_file.txt', 'w')
=> #<File:0xaca10>
irb(main):003:0> t.puts 'Write some content'
=> nil
irb(main):004:0> t.close
=> nil
```

The puts method continues to return nil, but take a look at a new file called test_file inside your home directory. It should now contain the text *Write some content*, proving that puts can easily print to a file, as well. Note that we use a filename that means *The file called .signature within the user's home directory*, which is the traditional location for email signature files. All that's left is to write a standard header at ❽, add the randomly-chosen quotation, and then close the signature file.

If you use a Unix-like operating system, you can put a call to this program in a crontab,[1] as I do on my Debian machine. Windows users can modify the script to write a signature file with whatever name they choose, and then change the settings of their email program to use that signature file.

Running the Script

This is run with `ruby -w random_sig.rb` (to assume the default `sig_quotes.txt` file), or `ruby -w random_sig.rb` *some_file*, replacing *some_file* with the name of your preferred version of `sig_quotes.txt`.

The Results

Here are my results. The `$` denotes a bash prompt on my GNU/Linux system. I add an additional `cat ~/.signature` (which just shows the contents of `~/.signature`) to show the results, since the script writes to that file instead of printing to the screen.

```
$ ruby -w random_sig.rb extras/sig_quotes.txt ; cat ~/.signature
Kevin Baird | kcbaird@world.oberlin.edu | http://kevinbaird.net/
Those who do not understand Unix are condemned to reinvent it, poorly.
$ ruby -w random_sig.rb extras/sig_quotes.txt ; cat ~/.signature
Kevin Baird | kcbaird@world.oberlin.edu | http://kevinbaird.net/
"You cannot fight against the future. Time is on our side."
- William Ewart Gladstone
```

Hacking the Script

Take a look at the Windows source code below, and try to figure out the changes before continuing on to my explanation.

```
#!/usr/bin/env ruby
# random_sig-windows.rb

❶ home = "#{ENV['HOMEDRIVE']}" + "#{ENV['HOMEPATH']}"
❷ filename = ARGV[0] || (home + '\\scripts\\sig_quotes.txt')
quotations_file = File.new(filename, 'r')
file_lines = quotations_file.readlines()
quotations_file.close()
quotations      = file_lines.to_s.split("\n\n")
random_index    = rand(quotations.size)
quotation       = quotations[random_index]
❸ sig_file_name   = home + '\.signature'
signature_file  = File.new(sig_file_name, 'w')
signature_file.puts 'Kevin Baird |   kcbaird@world.oberlin.edu |   http://
kevinbaird.net/'
signature_file.puts quotation
signature_file.close()
```

---

[1] A crontab is just a way for Unix machines to schedule operations. If you use a Unix-like operating system, just execute `man crontab` at the shell. If you use Windows, you can use Windows Scheduler with a batch file.

The only significant differences relate to the filesystem, which is how the operating system and programs access your machine's hard drive, CD-ROM drive, and so on. Windows uses a separate drive letter, which is represented by ENV['HOMEDRIVE'], and a path within that drive letter, which is represented by ENV['HOMEPATH']. Because of the greater complexity of the Windows definition of *home*, we have put it into a variable in this version of the script at ❶. The only other differences are the use of backslashes rather than forward slashes at ❷ and ❸.

#3 The 99 Bottles of Beer Song (99bottles.rb)

This script demonstrates basic Object Orientation by singing (okay, printing) the "99 Bottles of Beer" song. The content of the example may be a bit contrived, but the program itself reveals a great deal about naming conventions in Ruby. We'll be defining a Wall, on which there are bottles, the number of which repeatedly drops by one.

Here's the code. Classes are the basic building blocks in Ruby, so it's worthwhile for anyone curious about the language to understand them in some depth. We've already seen some built-in classes (String, Integer, and Array), so they're not a fundamentally new concept for you at this point. What is new is the ability to define completely novel classes of your own, as we do below.

The Code

```
#!/usr/bin/env ruby
# 99 bottles problem in Ruby
```

Classes
```
❶ class Wall
```

Instance Variables
```
❷    def initialize(num_of_bottles)
        @bottles = num_of_bottles
❸    end
```

```
     =begin rdoc
     Predicate, ends in a question mark, returns <b>Boolean</b>.
     =end
```

Predicate Methods
```
❹    def empty?()
        @bottles.zero?
     end
```

Destructive Methods
```
❺    def sing_one_verse!()
        puts sing(' on the wall, ') + sing("\n") + take_one_down! + sing(" on the
wall.\n\n")
     end
```

```
❻   private

    def sing(extra='')
❼     "#{(@bottles > 0) ? @bottles : 'no more'} #{(@bottles == 1) ? 'bottle' :
    'bottles'} of beer" + extra
    end

=begin rdoc
Destructive method named with a bang because it decrements @bottles.
Returns a <b>String</b>.
=end
❽   def take_one_down!()
      @bottles -= 1
      'take one down, pass it around, '
    end

end
```

How It Works

We define classes using the keyword *class* followed by whatever name we choose, which we do at ❶ for the class Wall. Classes must start with an uppercase letter, and it is traditional to use mixed case, as in *MultiWordClassName*. Our class is called *Wall*, which conjures up a real-world object in a reader's mind. This is the wall in the song on which the bottles sit.

It is also traditional to define a class in a file with the same name by using all lowercase letters and underscores between the words, if the name consists of multiple words (i.e., multi_word_class_name.rb). This is just a convention, but it is a widely followed one, and if you decide to use Rails, using this convention will make your life much easier.

If our wall just sat there and did nothing, there would be little point in creating it. We want our wall to be able to take some sort of action. These actions are methods, just like those we've already encountered. We've already defined functions with the def keyword. Now we'll do so within a class—this attaches the function we're defining to that class, making it a *method* of that class.

Every class should have a method called initialize, which is what that class uses when it creates itself. From the outside, we call the method new, but the class itself uses the name initialize. (We'll talk about why that distinction exists shortly.) Our wall's initialize method, defined at ❷, takes one argument called num_of_bottles. It then sets the value of a variable called @bottles equal to whatever num_of_bottles is. Why does @bottles have the @ sign in front of it? The @ sign is how Ruby indicates that something is what's called an *instance variable*.

An *instance variable* is just a characteristic of some thing. If we have a class called Person, each person could have characteristics like a name, an age, a gender, and so on. These characteristics are all good examples of instance variables, because they could (and do) differ from person to person. Just as a Person has an age, a Wall has a certain number of bottles on it. Our wall happens to have 99 bottles on it, because we've told it to have that many. Let's try a different number of bottles in irb. You can bring external content into an irb session with the -r command-line flag, which stands for *require*.

```
$ irb -r 99bottles.rb
irb(main):001:0> other_wall = Wall.new(10)
=> #<Wall:0xb2708 @bottles=10>
```

We can see from the returned value that @bottles is set to 10 in the case of our new variable, other_wall. Both wall and other_wall are examples (or instances) of the class Wall. They differ in key ways, such as the number of bottles they hold.

All we want to do when we create a new wall is set its number of bottles, so at ❸ we declare the end of the method after setting the value of @bottles. After we've created our wall, we'll ask the wall if it has any bottles left. We will implement this with a method called empty?, which we define at ❹. Note the question mark, which is a perfectly legitimate part of the method's name. Ruby has inherited a tradition from its ancestor Lisp of naming methods with a question mark when they return either *true* or *false*. Such methods that only return a Boolean are called *predicates*. It should be clear that a wall is either empty or not empty, so the empty? method is a predicate, since it will return either true or false.

We also include some RDoc at ❹, before the definition of the empty? method. The way to indicate RDoc comments is to have the text =begin rdoc flush left, with no whitespace before it. Ruby will consider everything after =begin rdoc and before =end, also flush left with no preceding whitespace, to be a comment meant to be read by a human, not something to be executed. RDoc allows HTML-like tagging, as shown in the boldfaced Boolean in our script. RDoc also allows a variety of other markup options, which we'll discuss in greater detail later.

The instance variable @bottles is a number, represented as an instance of Integer in Ruby. Integers have a built-in method called zero?, which simply tells us whether or not that Integer is zero. This is an example of a predicate that was already there for us to use, and it follows the question mark naming convention. Our definition of empty? for the class Wall also uses parentheses to show that it doesn't accept any arguments. It's often a good idea to refer to methods using parentheses, even in cases like this where there are no arguments involved. The main reason for doing so is to make it clear that you're dealing with a method and not a variable. Since you can define both methods and variables, and both are made of lowercase letters, the parentheses help Ruby distinguish between the two.

A song is made to be sung, so we want to tell the Wall how to do so. We'll define a method at ❺ called sing_one_verse!. Just as empty? uses a question mark, sing_one_verse! ends with an exclamation point (also called a *bang*), which indicates that the method is destructive. *Destructive* methods change the state of their object, which means that they perform some action on their object that persists after the method has been called.

The verse that sing_one_verse! has the responsibility to output has some internal repetition, so it only makes sense to break up that repetition and abstract it. We do this with the sing method, which takes an optional String argument called extra. This optional argument represents any additions to some boilerplate about the number of bottles remaining. The one-line expression at ❼, inside the sing method, has some things we haven't seen before.

Sometimes we want to have the value of an expression appear inside a String. This process is called *interpolation*, and Ruby does it, as we'll show here in irb:

Interpolation

```
irb(main):001:0> my_var = 'I am the value of my_var'
=> "I am the value of my_var"
irb(main):002:0> "my_var = my_var"
=> "my_var = my_var"
irb(main):003:0> "my_var = #{my_var}"
=> "my_var = I am the value of my_var"
irb(main):004:0> 'my_var = #{my_var}'
=> "my_var = \#{my_var}"
```

When we use double quotation marks and wrap an expression within #{}, the expression is evaluated before it is inserted into the String. When we use single quotation marks or omit the #{} wrapper, all the text simply appears literally, even if that text happens to be a valid expression, such as the name of a variable. The combination of double quotation marks and the #{} wrapper is a way to tell Ruby that you want interpolation to occur.

NOTE *If you want to have double quotation marks within a String that uses interpolation, you can use %Q, like this: %Q[I am an interpolating String. Call me "#{ 'Ishmael' }".]. Note that the delimiter does not have to be a bracket and could be conceivably any character. Common choices are [, {, and !.*

The sing method also does some testing based on the number of bottles left. This determines the specific output that it returns. Critical to this is the fact that we can interpolate any expression, not just variables. The first expression within the interpolation at ❼ is a test that checks if the value of @bottles is greater than zero. If it is, that first expression evaluates to @bottles, otherwise it evaluates to the String 'no more'. We do this with what we call the *ternary operator*. Let's look at the ternary operator a bit in irb as well.

Ternary Operator

```
irb(main):001:0> true ? 'I am true' : 'I am false'
=> "I am true"
irb(main):002:0> false ? 'I am true' : 'I am false'
=> "I am false"
```

The ternary operator examines whatever is to the left of the question mark; it evaluates to whatever immediately follows the question mark if the examined expression is true, and evaluates to whatever follows the colon otherwise. You can think of it as another way to implement flow control that is sometimes more convenient than an if test. The next expression at ❼ that uses a ternary evaluates to either the word *bottle* or the word *bottles*, as appropriate in English for the number of bottles the wall currently has. We then concatenate information that says that these are bottles of beer, rather than some other liquid, and add the extra argument. Since the argument defaults to the empty string, and concatenating the empty string onto something has no visible effect, we're safe when there is no argument.

NOTE   *Actually, this is just a ternary operator. It just happens to be the most common one, and therefore, it often gets special naming treatment. It is the only built-in ternary operator in Ruby.*

After singing a verse, we take a bottle of beer down with take_one_down!, the method defined at ❽, again named with a bang. We've grouped together the actions of taking a bottle away and reporting that fact, which seems to make sense, conceptually. Since Ruby methods return the last expression evaluated, this method returns the String 'take one down, pass it around, ', which gets incorporated into the entire verse inside sing_one_verse!.

We finish all of these method definitions with the end keyword, and use end again to finish the class definition. So we're done—except for the word *private*, which we define at ❻. To see how this works, let's open up irb again and instantiate a new Wall.

```
$ irb -r 99bottles.rb
irb(main):001:0> wall = Wall.new(99)
=> #<Wall:0xb7d2e628 @bottles=99>
irb(main):002:0> wall.sing
NoMethodError: private method 'sing' called for #<Wall:0xb7d2e628 @bottles=99>
        from (irb):2
        from :0
irb(main):003:0> wall.take_one_down!
NoMethodError: private method 'take_one_down!' called for #<Wall:0xb7d2e628 @bottles=99>
        from (irb):3
        from :0
irb(main):004:0> wall.empty?
=> false
```

The only class that can access methods that we've defined after the appearance of the word *private* is the class itself. The other methods that can be accessed from the outside are called *public* methods. Why the distinction? It allows us to define an interface for an object that doesn't change. We can mess around under the hood and change everything about how the class actually accomplishes its responsibilities, while no one outside the class has any idea that anything has changed.

Using classes in this way is especially useful when working on larger projects with other programmers. You can define your class, complete with public methods that your other team members know about, and write little stub versions of those methods that return legal values with some temporary hard-coded approach. This allows your colleagues to start work on their classes, which might depend on the output of your class' methods, even before you have written the real versions of those methods. This is very convenient.

By the way, the new versus initialize distinction we saw earlier is a public versus private distinction. The initialize method is automatically private, and the (public) new method of any object automatically calls the (private) initialize method of that same object. That's why we create an initialize method when we write completely new classes.

Running the Script

Let's try this one out in irb with irb -r 99bottles.rb. Note that this will output all 99 verses of this song, so don't be surprised when you see it happen.

The Results

```
$ irb -r 99bottles.rb
irb(main):001:0> wall = Wall.new(99)
=> #<Wall:0xb3040 @bottles=99>
irb(main):002:0> wall.sing_one_verse! until wall.empty?
```

Here's a brief section of the output:

```
99 bottles of beer on the wall, 99 bottles of beer
take one down, pass it around, 98 bottles of beer on the wall.

98 bottles of beer on the wall, 98 bottles of beer
take one down, pass it around, 97 bottles of beer on the wall.

97 bottles of beer on the wall, 97 bottles of beer
take one down, pass it around, 96 bottles of beer on the wall.
...
2 bottles of beer on the wall, 2 bottles of beer
take one down, pass it around, 1 bottle of beer on the wall.

1 bottle of beer on the wall, 1 bottle of beer
take one down, pass it around, no more bottles of beer on the wall.

=> nil
```

#4 Sound File Player (shuffle_play.rb)

In this script, we'll make a program that plays music files in a shuffled order. We explored classes in the previous example, and we'll learn more about them here. What happens when we want to have a class that is very similar to an existing class? We have several options.

NOTE   *This version is fairly Unix-centric. You can download a Windows version that uses the Winamp player at http://www.nostarch.com/ruby.htm.*

In Ruby, we know that everything is an object, which is just another way of saying that it's a member (or instance) of a class. We know about well-defined classes like Arrays, Strings, Integers, and so on. All of these are what we call *open classes,* meaning that we can add code to existing classes. For example, we could change all of the Arrays in our programs so that they have a new method, and that change would affect any and all Arrays. We don't have to create a new special type of Array to add this hypothetical new method.

NOTE *Old hands at Object Orientation will recognize the creation of a new type of class that is otherwise similar to an existing class as using* inheritance. *We'll address inheritance in Ruby in a later chapter.*

Our shuffle player will need to deal with a list of files. The built-in class Array is very well-suited to acting as a list of items, so we'll base our player around an Array of files. In doing so, we'll also add some behavior to all Arrays that will make it easier to deal with the shuffled playback we want to implement.

The Code

Open Classes

Blocks; The sort_by Method

The replace Method

```
#!/usr/bin/env ruby
# shuffle_play

class Array

=begin rdoc
Non-destructive; returns a copy of self, re-ordered randomly.
=end
❶   def shuffle()
sort_by { rand }
    end

=begin rdoc
Destructive; re-orders self randomly.
=end
❷   def shuffle!()
       replace(shuffle)
    end

=begin rdoc
While we're here, we might as well offer a method
for pulling out a random member of the <b>Array</b>.
=end
❸   def random_element()
       shuffle[0]
    end

end # Array

###

class ShufflePlayer

❹   def initialize(files)
       @files = files
    end
```

```
        =begin rdoc
        Plays a shuffled version of self with the play_file method.
        =end
❺    def play()
          @files.shuffle.each do |file|
            play_file(file)
          end
        end

❻    private

        =begin rdoc
        Uses ogg123, assumes presence and appropriateness.
        =end
        def play_file(file)
❼      system("ogg123 #{file}")
        end

      end # ShufflePlayer

      ###

❽  sp = ShufflePlayer.new(ARGV)
    sp.play()
```

The each Method (left margin, at ❺)

The system Method (left margin, at ❼)

How It Works

We use two different class definitions in this example: one in which we open the Array class to add behavior to it, and another in which we create a completely novel class called ShufflePlayer. One key method that we add to the Array class at ❶ is shuffle. Arrays already have two methods that are very handy: sort_by and rand. You'll notice that sort_by is followed by the opening brace character ({), then the rand method, then the closing brace (}). This content between the opening and closing braces is a *block*, which is central to how Ruby transforms or iterates over collections of data, like Arrays (among other things). The sort_by method is a sorting operation that takes a block argument, which determines the manner in which the sorting should occur. By calling the rand method within our block, we ask our Array to sort its elements randomly, which is how Arrays accomplish the shuffle method after Ruby reads this method definition.

NOTE   *Perlers (or JAPHs) might be interested to know that sort_by uses a Schwartzian Transform under the hood. Also, the numbers generated by random are technically* pseudo-random, *not truly random. The difference isn't critical for the purposes of this script.*

All Arrays can now shuffle themselves in our code. This is all we need for our Array, but since this book is about informing people about Ruby as much as it is about accomplishing tasks like playing shuffled audio files, we'll continue the discussion. Our Arrays will also be able to shuffle themselves with a method defined at ❷ called shuffle!, similar to but distinct from the method called shuffle (without the bang). You recently learned that methods with an ending bang are destructive, meaning that they change state in the calling object. We accomplish this change of state by using the `replace` method, which transforms the calling object into whatever argument it receives. The `shuffle` method returns a shuffled version of the calling Array. Since we pass that shuffled Array into the `replace` method, it is a very simple way to create a destructive method called `shuffle!`, which is precisely what we've done.

It's very easy to add the `random_element` method, as well, which we do at ❸. Since a shuffled version of an Array is in a random order (by definition), returning any member out of that shuffled Array will produce a random element. Here we return the first element, but we could return the last element, or any other element. Returning the first element is a good choice, though, because an Array with any members at all will definitely have a first member.

With a few short methods, we've dramatically added to the capabilities of all Arrays. We'll make use of those capabilities within our new `ShufflePlayer` class. Since `ShufflePlayer` is a completely new class, we need to define its `initialize` method (❹), which takes an argument called `files` and assigns it into an instance variable called `@files`. If you look at ❽, near the end of the program, you see that we instantiate a new `ShufflePlayer` with `ARGV` as the files argument.

Once a `ShufflePlayer` exists, we want it to play files in shuffled order. We do so with the `play` method, defined at ❺. Within `ShufflePlayer`, `@files` is an Array of filenames. We opened up the Array class, adding the `shuffle` method to all Arrays. Therefore, `@files` can call the method `shuffle` on itself. Since it's a public method, other objects can call `shuffle` on Arrays, as well. That's what `ShufflePlayer` does in our example. Since the return value of the `shuffle` method is also an Array, it can also call all of the methods of an Array, including `shuffle` again. Instead of reshuffling, however, we'll call a method called `each`, which takes a block describing what to do to or with each element of the Array.

We delimit blocks with braces, right? Sometimes. We could have implemented our play method like this:

```
def play()
  @files.shuffle.each { |file| play_file(file) }
end
```

However, I chose to do it as I did to demonstrate the different ways you can use blocks in your code. Blocks can either start with { and end with }, or start with `do` and end with `end`. Different Ruby coders have different ideas about how best to notate blocks, but the convention seems to be that the brace delimiters are more appropriate for one-line blocks, and the `do` and `end` delimiters are more appropriate for multi-line blocks. This is the convention I will use in this book, and the one I use in my personal code. Ruby itself, however, doesn't really care.

NOTE   *The different ways of delineating blocks have different precedences, for those who are curious. This means that Ruby will evaluate blocks delineated with { and } before evaluating blocks delineated with do and end. This fits well with how they are commonly used.*

Note that when we call each, we have the word *file* within two pipe characters. Ruby coders who like American football sometimes call this the *goalpost*. The *goalpost* just tells the code within the each method what each element should be called within the block. Conceptually, it resembles an argument to a method, and later in the book, we'll blur that distinction even more. In this case, we're asking the ShufflePlayer to loop through each element of @files, call that element file, and call some method called play_file, taking file as an argument.

Since we never need to call play_file from the outside, we can make it a private method, as shown at ❻. All play_file does is take an argument called file and use a method called system at ❼ in order to play that file argument using the ogg123 program. As you might guess, system goes outside of Ruby and asks the operating system to do something—like play an audio file.

NOTE   *I have a large number of files in Ogg Vorbis audio format, so I use the ogg123 program to play them. You can certainly replace ogg123 with mpg321 or any other command-line audio player.*

The play_file method makes several assumptions, of course. It assumes that every file it's asked to play will be playable with ogg123. It assumes that a command like ogg123 *some_file_name* will be understandable by the operating system. Most glaringly, it assumes that there is a program called ogg123 on the computer that runs this program. I wrote this program to play audio files on my computer at work, where it was safe for me to make these assumptions. This allowed the program to be much shorter, because it didn't have to worry about checking for the existence of ogg123, and so on.

Running the Script

You run this script as either ruby -w shuffle_play.rb *some_ogg_files* or ./shuffle_play.rb *some_ogg_files*.

The Results

Now that I have explained our script, let's try it out. These examples are within a bash shell in Linux, and use the long-winded version of shuffle_play.rb. The specific output you'll see will depend heavily on the files you choose to play (represented by *some_ogg_files* in "Running the Script" above). Since the shuffling is pseudo-random, successive runs will also probably be different, even on the same set of files.

```
$ ./shuffle_play.rb ~/Documents/Audio/Music/Rock/King_Crimson/Discipline/*.ogg

Audio Device: OSS audio driver output

Playing: /home/kevinb/Documents/Audio/Music/Rock/King_Crimson/Discipline/03-Matte_Kudasai.ogg
Ogg Vorbis stream: 2 channel, 44100 Hz
```

```
Title: Matte Kudasai
Artist: King Crimson
Album: Discipline
Date: 1981
Track number: 03
Tracktotal: 07
Genre: Prog Rock
Comment: Belew, Fripp, Levin, Bruford
Comment: Belew, Fripp, Levin, Bruford
Copyright 1981 EG Records, Ltd.
Musicbrainz_albumid:
Musicbrainz_albumartistid:
Musicbrainz_artistid:
Musicbrainz_trackid:
Time: 00:05.74 [03:43.52] of 03:49.25 (164.5 kbps) Output Buffer 96.9%
```

Or on another directory:

```
$ ./shuffle_play.rb ~/Documents/Audio/Music/Jazz/The_Respect_Sextet/
The_Full_Respect/*.ogg

Audio Device: OSS audio driver output

Playing: /home/kevinb/Documents/Audio/Music/Jazz/The_Respect_Sextet/
The_Full_Respect/08-Carrion_Luggage.ogg
Ogg Vorbis stream: 2 channel, 44100 Hz
Title: Carrion Luggage
Artist: The Respect Sextet
Album: The Full Respect
Date: 2003
Track number: 08
Tracktotal: 18
Genre: Jazz
Composer: Red Wierenga
Copyright 2003 Roister Records
License: http://respectsextet.com/
Time: 00:20.64 [05:15.00] of 05:35.64 (151.4 kbps) Output Buffer 96.9%
```

In these examples, the bash shell expands the filenames from *.ogg before it ever gets to Ruby. All of those files are the arguments to our ShufflePlayer, which then plays them all in shuffled order, meaning that once it's done with one file, it continues on to all the others without repeating any files. We'll look at another approach to shuffled playback of audio files in two programs designed for radio station use later in the book.

Hacking the Script

Incidentally, if you're interested in shorter programs, this entire program could be replaced by these two lines:

```
#!/usr/bin/env ruby
ARGV.sort_by { rand }.each { |f| system("ogg123 #{f}") }
```

You could just have the second line if you always called the program as an argument to the Ruby interpreter, like

```
ruby short_shuffle.rb some_file.ogg
```

I don't think that extreme brevity at the expense of clarity is a goal to strive for, however, and I won't be coding toward that end in this book. Brevity is particularly inappropriate for a book that means to teach people about programming, except to demonstrate alternative formats for the same functionality, as done here.

Chapter Recap

What was new in this chapter?

- Dates
- Constants versus magic numbers
- Expressions with the || operator
- `ENV['HOME']`
- External file access, both reading and writing, using `File.new`
- Splitting Strings into Arrays
- Printing with `puts`
- Generating (pseudo-)random numbers
- Running Ruby programs at the command line
- Defining and instantiating new Classes
- Instance variables: `@i_am_an_instance_variable`
- Ruby method naming conventions: predicate?, destructive!
- Introduction to RDoc
- Expression interpolation within Strings: `"#{interpolate_me}"`
- Ternary operator: `(expression ? if_true : if_false)`
- Access control
- Open classes
- Using `ARGV`
- Using the each method with blocks
- The system method

That's a great deal of non-trivial information. If you're relatively new to programming, have made it this far, and feel fairly comfortable with the content up to this point, you've accomplished something significant and praiseworthy. Congratulations. If you're an old hand, hopefully this chapter has given you a good idea of how Ruby does some things you've already done in other languages.

3

PROGRAMMER UTILITIES

This chapter is primarily geared toward tools that reveal more about Ruby, making the programmer's job both easier and more interesting. We'll revisit a few topics we broached in a cursory fashion earlier in the book, this time giving them more attention.

#5 What Is Truth? (boolean_golf.rb)

Back in Chapter 1, we talked about how various languages convert data from one type to another. You'll remember that this process is called *casting*, and Ruby generally requires programmers to do this explicitly, while some other languages provide shortcuts that implicitly cast data.

The one major exception to this policy in Ruby is the *Boolean* type, which is either true or false. However, we noted earlier that you can also use a to_b method, making data conversion in Ruby completely consistent, in that it is always explicit. We'll be doing a variation on the notion of the to_b method in the program below, which we call boolean_golf.rb. The name is inspired by a practice in the Perl community in which programmers try to accomplish a given task with as few keystrokes as possible—they score it like golf. This script accomplishes its task as succinctly as possible, without being illegibly terse.

The Code

```
#!/usr/bin/env ruby
# boolean_golf.rb

=begin rdoc
This is intended merely to add handy true? and false? methods to every
object. The most succinct way seemed to be declaring these particular
methods in this order. Note that to_b (to Boolean) is an alias to the
true?() method.
=end
```

Superclasses
```
class Object
```

❶
```
  def false?()
    not self
  end
```

❷
```
  def true?()
    not false?
  end
```

**Meta-
programming;** ❸
Symbols
```
  alias :to_b :true?

end
```

How It Works

This program takes advantage of Ruby's support for open classes and adds new behavior to the Object class. Object is what old hands at Object Orientation call a superclass. *Superclasses* are ancestors of other classes. In Ruby, Object happens to be the ultimate superclass, because it's the ancestor of every other class in Ruby. This status means that methods you add to Object will be available to every single variable of any kind, at any time afterwards. This is extremely powerful, as you might expect.

The methods we're adding are the explicit casting to Boolean methods already discussed. When we introduced the concept, we called our hypothetical method to_b. The program above has that method, but gets to it in a roundabout way. The first method defined in the program (at ❶) is false?. Remember that a method that returns a Boolean is a *predicate*, and Ruby follows the Lisp tradition of naming predicates so that they end in question marks. The false? method uses Ruby's implicit Boolean casting inside itself— it just forces its calling object into an implicit Boolean test with the not operator, which also reverses the Boolean value. Therefore, false? is the opposite of to_b.

Let's show that in irb:

```
$ irb -r boolean_golf.rb
irb(main):001:0> true.to_b
=> true
irb(main):002:0> false.to_b
=> false
irb(main):003:0> nil.to_b
=> false
irb(main):004:0> true.false?
=> false
irb(main):005:0> false.false?
=> true
irb(main):006:0> nil.false?
=> true
```

You can see that to_b reports whether its calling object is considered true by Ruby. The false? method does the opposite—it returns false when Ruby considers the calling object true, and true when Ruby considers the calling object false. You can also try calling these methods on other objects, as well as calling the true? method (❷) on these and any other values. You'll find that true? returns the same values as the to_b method. This program defines true? in a similar manner to false?, except instead of reversing self, it reverses the output of false?.

The methods true? and false? look familiar because they've been defined in the usual way. At ❸, we define to_b in a different way. Ruby gives us a the option of doing what's called *metaprogramming*, which allows us to manipulate our objects while we're still in the process of defining them. In this case, we're defining to_b as an alias to the method true? that we just created. The code is quite readable, isn't it? You might be curious about why we precede the names of the methods with a colon. In this use of alias, :true? and :to_b are instances of the Symbol class, which are preceded with a colon. We'll talk about Symbol in later chapters. At the moment, just remember that we define aliases with the keyword alias, the Symbol version of the new name (with an initial colon), and the Symbol version of the old name (with an initial colon), in that order. We'll show that in our existing irb session.

NOTE   Metaprogramming *is a general term for writing programs that create or manipulate other programs. In our case, we write a program that manipulates itself, which is perhaps a little conceptually weird. It's very powerful, however, and is used extensively in Rails. Technically, a compiler or interpreter is an example of metaprogramming, because it allows you to write a short program in a high-level language (like Ruby), which creates a program in a lower-level language (usually C) under the hood, which is then executed. Another example of a different sort of metaprogramming in this book is a script called* methinks_meta.rb, *which we'll see in "#35 Mutating Strings into Weasels (methinks.rb)" on page 168.*

Hacking the Script

In this irb session, we just make a not-terribly-useful alias for to_i with the cumbersome name make_me_into_an_integer. However, it does nicely demonstrate how to define aliases. We have accomplished several tasks. We added new methods to every single object in Ruby. These methods allow us to be completely pedantic about Boolean casting—in other words, we now have methods for explicit casting into Boolean values. While doing so, we refreshed our knowledge of method naming conventions and also learned a bit about both aliases and metaprogramming.

```
irb(main):007:0> class String
irb(main):008:1> alias :make_me_into_an_integer :to_i
irb(main):009:1> end
=> nil
irb(main):010:0> '5'.make_me_into_an_integer
=> 5
```

Running the Script

The easiest way to run this is with irb.

```
$ irb -r boolean_golf.rb
irb(main):001:0> true.true?
=> true
irb(main):002:0> true.false?
=> false
irb(main):003:0> nil.false?
=> true
```

The Results

This library file only returns either true or false, as demonstrated above.

#6 Making a List (array_join.rb)

In the previous script, we added new methods to allow explicit Boolean casting to every Object in all of Ruby. In this example, we create a new method that is a slight variation on a method that already exists. In this case, we're altering the way that Arrays can represent themselves as Strings.

When we talk about lists in natural speaking, we often separate the last item from the item before it with the word *and*. This is not how Ruby handles Arrays by default. Let's verify that in irb:

The join Method

```
irb(main):001:0> a = [0, 1, 2]
=> [0, 1, 2]
irb(main):002:0> a.join(' ')
=> "0 1 2"
irb(main):003:0> a.join(', ')
```

```
=> "0, 1, 2"
irb(main):004:0> a.join('')
=> "012"
```

We're creating a variant of the method join, which is available to all Arrays and whose behavior we see above in the irb session. It takes the items of the Array, concatenating them together into a String, with the argument to the join method between each item, but not before the first item or after the last item. That's the behavior of join. How can we make our own join that adds the String and before the last item? Here's how.

The Code

```ruby
#!/usr/bin/env ruby
# array_join.rb

class Array

❶    def my_join(separator1=', ', separator2=' and ')
       modified_join(separator1, separator2)
     end

❷    protected

❸    def modified_join!(separator1, separator2)
       last_one = self.pop()
       join(separator1) + separator2 + last_one.to_s
     end

❹    def modified_join(separator1, separator2)
       self.dup.modified_join!(separator1, separator2)
     end

end
```

Protected Methods ❷

The pop Method ❸

The dup Method ❹

How It Works

In our open class modification of Array, we define a new method at ❶ called my_join that takes two separator arguments. It calls another method, modified_join, with whatever our two separator arguments are.

The modified_join method hasn't been defined yet and doesn't need to be called except within the my_join method. You might think that it can be a private method, and so would expect to see the word *private* before the method definition. Instead, at ❷ you see the word *protected*. Why couldn't it just have been *private*? We'll find out very shortly.

The modified_join method is defined at ❹ simply as calling the new destructive method modified_join! on a duplicate of the calling object. We get a duplicate of the calling object simply by using the dup method. We define the destructive method modified_join! at ❸. It takes two separator arguments, just like all of our new methods in this program. It defines a new local variable called last_one, which is the value of the object calling the method pop on itself. *Pop* is a standard term in many languages for the operation of removing the last item from an Array. Here's an example of popping in action, continuing our existing irb session:

```
irb(main):005:0> a
=> [0, 1, 2]
irb(main):006:0> a.pop
=> 2
irb(main):007:0> a
=> [0, 1]
irb(main):008:0> a.pop
=> 1
irb(main):009:0> a
=> [0]
irb(main):010:0> a.pop
=> 0
irb(main):011:0> a
=> []
```

You can see that the Array called a is modified whenever it calls the method pop on itself. Why, you might ask, isn't this method called pop!, since it's destructive? That's a good question. The answer is convention—*pop* is an established term for this operation from languages that precede Ruby. If this convention bothers you, just remember that Ruby has ancestors, just like a real human spoken language does. Think about the spelling rules in English. They make little sense after the fact, but make perfect sense when you realize that English is the product of Norman soldiers trying to pick up Saxon barmaids a thousand years ago.

Ruby depends on its ancestors similarly to how a spoken language does, and given the choice between breaking either the convention of naming destructive methods with exclamation marks or of agreeing with precedent from other languages, Matz has decided to make Ruby play nicely with others.

Now we have our last item in a separate variable called last_one, and since pop is destructive, that item has been removed from the calling Array after pop has occurred. We're satisfied with the way the original version of join works on all items before the last one, so we can just call the plain old join on those items. We add our second separator, and then add our last item that we popped off, making sure that it is a String (and therefore willing to be concatenated) by calling the to_s method on it.

So what was all that business about using protected instead of private? The reason we used protected is that inside the (non-destructive) modified_join method, our Array doesn't call the (destructive) modified_join! method on itself. Instead, it calls modified_join! on a duplicate of itself. It's no longer the same object, and the duplicate won't allow another instance to call one of its private methods. So what do we do? Should there be a way for an Array to call a method on another Array that isn't available to an Integer, a String, or a Symbol? There is, and that's exactly what the protected access control keyword is for. Below is some irb action showing how the program works.

Running the Script

```
$ irb -r array_join.rb
irb(main):001:0> a = [0, 1, 2]
=> [0, 1, 2]
irb(main):002:0> a.join(', ')
=> "0, 1, 2"
irb(main):003:0> a.my_join(', ')
=> "0, 1 and 2"
irb(main):004:0>
```

Hacking the Script

Once you've tried that and are comfortable with it, change protected to private and try to run it again. It should fail on you, as shown here.

```
$ irb -r array_join.rb
irb(main):001:0> a = [0, 1, 2]
=> [0, 1, 2]
irb(main):002:0> a.join(', ')
=> "0, 1, 2"
irb(main):003:0> a.my_join(', ')
NoMethodError: private method 'modified_join!' called for [0, 1, 2]:Array
        from ./array_join.rb:14:in 'modified_join'
        from ./array_join.rb:7:in 'my_join'
        from (irb):3
        from :0
irb(main):004:0>
```

That private method error is the reason we want our non-public methods in this program to be protected, rather than private. That should give you basic understanding of Ruby's access control: public, private, and protected.

#7 Command-Line Interface (uses_cli.rb and simple_cli.rb)

The program uses_cli.rb understands command-line options, which are configuration options that you can use to make the script behave in different ways, depending on the specific values chosen. It uses specific options that have become somewhat standard, such as -h or --help. Options in the form with a single hyphen and a single letter are *short options*, while those with a double hyphen and a full word are (unsurprisingly) called *long options*. Let's look at the code for uses_cli.rb.

NOTE   *I think there is enough pedagogical value to rolling your own command-line parser to make it worthwhile, especially in a book like this. However, I should note that there are two fine built-in CLI parsers in Ruby: GetOptLong (Motoyuki Kasahara, http://www.sra.co.jp/people/m-kasahr/ruby/getoptlong) and OptionParser (Nobu Nakada, http://optionparser.rubyforge.org). I only include the URLs for information purposes; they are built in to the Ruby Standard Library, so you don't need to download them.*

The Code

```
#!/usr/bin/env ruby
# use_cli.rb

=begin rdoc
Please refer to the SimpleCLI Class for documentation.
=end
```

Require ❶ `require 'simple_cli'`

❷
```
cli = SimpleCLI.new()
cli.parse_opts(ARGV)
```

There isn't a whole lot here, and the script gives us almost no information, except at ❷, where it suggests that we need to look inside the SimpleCLI class for documentation. Why the redirection? For an example this straightforward, it's a fair question. The Holy Grail of computer programming is the notion of reusable code. There are many ways to accomplish that end, but one of the most enduringly successful ways is to have external libraries of functions that are reasonably abstract, which is the role played by the simple_cli.rb file in our example. Some other specific file can then use that library file, as we do at ❶ in uses_cli.rb with the *require* keyword, which takes a String argument that is the name of an external file without the .rb extension. This makes the code in that external file available to the file doing the requiring—it's analogous to running irb with the -r flag. Therefore, at ❷ we can easily instantiate an instance of SimpleCLI that we call cli, to which we pass all of the command-line options used by uses_cli.rb.

If we want to understand how SimpleCLI works, we'll have to look at its code. Note that some of the methods in SimpleCLI are *stubs*, meaning that they don't do anything worthy of real production code, but they demonstrate that the options are being parsed appropriately. If you find this example useful as a scaffold or guide for your own code that you want to take command-line options, you simply replace both the types of options and their specific implementations as your needs dictate. These are only examples. Here, we instantiate SimpleCLI and then call its parse_opts method with every command-line option used in uses_cli.rb. Let's see what that method does by looking at simple_cli.rb.

NOTE   *The help and version command-line options have become fairly standardized, and their inclusion is generally appreciated.*

```
#!/usr/bin/env ruby
# simple_cli.rb

=begin rdoc
Parses command line options.
=end
class SimpleCLI
```

❶ # CONSTANTS

Hashes

```ruby
OPTIONS = {
  :version => ['-v', '--version'],
  :help    => ['-h', '--help'],
  :reset   => ['-r', '--reset'],
}
```

Here Docs ❷

```ruby
USAGE =<<END_OF_USAGE

This program understands the following options:
  -v, --version : displays the current version of the program
  -h, --help    : displays a message with usage instructions
  -r, --reset   : resets the program

With no command-line options, the program performs its default behavior.

END_OF_USAGE

VERSION = "Some Project version 0.01 (Pre-Alpha)\n"

# METHODS
```

❸
```ruby
def parse_opts(args)
  return option_by_args(args[0]) if understand_args?(args)
  # options are not understandable, therefore display_usage
  display(USAGE)
end
```

❹
```ruby
private
```

❺
```ruby
def display(content)
  puts content
end

def do_default()
  puts 'I am performing my default behavior'
end
```

❻
```ruby
def option_by_args(arg)
  return display(VERSION) if OPTIONS[:version].include?(arg)
  return display(USAGE)   if OPTIONS[:help].include?(arg)
  return reset()          if OPTIONS[:reset].include?(arg)
  do_default()
end

def reset()
  puts 'I am resetting myself.'
end
```

❼
```ruby
def understand_args?(args)
  # works in Ruby1.8
  OPTIONS.keys.any? { |key| OPTIONS[key].include?(args[0]) }
```

**The any?
Method**

```
❽ =begin works in Ruby1.6
      return true unless args
      return true unless args[0]
      return true if args[0].size.zero?
      OPTIONS.keys.each do |key|
        return true if OPTIONS[key].include?(args[0])
      end
      return false
=end
    end

  end
```

The include?
Method

How It Works

This file, simple_cli.rb, is a basic definition of a class called SimpleCLI, of course, with RDoc before the class definition and some useful constants right away at ❶. We've seen constants before, but we declare these constants inside of a class definition. This is actually the preferred way to use constants in Ruby. You often want to encapsulate methods inside an object, and the same is true for constants. Your code for some physics calculation cares about the speed of light, whereas your payday notification program cares about the number of days in a pay period. In our case, the command-line parser cares about what OPTIONS it can understand and the USAGE message it should report.

The OPTIONS constant is a new type of data structure called a Hash. *Hashes* are lookup tables, and are very similar to functions, in a way. You pass something into a Hash, and you receive one thing from it. That one thing never changes unless you either change what you pass into the Hash, or you change the internals of the Hash. As you can see, you declare a Hash with braces. The items to the left of the => are the *keys* of the Hash, while the items to the right of the => are the *values* of the Hash. If you pass in one of the keys, the Hash will return the matching value.

NOTE *Note that the one thing you receive could be a composite data type. For example, in our OPTIONS Hash, the values you receive are Arrays. The point is that you'll always receive the same Array for a given input value.*

Let's demonstrate in irb. The way to refer to a constant within a class is with the syntax Class::CONSTANT, so let's do that. Keep in mind that the Array ["-v", "--version"] is the value of SimpleCLI:: OPTIONS class associated with the key :version. That means that if you pass in the Symbol :version, you receive the Array ["-v", "--version"].

```
$ irb -r simple_cli.rb
irb(main):001:0> SimpleCLI::OPTIONS[:version]
=> ["-v", "--version"]
irb(main):002:0> SimpleCLI::OPTIONS[:help]
=> ["-h", "--help"]
irb(main):003:0> SimpleCLI::OPTIONS[:reset]
=> ["-r", "--reset"]
```

It works. If you compare our results in irb with the declaration of the Hash in the code, you shouldn't be surprised by what we got. Hashes are critically important data structures. I am particularly fond of defining them as constants within a class, so you'll see this practice repeated many times in the course of the book.

NOTE *There are several reasons why I often have Constants within a class that are Hashes. They're within a class because they need to be accessible within that class, but not outside it. The reason they're often Hashes is that I often find (for whatever reason) that simple lookup tables are useful data structures to have. After you've read some of the functional programming information, you may find it interesting to define both lambdas and Procs as class constants as well. I find myself often doing so.*

The declaration of the USAGE constant at ❷ looks a bit odd, with the equals sign followed by two left arrows. However, this is a very useful tool for multi-line text called a here doc. With a here doc declaration, the programmer can say that an expression should continue across multiple lines until a specific marker is reached—END_OF_USAGE, in this case. This is very handy for large amounts of verbatim text that you would otherwise have to build using multiple print or puts statements.

Next is a more straightforward constant called VERSION, which is a regular String. Its definition uses double-quote characters, because we want a newline character (notated by \n) at the end. The following two statements would print the same thing; the \n is just the way to include the newline within the String.

```
puts 'Some Project version 0.01 (Pre-Alpha)'
print "Some Project version 0.01 (Pre-Alpha)\n"
```

We have our constants, so let's move on to our methods. The main one (and in fact, the only public one) is parse_opts, defined at ❸. It parses options, and its implementation should be fairly readable at this point. It returns the result of calling the option_by_args method if it understands the args, and otherwise passes its own USAGE message into the display method. I like method names that tell you what they're supposed to do. If you care about the details, you can look inside to learn more, but the name should give you the basic information you need up front.

All of our methods, other than parse_opts, are private (❹), because they only need to be called by a SimpleCLI instance on itself. The display, do_default, and reset methods starting at ❺ should be pretty straightforward to you. These are the methods that you would change to do something more useful in real production code. The major logic of the class occurs in the remaining methods option_by_arg (❻) and understand_args? (❼). We know understand_args? is a predicate by the question mark at the end of its name, so it will be returning either true or false.

The option_by_args method checks each key of the OPTIONS constant, and if it finds a match, returns with the appropriate behavior. This means that it will not continue checking keys after it finds a match, so the order of the keys is important. It checks for matches using an Array predicate method called include?, which simply returns true if the argument is found in the Array and false if it is not. This makes it very easy to have command-line aliases like -v and --version which mean the same thing, because either one will cause include? to return true. If option_by_args gets no matches, it performs its default behavior.

Key to all of this is whether or not the instance of SimpleCLI understands it arguments. In Ruby1.8, which this book assumes you're using, it's easy to determine that question using another predicate method called any?. It takes a block and returns true if the contents of that block evaluate to true for any of the elements of the calling object, which is usually an Array. Let's demonstrate in irb:

```
$ irb
irb(main):001:0> a = [0, 1, 2]
=> [0, 1, 2]
irb(main):002:0> a.any? { |i| i > 1 }
=> true
irb(main):003:0> a.any? { |i| i > 2 }
=> false
```

In our case, we're checking if it's true that the Array value returned from the OPTIONS Hash includes the first argument to the understand_args? method for any of the keys of the OPTIONS Hash. As you can see, Hashes have a method called keys that returns all of their keys as a single Array. If our any? test returns true, that means that SimpleCLI knows how to react to the argument it received. The nice thing about this setup is that to make SimpleCLI understand more options, we just add more data to the OPTIONS Hash. The understand_args? method never has to change, only its input does. Programmers call this *data-driven programming*, and generally think highly of the practice.

That's our command-line parsing example. Let's run this using the options shown. Just like in irb, I'll show the output.

Running the Script

```
$ ./uses_cli.rb -r
I am resetting myself.
$ ./uses_cli.rb -v
Some Project version 0.01 (Pre-Alpha)
$ ./uses_cli.rb -h

This program understands the following options:
  -v, --version : displays the current version of the program
  -h, --help    : displays a message with usage instructions
  -r, --reset   : resets the program

With no command-line options, the program performs its default behavior.
```

```
$ ./uses_cli.rb
I am performing my default behavior
$ ./uses_cli.rb --reset
I am resetting myself.
$ ./uses_cli.rb --version
Some Project version 0.01 (Pre-Alpha)
$ ./uses_cli.rb --help

This program understands the following options:
  -v, --version : displays the current version of the program
  -h, --help    : displays a message with usage instructions
  -r, --reset   : resets the program

With no command-line options, the program performs its default behavior.
```

Hacking the Script

I mentioned Ruby1.8, which provides the any? method. One of the machines I used while writing this book only has Ruby1.6. I've included some alternative code inside a modified RDoc section at ❽ to show just how convenient it is to have any? available to us. As you can see, RDoc can be useful for things other than final comments.

#8 Palindromes (palindrome.rb and palindrome2.rb)

I'm rounding out this chapter with a few shorter examples pertaining to palindromes, which are bits of text that are the same when reversed as they are when read normally. Usually, we allow cheating to ignore spaces, capitalization differences, and punctuation, so *A man, a plan, a canal, Panama* qualifies as a palindrome under those conditions. While working on this book, I was reading another programming book that contained a discussion about palindromes. "Great!" I thought. "I'll add a palindrome? predicate method to all Strings. It'll be a nice simple bit to have in the chapter in which I talk about text." So I started thinking about breaking Strings into individual characters, writing a method that would compare characters an equal distance from each end of the String, and all the other things you'd need to do in some other languages. Then I realized how easy it is to implement this method in Ruby.

The Code

The reverse
Method

```
class String

  def palindrome?()
    (self == self.reverse)
  end

end
```

How It Works

That's it. Such an easy solution was staring me in the face the whole time. Strings can reverse themselves, and the definition of a palindromic String is that it is the same as itself reversed. This is when I realized that this example belongs in this chapter, because of the incredible relative ease of this task and what it implies about programmers being able to roll their own libraries.

Easy as it was to do, this version of a palindrome isn't entirely satisfactory. For one thing, it doesn't work for our example sentence. We need a version of the palindrome? predicate that is a bit more complex. Here it is. I'm placing the "Hacking the Script" subsection earlier in this section because I use it to demonstrate some ideas in the "Running the Script" and "Results" subsections, as I hope will become clear.

Hacking the Script

The file palindrome2.rb is a bit more complex, as you'll see. But given what it does, it's still pretty simple in Ruby, compared to some other languages.

```
#!/usr/bin/env ruby
# palindrome2.rb

=begin rdoc
Gives every <b>String</b> the ability to identify whether it is a
a palindrome. This version ignores all non-alphabetic characters,
making it suitable for longer text items.
=end

class String

❶    DUAL_CASE_ALPHABET = ('a'..'z').to_a + ('A'..'Z').to_a

=begin rdoc
Contrast this with some other languages, involving iterating through each
string index and comparing with the same index from the opposite end.
Takes 1 optional Boolean, which indicates whether case matters.
Assumed to be true.
=end
❷    def palindrome?(case_matters=true)
       letters_only(case_matters) == letters_only(case_matters).reverse
     end

     private

=begin rdoc
Takes 1 optional Boolean, which indicates whether case matters.
Assumed to be false.
```

```
=end
```

❸
```
  def letters_only(case_matters=false)
    just_letters = split('').find_all do |char|
      DUAL_CASE_ALPHABET.include?(char)
    end.join('')
    return just_letters if (case_matters)
    return just_letters.downcase
  end

end
```

This file has the shebang telling us that it should be run in Ruby, even though it is a library file, rather than a file that will be directly executed. Why is that? The main reason is that it would otherwise start with RDoc, which we wouldn't want bash to try to interpret. With the shebang, this will automatically be run by Ruby if it is accidentally executed at the command line. If you're extra paranoid, you could add the first line to `palindrome.rb`, as well.

NOTE   Shebang *is the standard Unix geek pronunciation of #!, which one often finds at the beginning of scripts.*

In this program, we want to be able to test palindromes such that we ignore all non-letters and also have the ability to ignore case if we choose to. This is easy enough to do. Our new String has a private method called `letters_only` that does what you expect it to: It compiles a new String consisting only of those characters that pass `DUAL_CASE_ALPHABET.include?`, where `DUAL_CASE_ALPHABET` (❶) is an Array of all letters, both upper- and lowercase. If it receives a `case_matters` argument that is true, it returns those letters as they are, otherwise it returns an all-lowercase version of those letters, which we accomplish with the `downcase` method. The `split` method breaks a String into chunks (each character, in this case), and the `join` method sews them back together with a delimiter, which in this case is the empty String.

The `letters_only` method at ❸ is handy enough that in our `palindrome?` predicate (❷), all we need to do is compare its output to the reverse of its output, and we have our more flexible palindrome detector. Let's see it in action.

Running the Script

I have written a test program called `test_palidrome.rb` that I keep in a separate directory called tests/. Here is the file, followed by a bash session in which I run it.

```
#!/usr/bin/env ruby
# test_palindrome.rb
puts "Band\tPal?\tpal?"
bands = %w[abba Abba asia Asia]
bands.each do |band|
  puts "#{band}\t#{band.palindrome?}\t#{band.palindrome?(false)}"
end
```

The Results

```
$ ruby -r palindrome2.rb tests/test_palindrome.rb
Band    Pal?    pal?
abba    true    true
Abba    false   true
asia    false   false
Asia    false   false
```

I started thinking about musical groups that both start and end with the letter *A*. I didn't get very far—but far enough to demonstrate the program, anyway. Note that we require palindrome2.rb at the command line, rather than with an explicit require keyword inside test_palindrome.rb. We can also do testing in irb, of course.

```
$ irb -r palindrome2.rb
irb(main):001:0> 'Ika Yaki'.palindrome?
=> false
irb(main):002:0> 'Ika Yaki'.palindrome?(false)
=> true
irb(main):003:0> 'ika yaki'.palindrome?
=> true
```

We see that Japanese grilled squid (Ika Yaki) is either properly recognized as a palindrome or not, depending on the parameters we tell the palindrome? predicate to use. These String-related operations should get us properly prepped for the next chapter, which deals with text manipulation in greater detail. Before, that, however, we should review what was new in this chapter.

NOTE   *If you try ruby -r palindrome.rb tests/test_palindrome.rb, the test script will fail. Can you figure out why? The reason has to do with arguments.*

Chapter Recap

What was new in this chapter?

- Making new predicates for explicit Boolean casting
- Method aliases
- Superclasses
- Metaprogramming
- The Symbol class
- Arrays and the join method
- The protected level of access control
- The dup and pop methods
- Making command-line interface flags
- Library files for reusable code
- Class constants
- The Hash class
- Hash keys and values
- The here doc declaration
- Newline characters within Strings
- Using Array.include? to test for membership
- The any? predicate
- The Hash.keys method
- A bit on Ruby1.8 vs. Ruby1.6 and the any? predicate
- Palindromes and reversing Strings
- Extracting the letters from Strings
- Changing the case of Strings

That's even more than the last chapter, which was hardly holding your hand. Congratulations again. Let's move on to some more complex treatment of Strings in the next chapter.

4

TEXT MANIPULATION

Text is the basic format for storing configuration data, web content, email, as well
as data written in XML (eXtensible Markup
Language) and YAML (YAML Ain't Markup
Language) which we'll be looking at in greater detail
later. It's important for a programming language to deal with text easily
and efficiently. Luckily, Ruby meets this requirement. This chapter includes
several scripts that demonstrate Ruby's approach to some common text-
oriented problems.

#9 End-of-Line Conversion (dos2unix.rb)

If you've never had to deal with end-of-line (EOL) differences among
operating systems, consider yourself fortunate. Microsoft, Apple, and the
various Unix-like operating systems (such as the BSDs and GNU/Linux
systems) all disagree about how a text file should show the end of a line. This is
further complicated by Apple's transition to a Unix-like operating system
with Mac OS X, which is very similar to FreeBSD. Unix-like systems mark the

end of a line with the *line feed* character (also called *newline*); in interfaces that predate the cathode-ray tube (CRT), this character indicated that the paper should move up a line so that there would be more blank paper on which to print. On the other hand, older Macintosh systems (pre–Mac OS X) indicated the end of a line with the *carriage return* character, which indicated that the printer should move back to the left side to start printing again (this assumes you are using a language that is written left to right, like English). Windows (and DOS) systems, on the third hand, mark the end of a line with a carriage return followed by a line feed.

NOTE   *Some Internet protocols also use the Windows EOL convention, despite often being hosted on Unix-like machines. Go figure.*

Why the difference? One could argue that the Windows approach makes the most sense—if we're modeling the physical action of something like a typewriter, then both a carriage return and a line feed would be needed. However, the Unix-like and Macintosh approaches have the benefit of only using one character. This is an important savings, given how often newlines appear in text documents, and it was even more important in the early days of computers when both RAM and storage were much more limited and expensive than they are now.[1]

Today, most text editors and similar programs can deal with these differences without too much difficulty, so the end-of-line compatibility problem is generally no more than a nuisance. But why put up with a nuisance when you don't have to? We can write a Ruby program that converts DOS or old-style Mac EOLs to Unix EOLs for us.

The Code

```
#!/usr/bin/env ruby
# dos2unix.rb
# converts line feeds from DOS (or old-style Mac) to Unix format
❶ ARGV.each do |filename|
    contents_file = File.open(filename, 'r')
❷   contents = contents_file.read()
    contents_file.close()
❸   contents.gsub!(/\r\n?/, "\n")
    replace_file = File.new(filename, 'w+')
❹   replace_file.puts(contents)
    replace_file.close()
  end
```

Regular Expressions

How It Works

My pro-Unix biases are clear from both the name and purpose of this program. Let's see what it does. At ❶, we start looping through the arguments to the script, calling each filename in turn. We open and close that argument

---

[1] This is also the reason many Unix commands are so short: rm for *remove*, cp for *copy*, and so on.

(currently called filename) as we've done before, reading its contents into the creatively named variable contents. We do some magic with gsub! at ❸, and then write contents into a new file (❹) called replace_file. What's the magic at ❸? Let's look at it again.

```
contents.gsub!(/\r\n?/, "\n")
```

We're calling a method called gsub! on our contents String. We know that gsub! (which stands for *global substitution*) is a destructive method because of its exclamation-mark ending, and it looks like it takes two arguments. The first argument is enclosed in regular slashes, and the second argument is a newline String. The first argument is a *regular expression*, which is a special kind of variable that can describe the contents of a piece of text without knowing everything about it. Regular expressions (*regexes* for short) allow you to test for conditions like *Does this text consist entirely of digits?*, which you could imagine might be useful before using the to_i method of a String. Regexes also allow tests like *Are there exactly seven words in the text?* or *Do all words in this text start with a capital letter?*, as well as many others.

Regexes accomplish tasks by defining descriptors for characters as well as groupings and the number of occurrences of those characters. As you can see in the code, regexes are delineated with slashes. This practice of using slashes is not specific to Ruby; it is common in other languages as well. The question mark in the regex does not mean a literal question mark appearing in the text; instead, it means that whatever preceded it is optional, occurring zero or more times. Let's try out some regexes in irb. We'll use a new operator called =~, which is similar to ==. Instead of testing for exact equality, though, it tests whether or not the regular expression matches any part of the String we call it on. It returns the first point at which a match occurs if the question the regex represents (i.e., *Does this text consist entirely of digits?*) is true for that String; it returns nil if there is no match.

```
irb(main):001:0> letters = 'abcde'
=> "abcde"
irb(main):002:0> letters =~ /a/
=> 0
irb(main):003:0> letters =~ /b/
=> 1
irb(main):004:0> letters =~ /e/
=> 4
irb(main):005:0> letters =~ /x/
=> nil
```

We have our String, letters, which is just the first five letters of the alphabet. We then test whether the letter *a* appears anywhere in letters. It does, right at the beginning, so our test returns zero. Why? Because that is the index within the String where the first match occurs—remember that we start counting with zero, not one. Since the next letter is *b*, when we test for the presence of *b* within letters, we should get a result that is one higher than the value when we tested for *a*. We do. Jumping ahead to the letter *e*, we have a match at the last index, which is the fifth letter and has the index of four, again because we start counting with zero. When we test for a letter that does not appear in letters, we get the return value nil.

That's simple matching. Now let's use that question mark.

```
irb(main):006:0> letters =~ /aa?/
=> 0
irb(main):007:0> letters =~ /ax?/
=> 0
```

At first, line six seems similar to line two. Line seven is more interesting, in that the optional second letter is a new letter that does not appear in letters at all. In both cases, the second letter precedes a question mark, which makes it optional. On line six, we are asking if our String (consisting of the first five letters) has an *a* followed by zero or more *a*s. It does, starting at index zero, so that is our return value. We then ask if our String has an *a* followed by zero or more *x*s. It does, starting at index zero. Let's continue.

```
irb(main):008:0> letters =~ /ab?/
=> 0
irb(main):009:0> letters =~ /bc?/
=> 1
irb(main):010:0> letters =~ /b?/
=> 0
```

Line eight asks if letters has an *a* followed by any optional *b*s, which it does at index zero. Line nine asks if letters has a *b* followed by any optional *c*s, which is does at index one. Line ten asks if letters has any optional *b*s, which it does at index zero. The lesson is clear—matching optional characters is very enthusiastic, and the complete absence of a character matches zero or more occurrences of any character. Be very careful with your use of the question mark, especially as a regex argument used by a destructive method. Here's another demonstration of a match for zero occurrences of a character:

```
irb(main):011:0> letters =~ //
=> 0
```

There's nothing at the beginning of letters. Matching on nothing is conceptually odd, but it can be very useful when you want to break a String into an Array of each of its characters. You may recall we used the split method matching the empty string in our script palindrome2.rb (Chapter 3) to deal with each letter in the String in turn.

Now we've done our matching. I said earlier that gsub stands for *global substitution*, so let's do some substituting, again in irb.

The gsub Method

```
irb(main):012:0> letters.gsub(/a/, 'x')
=> "xbcde"
irb(main):013:0> letters.gsub(/ab?/, 'x')
=> "xcde"
irb(main):014:0> letters.gsub(/ac?/, 'x')
=> "xbcde"
```

You can see that `gsub` finds the portion of the String that matches the first argument and returns a result in which the first argument is replaced by the second argument. Now let's review the differences between destructive and non-destructive methods, as they relate to these substitutions.

```
irb(main):015:0> letters
=> "abcde"
irb(main):016:0> letters.gsub!(/ac?/, 'x')
=> "xbcde"
irb(main):017:0> letters
=> "xbcde"
```

The non-destructive version leaves the original `letters` alone, as you'd expect, while the destructive version makes permanent changes to `letters`. The `gsub!` method also returns `nil` if it is unable to comply, as shown in irb:

```
 irb(main):001:0> foo = 'abcd'
=> "abcd"
irb(main):002:0> foo.gsub(/a/, 'b')
=> "bbcd"
irb(main):003:0> foo.gsub!(/a/, 'b')
=> "bbcd"
irb(main):004:0> foo.gsub(/a/, 'b')
=> "bbcd"
irb(main):005:0> foo.gsub!(/a/, 'b')
=> nil
```

This interlude barely scratches the surface of regular expressions—they're tremendously useful. I'll certainly explain the specific regexes used in the scripts in this book, but there's a lot more to learn about them. If you want to explore regular expressions further, an excellent resource is Jeffrey Friedl's *Mastering Regular Expressions* (O'Reilly, 2006) and its companion website, http://regex.info. This is the definitive text on the subject of regular expressions. It has a slight Perl bias, although its respect for Ruby seems to increase with every new edition. Since the implementation of regular expressions in many languages (including Ruby) is inspired by Perl, the Perl-specific content is easily transferable to Ruby, largely because the two languages' treatment of regular expressions is so similar in the first place.

How does all this relate to our script, `dos2unix.rb`? The \r String stands for the carriage return character—the one used on older Macintosh systems to indicate a line break. The \n String is the newline character, which is used on Unix-like systems and after a carriage return on Windows systems to indicate a line break. This substitution finds all occurrences of a carriage return, as well as any optional newlines that follow it, and replaces them with a single newline.

Running the Script

Execute this as `ruby -w dos2unix.rb file_to_modify`.

The Results

When I look at my sample file extras/DOS_file.txt in my text editor of choice (vim), it looks like this:

```
I am a DOS file.^MI am a DOS file.
```

The ^M is how vim displays a \r character on my system. After running the script with ruby -w dos2unix.rb extras/DOS_file.txt, the results are

```
I am a DOS file.
I am a DOS file.
```

Hacking the Script

What if you want to convert to one of the other line break formats? To convert a file to Windows EOL format, you can replace the line at ❸ in dos2unix.rb with the following line, which essentially means *Replace all occurrences of either a carriage return or a newline with a carriage return followed by a new line.*

```
contents.gsub!(/(\r|\n)/, "\r\n")
```

For a nostalgic Mac that wants to go back to its pre–OS X line breaks, you can convert to the old Apple format by replacing the line at ❸ with this line; this will replace all optional carriage returns followed by a mandatory new-line with just a carriage return.

```
contents.gsub!(/\r?\n/, "\r")
```

The parentheses in a regex are similar to the parentheses in Ruby—they indicate a grouping that should be considered a single entity. The *pipe* character (also called the *vertical bar*) in a regex indicates a choice between what is on either side of it.

NOTE *Subexpressions that are grouped together by parentheses within a regular expression are also captured into specific variables, depending on the programming language's implementation of regular expressions. You can read more in Friedl's book if this topic interests you.*

You can also accomplish a DOS-to-Unix EOL conversion with a one-liner:

```
ruby -pi -e 'gsub(/\r\n?/, "\n")' some_file
```

Sometimes a quick-and-dirty solution is all you need. If you're curious about the implementation of this one-liner, you can consult the Ruby man page (man ruby) for more about the -p flag (which provides a shortcut for dealing with the lines of a file), the -i flag (which specifies in-place editing of a file), and the -e flag (which specifies that a command should be executed).

#10 Showing Line Numbers (line_num.rb)

Another useful trick when dealing with text files is the ability to automatically add line numbers to them. Here's a script that does just that.

The Code

```
#!/usr/bin/env ruby
# line_num.rb
```
❶
```
def get_lines(filename)
  return File.open(filename, 'r').readlines
end
```

sprintf Formats

❷
```
def get_format(lines)
  return "%0#{lines.size.to_s.size}d"
end
```

The each_with_index and sprintf Methods

❸
❹
❺
❻
```
def get_output(lines)
  format = get_format(lines)
  output = ''
  lines.each_with_index do |line,i|
    output += "#{sprintf(format, i+1)}: #{line}"
  end
  return output
end

print get_output(get_lines(ARGV[0]))
```

How It Works

The get_lines method (❶) should look familiar at this point, since we've covered some very similar methods earlier in the book. This method returns an Array of lines based on the contents of an input filename. The get_format method (❷), on the other hand, behaves a bit differently. It returns a single String with the form "%0xd", where x is the number of characters taken up by the String representation of the number of members of the lines Array. Let's explore the methods a bit in irb:

```
irb(main):001:0> def get_format(lines)
irb(main):002:1> return "%0#{lines.size.to_s.size}d"
irb(main):003:1> end
=> nil
irb(main):004:0> has10items = [0, 1, 2, 3, 4, 5, 6, 7, 8, 9]
=> [0, 1, 2, 3, 4, 5, 6, 7, 8, 9]
irb(main):005:0> get_format(has10items)
=> "%02d"
irb(main):006:0> has100items = has10items * 10
=> [0, 1, 2, 3, 4, 5, 6, 7, 8, 9, 0, 1, 2, 3, 4, 5, 6, 7, 8, 9, 0, 1, 2, 3, 4,
5, 6, 7, 8, 9, 0, 1, 2, 3, 4, 5, 6, 7, 8, 9, 0, 1, 2, 3, 4, 5, 6, 7, 8, 9, 0,
1, 2, 3, 4, 5, 6, 7, 8, 9, 0, 1, 2, 3, 4, 5, 6, 7, 8, 9, 0, 1, 2, 3, 4, 5, 6,
```

Multiplying Arrays

```
7, 8, 9, 0, 1, 2, 3, 4, 5, 6, 7, 8, 9, 0, 1, 2, 3, 4, 5, 6, 7, 8, 9]
irb(main):007:0> get_format(has100items)
=> "%03d"
```

You can see that the numeral part of the format changes; it is always equal to the digits taken up by the size of the Array. Incidentally, you can also see how the Array class implements multiplication. One way would have been to multiply each member of the Array by the operand outside of the Array, but that would only work when each member of the Array knows how to be multiplied by something. Instead, the Array just duplicates itself as many times as the value of the operand. If you multiply an Array by one, you should get an equivalent Array.

```
irb(main):008:0> has10items * 1
=> [0, 1, 2, 3, 4, 5, 6, 7, 8, 9]
irb(main):009:0 (has10items * 1) == has10items
=> true
```

We see that we do.

The get_output method (❸) starts by establishing the necessary format and setting a variable called output to the empty String. You can guess that we'll be concatenating other Strings onto it.

We do that at ❺ with a new Array method called each_with_index. This method is very similar to the each method that we've already seen, except that it also gives us the appropriate index number. We'll call the given element of lines by the name line, and we'll refer to the index number as the letter i. We then use a new method called sprintf that formats data into Strings (❻). It takes two arguments: the first is the format to use, and the second is the data to be formatted. We want to format the index number i using the output of the get_format method.[2] The purpose of this operation is to calculate the number of digits needed for the maximum line number we'll be displaying (the width), and format each line number according to that width. This formatting ensures a prettier output.

Each line of our output consists of sprintf's output, a colon, a space, and the original line. All of this happens with the first argument on the command line.

Running the Script

You can run with ruby -w line_num.rb *some_file*, replacing *some_file* with the file to which you want to add line numbers.

The Results

```
$ ruby -w line_num.rb line_num.rb
01: #!/usr/bin/env ruby
02: # line_num.rb
```

---

[2] Actually, we format the value of $i + 1$; we want to call the first line number one, but the index value is zero, because computers start counting with zero.

```
03:
04: def get_lines(filename)
05:    return File.open(filename, 'r').readlines
06: end
07:
08: def get_format(lines)
09:    return "%0#{lines.size.to_s.size}d"
10: end
11:
12: def get_output(lines)
13:    format = get_format(lines)
14:    output = ''
15:    lines.each_with_index do |line,i|
16:      output += "#{sprintf(format, i+1)}: #{line}"
17:    end
18:    return output
19: end
20:
21: print get_output(get_lines(ARGV[0]))
```

If your text file has one 100 or more lines, the pre-colon portion of this output will automatically add as many characters as needed to accommodate its new requirements. That's all there is to it.

#11 Wrapping Lines of Text (softwrap.rb)

Sometimes you may have a text file that you want to perform whitespace compression on, such as converting all repeated spaces into a single space. The script below assumes that all double line breaks should be preserved and that all single line breaks should be converted into spaces. Each group of repeated spaces should also be converted into a single space. Let's dive right in.

The Code

```
#!/usr/bin/env ruby
# softwrap.rb

=begin rdoc
"Softwrap" a filename argument, preserving "\n\n"
between paragraphs but compressing "\n" and other
whitespace within each paragraph into a single space.
=end
❶ def softwrap(filename)
❷   File.open(filename, 'r').readlines.inject('') do |output,line|
❸     output += softwrap_line(line)
❽   end.gsub(/\t+/, ' ').gsub(/ +/, ' ')
end # softwrap
```

The `inject` Method

```
=begin rdoc
Return "\n\n" if the <b>String</b> argument has no length after being
chomped (signifying that it was a blank line separating paragraphs),
otherwise return the chomped line with a trailing space for padding.
=end
❹ def softwrap_line(line)
❺   return "\n\n" if line == "\n"
❻   return line.chomp + ' '
    end # softwrap_line

❼ puts softwrap(ARGV[0])
```

We define a softwrap method (❶) that takes a filename argument and
then call softwrap on the first command-line argument to the script. The
script then calls the readlines method upon the opening of a file, as we've
done many times already. Usually, as in the previous script, we would assign
that result into an Array of lines. This time, we call a new method called
inject that you can see takes an argument (the empty String, in our example)
and a block; we define two variables within the block in the process (❷).

In our example, we're calling those two variables output and line. The
name line is familiar enough. The name output is apt, as the inject method
assumes that the first block-level variable should start with the value of the
argument to inject that preceded the block—the empty String, in this case.
The inject method is remarkable in that modifications of the output variable
persist from each iteration to the next. At ❸ we append softwrap_line(line)
onto output each time through the iterations within inject, and the appends
are remembered each time. The inject method is very useful for any sort of
appending or successive operations. Let's look at how it operates on some
numbers in irb.

```
irb(main):001:0> nums = [1, 2, 3, 4]
=> [1, 2, 3, 4]
irb(main):002:0> nums.inject(0) { |sum,number| sum += number }
=> 10
irb(main):003:0> nums.inject(0) { |product,number| product *= number }
=> 0
irb(main):004:0> nums.inject(1) { |product,number| product *= number }
=> 24
```

On line one we define a variable that holds the digits from one to four.
One operation that inject seems well suited for is adding a list of numbers;
we do that on line two. The inject method can handle any operation, though,
so let's try multiplication on line three. When we do this, we get a result of
zero. The reason is that our initial value for product is zero, so any multiplication after that will get us nowhere. On line four, we set the initial value to
one, which is more appropriate for multiplication, and we get a result that
makes sense.

The inject method is your first real taste of *functional programming*, a style
of programming in which operations are treated as mathematical functions
and side effects are minimized. We'll see much more of inject and similar

methods in later chapters. For now, all we need to concern ourselves with is the fact that it collects each line, passes line through the softwrap_line function, and then appends the result onto output.

NOTE   *Remember that* side effects *are persistent changes made to something (anything) apart from the value returned. In Ruby, methods that have side effects generally end with an exclamation mark, as we've seen already. Methods with no side effects return some value that you requested, but leave the object on which the method was called in the same state it was in before you called the method.*

What does softwrap_line do? The name suggests that it performs the soft-wrapping operation (however we are about to define it) on one line at a time.

The method definition starts at ❹, where it takes in a line. At ❺, we return right away if our new line variable is only a carriage return, since this would indicate a real break that we want to preserve. In all other cases, we return the chomped line plus a space character (❻), which is how this script implements the actual wrapping. We do this softwrap_line operation on every line, appending it onto the inject's output variable at ❸ as described earlier. Our block for inject is of the do/end variety, rather than one that uses the brace characters.

We see something new at ❽—a method called on the keyword end.[3] There's no reason we shouldn't see this, though. Everything in Ruby is a object, and the the result of our inject method is whatever has accumulated into its output variable. In our script, it's a String, so the value of our inject block can respond to any String methods, such as gsub.

The first gsub at ❽ searches for any grouping of tab characters (represented within the regular expression as "\t") and replaces the set of them with a space. The plus sign within the regular expression is similar to the question mark we've seen before, except that instead of meaning *Zero or more of the preceding thing* it means *One or more of the preceding thing*. This regular expression replaces one tab with one space, three tabs with one space, and so on. Let's try something similar in irb. I'll use letters rather than tabs in the irb example because they'll be easy to read in a printed book. The question mark was just for a review and to show the difference between it and the plus sign within a regular expression.

The + sign in Regular Expressions

```
irb(main):001:0> s = 'abcde'
=> "abcde"
irb(main):002:0> s.gsub(/ab+/, 'ba')
=> "bacde"
irb(main):003:0> s.gsub(/abb+/, 'ba')
=> "abcde"
irb(main):004:0> s.gsub(/abb?/, 'ba')
=> "bacde"
```

So we replace tabs (if there are any) with a space. The output of the first gsub is also a String, so it can respond to any String methods, such as another gsub. This time we want to replace any occurrences of one or more spaces

---

[3] More precisely, the method is being called on the result of the code concluded by end.

with a single space—basically just compressing the whitespace. The last line of the script at ❼ shows that we do all of this on the first `filename` argument to the script.

Running the Script

This script is run with `ruby -w softwrap.rb some_file`, where *some_file* is the file whose whitespace will be compressed. Note that this script does not modify the original file, but rather outputs the changed version, just like a non-destructive method in Ruby.

The Results

Here's the result of calling this script on itself:

```
$ ruby -w softwrap.rb softwrap.rb
#!/usr/bin/env ruby # softwrap.rb

=begin rdoc "Softwrap" a filename argument, preserving "\n\n" between
paragraphs but compressing "\n" and other whitespace within each paragraph
into a single space. =end def softwrap(filename) File.open(filename,
'r').readlines.inject('') do |output,line| output += softwrap_line(line)
end.gsub(/\t+/, ' ').gsub(/ +/, ' ') end # softwrap

=begin rdoc Return "\n\n" if the <b>String</b> argument has no length after
being chomped (signifying that it was a blank line separating paragraphs),
otherwise return the chomped line with a trailing space for padding. =end def
softwrap_line(line) return "\n\n" if line == "\n" return line.chomp + ' ' end
# softwrap_line

puts softwrap(ARGV[0])
```

Hacking the Script

The successive gsub calls on line ❽ could have been expressed with a more complex regular expression instead: `gsub(/(\t| )+/, ' ')`.

#12 Counting Words in a File (word_count.rb)

It's often handy to know the number of words in a file. Word count is a standard feature in word-processing programs, but if you're not using a word processor, obtaining a word count might not be so easy. I originally wrote this script when I was working on a project using an XML-based document production system called *DocBook* (http://www.docbook.org) and wanted to have a word count that roughly corresponded to those you could get from a word processor. The Unix command `wc` counts words, but the numbers it reported didn't necessarily match what a word processor might report; the main reason probably had to do with issues like whether words with fewer than a certain number of letters should count as a "word" in the word processor's counter. I knew the approximate ratio of the word processor's word count versus the output of wc (I call this the *fudge factor*), and I could certainly do the math, but I wanted something that would do all of this for me automatically. Let's take a look.

The Code

```ruby
#!/usr/bin/env ruby
# word_count.rb

class String

❶   def num_matches(thing_to_match)
        return self.split(thing_to_match).size - 1
    end # num_matches

end # String

❷ BAR_LENGTH    = 20

    # to match these calculations with the output of some word processors
❸ FUDGE_FACTOR = 0.82

❹ def word_count(files)
    output = ''
    total_word_count = 0
❺   files.each do |filename|
        file_word_count = word_count_for_file(filename)
        output += "#{filename} has #{file_word_count} words.\n"
        total_word_count += file_word_count
    end # each file
❻   return output +
        '-' * BAR_LENGTH + "\n" +
        "Total word count = #{total_word_count}" +
        " (#{(total_word_count * FUDGE_FACTOR)})"
    end # word_count

❼ def word_count_for_file(filename)
    f = File.new(filename, 'r')
    contents = f.read()
    f.close()
    spaces = contents.num_matches(' ')
    breaks = contents.num_matches("\n")
    false_doubles = contents.num_matches(" \n")
    double_spaces = contents.num_matches('  ')
    hyphens = contents.num_matches('-')
    false_doubles += double_spaces + hyphens
    words = spaces + breaks - false_doubles + 1
    return words
end # word_count_for_file

puts word_count(ARGV)
```

Multiplying Strings

How It Works

We start out by adding a new method called num_matches to the String class (❶). It simply returns the number of times the argument appears within the calling String. I also define top-level constants called BAR_LENGTH (❷), which is just for visual formatting, and FUDGE_FACTOR (❸), which I already noted is the ratio between the two different word-counting programs I was working with.

We then define the word_count method (❹), which takes the files argument. You'll notice on the last line of the script that this program takes an arbitrary number of filenames as its argument, which is different from our earlier scripts that would only deal with a single file at a time. The word_count method defines local variables called output and total_word_count, setting them to useful defaults for a String and an Integer, respectively. We then loop through the files (❺), assigning the proper values into file_word_count and output and accumulating each file_word_count into the total_word_count. The output variable now has a description of each file's count. We return that, followed by a line consisting of the hyphen character multiplied by the BAR_LENGTH constant (❻). Multiplication of Strings is very similar to multiplication of Arrays, which we've already seen. We add a String consisting of 20 hyphen characters to the overall expression returned. The returned expression closes with the total multiplied by the FUDGE_FACTOR constant in parentheses.

Before finishing with this script, we need to understand how it calculates the word count for each file. Let's examine the word_count_for_file function (❼). It opens by getting the contents out of the file being worked on. It then uses some quick-and-dirty calls to the num_matches method on the contents variable to get counts for spaces, line breaks, and so on. It then calculates the number of words in the contents String using those rough numbers.

There are more accurate ways to count words in a String, many of which use techniques described in Jeffrey Friedl's *Mastering Regular Expressions*. However, this script is intended for quick, approximate results, given that it uses a fudge factor. This script shows that just adding one new method to an existing class can be very handy even for a short, back-of-the-envelope task. We'll see more of that in later scripts, as well.

Running the Script

You can run this script with ruby -w word_count.rb *some_file*, where *some_file* is the file whose word count you want to compute.

The Results

Here is the result of calling this file on itself:

```
$ ruby -w word_count.rb word_count.rb
word_count.rb has 132 words.
--------------------
Total word count = 132 (108.24)
```

Notice how the script reports both the literal and fudged word counts.

#13 Word Histogram (most_common_words.rb)

And now for something that most word processors don't do: finding the most commonly used words in a document. Like the previous script, it adds an additional "helper" method to an existing built-in class to simplify the job for our new main method. Let's take a look.

The Code

```ruby
#!/usr/bin/env ruby
#most_common_words.rb

class Array
```
The grep Method
```ruby
❶    def count_of(item)
❷      grep(item).size
❸      #inject(0) { |count,each_item| item == each_item ? count+1 : count }
     end

end

❹    def most_common_words(input, limit=25)
       freq = Hash.new()
       sample = input.downcase.split(/\W/)
       sample.uniq.each do |word|
❺        freq[word] = sample.count_of(word) unless word == ''
       end
❻      words = freq.keys.sort_by do |word|
         freq[word]
```
The map Method
```ruby
       end.reverse.map do |word|
❼        "#{word} #{freq[word]}"
       end
❽      return words[0, limit]
     end

❾ puts most_common_words(readlines.to_s).join("\n")
```

How It Works

The new method of Array is called count_of (❶); it takes an argument called item and returns the number of times that item is found within the Array in question. The default implementation of this method (❷) uses an Array method called grep, which takes an argument and returns all elements that match that element. Since we want the count of items matching the condition (and not those items themselves), we call the size method on the return value of grep.

The line at ❸ shows a way to accomplish the same task using the inject method, which we've already covered.

At ❹ we define the most_common_words method; it takes a mandatory input argument and an optional limit argument, which defaults to 25. We define a new Hash variable called freq, which will store the frequency of each word.

We define an Array called sample, which consists of a case-insensitive input, broken at each whitespace portion (the \W in the regular expression means *any whitespace*). We loop through each unique word in the sample, adding its frequency to the freq Hash. I chose to skip the empty string, not counting it as a word (❺).

Once we've constructed the freq Hash, we want to use our limit argument. We loop through the keys of freq (which are the actual words themselves) and sort them by their frequency of appearance (❻). We want to see the most common words, rather than the least common words, so we reverse that sorted list, and map an operation onto it.

The map operation is very common in the world of functional programming. It's often used as an alternative to looping, so in Ruby, we'll often find that we want to use either the each method or the map method for a given task, depending on our needs. Generally, if you want to make destructive changes to a list of items, use each; if you want to make a new list of transformed items, use map. Let's try map in irb. I've been showing you lots of irb examples with digits, so now I'll show you a quick way to create an Array of them. Ruby has a class called *Range*, which indicates the items from a given starting point to a given endpoint. We'll use that class to construct an Array.

Ranges

```
irb(main):001:0> digit_range = 0..9
=> 0..9
irb(main):002:0> digit_range.class
=> Range
irb(main):003:0> digits = digit_range.to_a
=> [0, 1, 2, 3, 4, 5, 6, 7, 8, 9]
irb(main):004:0> digits.map { |num| num + 1 }
=> [1, 2, 3, 4, 5, 6, 7, 8, 9, 10]
irb(main):005:0> digits.map { |num| num + 10 }
=> [10, 11, 12, 13, 14, 15, 16, 17, 18, 19]
irb(main):006:0> digits.map { |num| num * 2 }
=> [0, 2, 4, 6, 8, 10, 12, 14, 16, 18]
irb(main):007:0> digits.map { |num| num ** 2 }
=> [0, 1, 4, 9, 16, 25, 36, 49, 64, 81]
irb(main):008:0> digits
=> [0, 1, 2, 3, 4, 5, 6, 7, 8, 9]
irb(main):009:0> digits.map! { |num| num ** 2 }
=> [0, 1, 4, 9, 16, 25, 36, 49, 64, 81]
irb(main):010:0> digits
=> [0, 1, 4, 9, 16, 25, 36, 49, 64, 81]
```

As you can see, map is very convenient for any sort of transformation of a list of items that can be expressed with a simple description, such as *double all of these things* on line six, or *square all of these things* on line seven. Remember that map is non-destructive (as shown on line eight) unless you call it with the exclamation mark (as shown on lines nine and ten). We'll map an operation onto the words, sorted in reverse order by frequency of appearance in our sample text. The operation to be mapped (❼) is the outputting of a String consisting of the word itself followed by a space character, followed by the frequency of that word.

All of this occurs within the assignment into the words variable on the same line as ❺, so each member of the Array called words is a String that is the result of the ❼ operation. At ❽, we return a subsection of the words Array, starting at the beginning, and limit it to a length equal to the limit argument. Since the output of the most_common_words method is an Array and we want to print it as a String, we do a join with a newline at ❾, making each Array item a separate line.

Running the Script

We call this script with ruby most_common_words.rb filename_to_analyze, calling readlines.to_s on the filename argument, which provides the input to analyze. Let's try it on itself.

The Results

```
$ ruby most_common_words.rb most_common_words.rb
word 9
end 6
freq 5
do 3
sample 3
most_common_words 3
count 3
item 3
0 2
count_of 2
words 2
input 2
def 2
limit 2
each_item 2
split 1
unless 1
1 1
downcase 1
map 1
rb 1
array 1
ruby 1
usr 1
each 1
```

Hacking the Script

Just as an aside, you could also implement count_of using this line:

```
dup.delete_if { |i| i != item }.size || 0
```

#14 Rotating Characters in a String (rotate.rb)

We'll close with a simple program that rotates the order of characters within a String. We'll accomplish this via a method that takes a character (meaning a String of length one) argument. The String to be rotated will try to keep rotating until the character argument appears at index 0. If the character is not found at all, it will return nil.

The Code

```
#!/usr/bin/env ruby
# rotate.rb

class String

❶    def rotate(char)
❷      return nil unless self.match(char)
❸      return self if (self[0] == char[0])
❹      chars = self.split(//)
        return ([chars.pop] + chars).join('').rotate(char)
      end

❻    def rotate!(char)
        replace(rotate(char))
      end

end
```

Recursion

How It Works

This program introduces a concept called *recursion*, which (like map) is used frequently in functional programming, often as an alternative to looping. A *recursive operation* is one that is partly defined in terms of itself. Let's explore the concept in our rotate.rb script.

The definition of the main rotate method that we add to the String object is at ❶. I said earlier that if the character argument (called char) is not found within the main String (here called self), the rotate method will return nil (❷). If char is the initial character within the String, we don't need to do any rotating, so it will return the main String under those conditions (❸). The numeral 0 within braces is not an anonymous Array—it's a method of self that returns the first character of a String. We call that method on both the self String and the single-character String char. When those two Strings are equal, we know that the self String starts with the requested rotation character.

NOTE   *We use an index of zero within the braces to return the first character in the String on line ❸ because Ruby (like many languages) starts counting indexes at zero, not one.*

We know that if we've gotten this far without returning, we have a String that is eligible for rotation (because it contains char), and needs to be rotated to match (because it doesn't start with char). We perform the rotation by defining a new variable called chars (❹), which is an Array of each character within the String. We use the pop method at ❺ to remove the last character from chars, remembering that pop is destructive (despite the lack of an exclamation mark, for historical reasons). The chars Array now contains all the characters except the one that was just popped off. If we add those Arrays together, putting the Array containing the popped character first, we've just created a new Array in which the last member has been moved from the end to the front, shifting all other members back.

We wrap the popped character in brackets so that we can more easily add the two Arrays (the popped off character and the remaining characters, respectively). Since the rotate method will eventually return a String, we join our Array elements with an empty String separator. This produces a String that has been rotated once. Are we done? Not really.

Recursion

The rotation works well, but it might not be enough. What if we need to rotate multiple characters before we find a match? There's an easy way to do that; it's called the rotate method—you know, the method we're still in the process of defining. We can just call rotate on our newly created String.

We already know that our newly created String will pass the test at ❷. We're mainly interested in whether or not it needs further rotation. That's the test at ❸. If only one rotation was needed, this second call to the rotate method will return the newly created String, and since the second call to rotate was within a return call on the line at ❺, the main call to rotate will return that value, as well.

If only one rotation was not enough to find a match, our second call to the rotate method will do the same shifting of characters (starting at ❹) that we just discussed, culminating in yet another call to rotate, this time on a String that has been rotated two characters' worth, and so on.

Each successive time rotate is called, the String to be operated on is one step closer to our desired result. This is very common in recursion, which we will be discussing in greater depth in later chapters. As you can see at ❻, we also define a destructive version called rotate!.

Running the Script

Let's look at some output using irb with irb -r rotate.rb.

The Results

```
$ irb -r rotate.rb
irb(main):001:0> 'I am a String.'.rotate('a')
=> "a String.I am "
irb(main):002:0> 'I am a String.'.rotate('S')
=> "String.I am a "
```

In each case, the String on which rotate is called has its characters shifted until the character asked for is the first character in the String. That's it for this chapter's scripts.

Chapter Recap

What was new in this chapter?

- End-of-line differences among operating systems
- Regular expressions, including the ? counter
- The `sprintf` method
- Multiplication of Arrays
- The `inject` method
- Regular expressions with the + counter
- Objects as the results of blocks
- Calling successive methods on the output of methods ("chaining" methods)
- Using new methods of Open Classes in quick scripts
- Multiplication of Strings
- The `grep` method
- The `map` method
- The Range class
- Recursion

That's quite a bit, including some important new functional concepts like recursion and a few very handy functional methods. You'll need these concepts as we move on. Let's proceed to some more complex treatment of numbers in Chapter 5.

5

NUMBER UTILITIES

Numbers are fundamental for all computers and programming languages, and Ruby is no exception. In this chapter's scripts, we'll deal with useful data that is primarily numeric but is otherwise quite diverse. We'll explore some pure math, following up with recursion, which I introduced in Chapter 4. We'll also do some type conversion, whereby numbers will be represented in different ways that are convenient for human users. We'll also do some unit conversion, specifically monetary units.[1] While doing all of this, we'll also delve further into metaprogramming, Hashes, using external libraries, and two distinct formats for data storage in external files: XML (eXtensible Markup Language) and YAML (YAML Ain't Markup Language). That's a lot of ground to cover, so let's get started.

---

[1] We'll make a temperature converter in Chapter 7, since it depends on concepts we haven't covered yet.

#15 Computing Powers (power_of.rb)

This is the most purely mathematical of this chapter's scripts, and it deals with exponentiation. Before we get too far into the script itself, let's use irb to explore how Ruby handles exponentiation:

Exponentiation

```
irb(main):001:0> 2 ** 2
=> 4
irb(main):002:0> 2 ** 3
=> 8
```

As you can see, the way to express "to the power of" in Ruby is with the double asterisk. Since both the number raised to some power and the power itself are expressions, they can also be more complex, like this:

```
irb(main):003:0> 2 ** (1 + 2)
=> 8
irb(main):004:0> 8 ** (1.0/3.0)
=> 2.0
```

You can raise a number (called the *base*) to a given exponent easily with the ** operator. As you can see in line four in the above code, when you want to reverse a traditional exponentiation, you can use a reciprocal power.

NOTE   *We use floating-point numbers for the exponent in* ❶, *because we don't want our expression to be rounded down to zero.*

If you have the base and the exponent, you can find the missing result. If you have the result of the exponentiation and the exponent, you can undo your operation to find the base by using the reciprocal of the exponent. What if you know the base and the result, and want to find the exponent? That's what this script is for. Let's take a look.

The Code

```
#!/usr/bin/env ruby
# power_of.rb

class Integer

=begin rdoc
Add a simple <b>Integer</b>-only method that reports the
exponent to which the base must be raised to get self.
=end
    def power_of(base)
        # return nil for inapplicable situations
        return nil   unless base.is_a?(Integer)
        return nil   if (base.zero? and not [0,1].include?(self))

        # deal with odd but reasonable
        # numeric situations
```

Recursion   ❶

The is_a?
Method   ❷

```
❸      return 1      if base == self
❹      return 0      if self == 1
❺      return false if base == 1
❻      return false if base.abs > self.abs

❼      exponent = (self/base).power_of(base)
❽      return exponent ? exponent + 1 : exponent
     end

   end
```

The abs Method ❻

How It Works

We want this operation to be a method that can be called on any Integer, so we take advantage of Ruby's open classes and simply add a new method. We have the standard boilerplate and RDoc up to the method definition at ❶, which shows that it takes an argument called base. The lines up to and including ❷ cause our power_of method to exit early under conditions that are not appropriate for it to do its job. We return the nil value when asked to find a power in relation to a base that isn't even an Integer, because that question is meaningless. We also return nil when the base is zero and the result is neither zero nor one, because zero raised to any power will always be either zero or one, making that question also meaningless.

There will certainly be other situations where our response is meaningful. We return 1 at ❸ if the base and the result of the exponentiation (self) are the same value, because any number to the power of one will be itself. We return 0 at ❹ if self is one, because any number raised to the zero power will equal one. This is confusing for many people. How can something multiplied by itself zero times be anything?

The answer lies in what's called the *multiplicative identity*, which is how mathematicians describe the fact that any number times one equals one times that number as well as that number itself. You can always assume with any standard multiplication that there could be any number of "times one" additions to your multiplication, and it won't matter. We can also see this in irb:

```
irb(main):005:0> (42 * 1) == (1 * 42)
=> true
irb(main):006:0> (1 * 42) == (42 * 1)
=> true
irb(main):007:0> (42 * 1) == 42
=> true
irb(main):008:0> (1 * 42) == 42
=> true
```

Since you can always assume a "times one" for anything multiplied by itself twice, or by itself once, you can similarly assume it for something multiplied by itself zero times, which is all raising something to the zero power means. Therefore, raising something to the zero power will result in a value of one.

At ❺, we return `false` if the base is one. This is because one can never be raised to a power that will result in a value other than one. How do we know that our result isn't one? Because we would have already returned a zero at ❹ if `self` was one. At ❻, we also return `false` if the absolute value of the `base` (acquired through calling `base.abs`) is greater than the absolute value of `self`. We do this because you can't raise a base to an Integer power and get a result with a smaller absolute value than your original base.

Everything from ❶ to ❻ deals with the odd cases—either meaningless situations or situations that let us know we're finished, otherwise known as *exit conditions*. What happens next? If a given number is a power of a given base, it means that that number divided by the base is also a power of the base, but the exponent will be one lower. Let's demonstrate in irb.

```
irb(main):009:0> 3 ** 3
=> 27
irb(main):010:0> 3 ** 2
=> 9
irb(main):011:0> 27 == 9 * 3
=> true
```

Three to the third power is 27, three to the second power is nine, and 27 is equal to nine times three. If we're trying to find an exponent and none of our base cases apply, we can simply divide `self` by the base, try to get the power of the new divided value relative to the same base, and remember to add one to our new result if it turns out to be an Integer.

That's exactly what we do at ❼ and ❽. We define a new variable called `exponent`, which is the result of calling the `power_of` method on `self` divided by `base`. The `exponent` variable will either be `nil`, `false`, or an Integer. How do we know this? Because we return either `nil` up to ❷, `false` at ❺ or ❻, or an Integer.

All Integers have true Boolean values, so we can test with our standard ternary operator, as we do at ❽. If `exponent` evaluates to `true`, it's an Integer (because both `nil` and `false` would evaluate to `false` in the Boolean ternary operation). We therefore `return` it, remembering to add one, because we've already divided by the `base` once. If `exponent` evaluates to `false`, we want to simply `return` that value: either `false` or `nil`.

What happens in our new call to `power_of` on `self` divided by the base at ❼? It goes through all the same tests from ❶ to ❻, and if none of those apply, it divides the new value of `self` by the `base` again, remembering to add yet another one to the eventual result. All of this happens inside each iteration of the `power_of` method—the first version of it up at the top level doesn't need to know or care about how many other iterations of `power_of` end up being called. This is what recursion is all about.

Running the Script

You can try out this script in irb by requiring it at the command line with `irb -r power_of.rb` or by entering `require 'power_of.rb'` once you're in irb. Remember that this script can only handle Integers, so `2.power_of(4)` will return `false`, rather than `0.5`.

The Results

Here is a sample irb session with some output.

```
$ irb -r power_of.rb
irb(main):001:0> 1.power_of(1)
=> 1
irb(main):002:0> 1.power_of(2)
=> 0
irb(main):003:0> 4.power_of(2)
=> 2
irb(main):004:0> 2.power_of(4)
-> false
```

#16 Adding Commas to Numbers (commify.rb)

A standard way of formatting numbers is to present them with commas (or some other delimiter) separating each group of thousands. Our next script does that by adding a method called commify to all numbers. You might think that we could do this by opening the Integer class and adding a new method to it, as we did in power_of.rb. This is certainly a reasonable approach, except that we may want to use commify on floating-point numbers as well. What's the solution?

Inheritance

The answer deals with an object-oriented concept called *inheritance*. We discussed this earlier in Chapter 3 when we added methods to the Object class. Inheritance is what allows all other classes to use methods of the Object class, because these other classes *inherit* from Object. Inheritance is a factor in our commify script as well. Let's examine the inheritance hierarchy of some number classes in irb.

The ancestors Method

```
irb(main):001:0> Integer.ancestors
=> [Integer, Precision, Numeric, Comparable, Object, Kernel]
irb(main):002:0> Float.ancestors
=> [Float, Precision, Numeric, Comparable, Object, Kernel]
irb(main):003:0>
```

We've used a method called ancestors that can be called not on an instance of a class, but on the class itself. It returns an Array of all of the ancestors of the class on which it is called (by *ancestors* I simply mean the classes from which it inherits). You may find it useful to consider inheritance through a biological metaphor, in which each class is a species and the ancestor classes are that species' ancestor species. We can see that both the Integer class and the Float class inherit directly from something called *Precision*.

Precision must be a class—some kind of number, right? Not exactly. Let's continue in irb.

```
irb(main):003:0> Integer.class
=> Class
irb(main):004:0> Float.class
=> Class
irb(main):005:0> Precision.class
=> Module
```

We see that Integer is a *class*, something that can be instantiated. So is Float. That's no surprise. 5 is an Integer, and 3.14 is a Float. But Precision is something called a Module, not a Class at all. What are Modules for?

Modules

Let's continue with our biological metaphor. Both humans and bats are mammals, so if we called `Human.ancestors` and `Bat.ancestors`, we would have significant overlap—humans and bats have shared ancestors, specifically earlier mammals. If we called `Bird.ancestors`, there would be less overlap with either of the others, because birds are not mammals. However, bats and most birds can fly, which you could think of as a method, in object-oriented terms. We could define `Bat.fly` and `Bird.fly` separately, but there is another option available to us.

We can thus define the ability to fly (along with related characteristics and behaviors) and add that ability to existing classes. That process is called *mixing in*, and it's how Ruby deals with the problem of assigning the same methods to different classes with distinct ancestor classes, like our Bat and Bird example.

We do this by defining the ability to fly as a module, perhaps called Flyable. Modules are similar to classes, except that they don't get instantiated. We'll write our own modules later in Chapter 10. For now, keep in mind that the Precision module adds behavior to both Integer and Float, just like our hypothetical Flyable. Flyable grants the ability to fly to those organisms it's mixed into, and Precision grants the ability to do precise calculations to those numbers it's mixed into.

Modules are open, just like classes, so we can add new behavior to the Precision module, just as we did earlier to the Object class. Let's take a look at the `commify.rb` script.

The Code

Modules

```
module Precision

❶   # What character should be displayed at each breakpoint?
    COMMIFY_DELIMITER = ','

    # What should the decimal point character be?
    COMMIFY_DECIMAL = '.'
```

```ruby
    # What power of 10 defines each breakpoint?
    COMMIFY_BREAKPOINT = 3

    # Should an explicit '0' be shown in the 100ths place,
    # such as for currency?
    COMMIFY_PAD_100THS = true

  =begin rdoc
  This method returns a <b>String</b> representing the numeric value of
  self, with delimiters at every digit breakpoint. 4 Optional arguments:

  1. delimiter (<b>String</b>): defaults to a comma
  2. breakpoint (<b>Integer</b>): defaults to 3, showing every multiple of 1000
  3. decimal_pt (<b>String</b>): defaults to '.'
  4. show_hundredths (<b>Boolean</b>): whether an explicit '0' should be shown
  in the hundredths place, defaulting to <b>true</b>.
  =end
```
```ruby
  def commify(args = {})

    args[:delimiter]        ||= COMMIFY_DELIMITER
    args[:breakpoint]       ||= COMMIFY_BREAKPOINT
    args[:decimal_pt]       ||= COMMIFY_DECIMAL
    args[:show_hundredths]  ||= COMMIFY_PAD_100THS

    int_as_string, float_as_string = to_s.split('.')

    int_out   = format_int(
      int_as_string,
      args[:breakpoint],
      args[:delimiter]
    )

    float_out = format_float(
      float_as_string,
      args[:decimal_pt],
      args[:show_hundredths]
    )

    return int_out + float_out
  end

  private
```
```ruby
  =begin rdoc
  Return a <b>String</b> representing the properly-formatted
  <b>Integer</b> portion of self.
  =end
  def format_int(int_as_string, breakpoint, delimiter)
    reversed_groups = int_as_string.reverse.split(/(\d{#{breakpoint}})/)
    reversed_digits = reversed_groups.grep(/\d+/)
    digit_groups    = reversed_digits.reverse.map { |unit| unit.reverse }
    return digit_groups.join(delimiter)
  end
```

```
      =begin rdoc
      Return a <b>String</b> representing the properly-formatted
      floating-point portion of self.
      =end
❼     def format_float(float_as_string, decimal_pt, show_hundredths)
        return ''  unless float_as_string
        output = decimal_pt + float_as_string
❽       return output unless show_hundredths
❾       output += '0' if (float_as_string.size == 1)
        return output
      end

    end
```

How It Works

Starting at ❶, we define some useful constants, just like we do for a class. Each definition is preceded by some comments explaining what the constant is for. I mentioned that the `commify` method will insert commas at every grouping of a thousand. This is customary in the United States, but many other countries use a period in place of a comma and use a comma to separate units from floating-point portions (for which the United States uses a period). These constants are preset for the US notation that is useful for me, since I live here, but you can easily customize them to match what's appropriate for your home country.

After some RDoc that explains the input parameters in the form of a single Hash, at ❷ we get to the definition of the `commify` method, our only public method. It accepts a Hash argument called `args` to override the default configuration constants, as shown at ❸. Note that the `||=` operation means that if `args` asks for an override (meaning it has a value in itself for the appropriate Symbol, such as `:delimiter` for the delimiter), we use what's in `args`. Otherwise, we fall back to the Module's appropriate constant. At ❹, we split the Integer and Float portions of `self`, although keep in mind that they are both instances of the String class, despite the fact that they represent numbers. Ruby allows us to assign into two different variable names at a time, as we do here.

NOTE *Symbols make great Hash keys, and that's a convention you'll see a great deal in both my scripts and in the whole Ruby community. You'd have a terrible time trying to do anything in Rails without respecting this convention. Symbols work particularly well for this job because they can be used as names or labels for things, and they take up an extremely small amount of memory.[2]*

We then define a variable called `int_out` and give it the value of a method called `format_int`. We do the same for `float_out`, and finally return the concatenation of those two Strings at ❺. You can see that the real work occurs within the formatting methods (`format_int` and `format_float`), both of which are private.

---

[2] My technical reviewer, Pat Eyler, wisely asked me to stress that the *reason* Symbols take up so little space is because each Symbol only takes up space once, and all subsequent instances merely refer to that same memory space again, instead of duplicating it, as would happen with a String or other type of object.

The format_int Method

The format_int method at ❻ is the more conceptually complicated of the two methods. Let's open irb again and step through this method's operations. First, let's define some variables representing the inputs to the method.

```
irb(main):001:0> int_as_string = '186282'
=> "186282"
irb(main):002:0> breakpoint = 3
=> 3
irb(main):003:0> delimiter = ','
=> ","
```

Next, let's split our String at the appropriate breakpoints, using a regular expression representing any group of digits that is the appropriate length. The notation {x} within a regular expression means *X instances of whatever is to the left*, so a{3} means *Three instances of the letter* a. We also use string interpolation so that we can use our breakpoint argument for the number of digits to break on. We want to go from right to left, so we'll use the reverse method prior to breaking up the String into an Array.

```
irb(main):004:0> reversed_groups = int_as_string.reverse.split(/(\d{#{breakpoint}})/)
=> ["", "282", "", "681"]
```

Then we want to extract only those Array members that are genuine number groups, which we can do easily enough with another regular expression /\d+/ (meaning *Consisting of one or more digits and nothing else*) and the grep method, which finds all members of an Array that match the regex argument that grep takes.

```
irb(main):005:0> reversed_digits = reversed_groups.grep(/\d+/)
=> ["282", "681"]
```

What else is wrong with our content at this point? Not only are the number groups in the wrong order, but the numbers within each group are also reversed. This is because we reversed the entire String before doing our split. Now we want to get everything in the right order. We can just reverse our Array, right?

```
irb(main):006:0> reversed_digits.reverse
=> ["681", "282"]
```

This won't work. It puts the groups in the right order, but the digits within each group are still reversed. We can use the map method to reverse each member of the Array instead.

```
irb(main):007:0> reversed_digits.map { |unit| unit.reverse }
=> ["282", "186"]
```

Oops. Now the digits within each set of three numbers are in the right order, but the groups are in the wrong order. We could define yet another variable like `reversed_digits` in a two-step operation, but why not take advantage of Ruby's ability to chain methods?

```
irb(main):008:0> digit_groups    = reversed_digits.reverse.map { |unit| unit.reverse }
=> ["186", "282"]
```

Now our digits groups are in the right order and have the correct internal ordering, as well.

Note that the two different calls to the `reverse` method in the irb example are completely different. One is a call to the Array method `reverse` on `reversed_digits` and the other is a call to the String method `reverse` on each digit group that we call `unit` within the `map` operation.

We still have an Array, and we want a String. This calls for a `join`, using the delimiter.

```
irb(main):009:0> digit_groups.join(delimiter)
=> "186,282"
```

Our `format_int` method now returns a String that is an altered version of our `int_as_string` argument. We break up `int_as_string` at the right point (breakpoint), insert the `delimiter` between our groups of digits, and make sure that everything stays in the right order. That's it for the integer component.

The format_float Method

We also want to be able to format floating-point portions of numbers, which we do with the `format_float` method at ❼. If there is no floating-point portion, it returns an empty String right away. Otherwise, it creates a new variable called `output` consisting of the `decimal_pt` argument concatenated with the `float_as_string` argument—remember that they're both Strings, so the plus sign means concatenation. If the configuration options are such that the hundredths place is not mandatory (you can tell from the `show_hundredths` argument), we can simply return the `output` variable at ❽. If we need to show the hundredths place and the floating-point portion is only a single character wide, we need to concatenate the String `'0'` onto the end of the output at ❾. Otherwise, we can simply return the `output` variable.

Type Testing

You'll remember that in `power.rb`, we had an early exit condition based on whether or not the base argument was an Integer at all. You'll also notice that in this script we don't test any of the numbers to find out whether or not they're real numbers. Why is that? The reason is that our new methods will be included in the Precision module, which is only mixed in to classes that represent some sort of number, like Integer and Float. Therefore, checks for numeric type are not necessary.

Running the Script

Let's try this out with a test script. Here are the contents of tests/test_commify.rb, which we'll run in the same directory as commify.rb with the command ruby -w tests/test_commify.rb 186282.437 at the shell.

```ruby
#!/usr/bin/env ruby
# test_commify.rb

require 'commify'

puts ARGV[0].to_f.commify()
alt_args = {
    :breakpoint => 2,
    :decimal_pt => 'dp',
    :show_hundredths => false
}
puts ARGV[0].to_f.commify(alt_args)
```

We call the commify method on the first argument after the script name, which in our case is the floating-point number 186282.437. First, we call it with the default parameters with regard to the delimeter character, breakpoint size, and so on. Then we call it with some modified configuration parameters, just to see how they work.

The Results

Here's the output I got:

```
186,282.437
18,62,82dp437
```

Yours should look the same. That's it for this script.

#17 Roman Numerals (roman_numeral.rb)

In the previous script, you learned how to change the representation of a number as a String so that it had commas (or some other desired delimiting character) in appropriate places for easier readability. One of the most traditional ways to represent a number as a String is as a Roman numeral. This script adds a new method to all Integers called to_roman. Let's see it in action in irb.

```
$ irb -r roman_numeral.rb
irb(main):001:0> 42.to_roman
=> "XLII"
irb(main):002:0> 1.to_roman
=> "I"
```

```
irb(main):003:0> 5.to_roman
=> "V"
irb(main):004:0> digits = (0..9).to_a
=> [0, 1, 2, 3, 4, 5, 6, 7, 8, 9]
irb(main):005:0> digits.map { |d| d.to_roman }
=> ["", "I", "II", "III", "IV", "V", "VI", "VII", "VIII", "IX"]
```

If you remember your Roman numerals, you will see that to_roman follows your expectations. It returns the empty string for zero and uses the *subtractive* approach of reporting four as *IV*, using a lower-value letter to the left of a higher-value letter to indicate subtraction. Let's look at the source code to see how it works.

The Code

```
class Integer

    # Base conversion Hash
❶   ARABIC_TO_ROMAN = {
        1000 => 'M',
         500 => 'D',
         100 => 'C',
          50 => 'L',
          10 => 'X',
           5 => 'V',
           1 => 'I',
           0 => '',
    }

    # Represent 4 as 'IV', rather than 'IIII'?
    SUBTRACTIVE_TO_ROMAN = {
        900 => 'CM',
        400 => 'CD',
         90 => 'XC',
         40 => 'XL',
          9 => 'IX',
          4 => 'IV',
    }

    # Use SUBTRACTIVE_TO_ROMAN Hash?
    SUBTRACTIVE = true

❷   def to_roman()
        @@roman_of ||= create_roman_of()
❸       return ''    unless (self > 0)
❹       return to_s if self > maximum_representable()
❺       base = @@roman_of.keys.sort.reverse.detect { |k| k <= self }
❻       return '' unless (base and base > 0)
❼       return (@@roman_of[base] * round_to_base(base)) + (self % base).to_roman()
    end

    private
```

Class Variables (❷)

The detect Method (❺ ❻)

```
=begin rdoc
Use constants to create a <b>Hash</b> of appropriate roman numeral values.
=end
```
❽
```
   def create_roman_of()
      return ARABIC_TO_ROMAN unless SUBTRACTIVE
      ARABIC_TO_ROMAN.merge(SUBTRACTIVE_TO_ROMAN)
   end
```

**The merge
Method**

```
=begin rdoc
What is the largest number that this method can reasonably represent?
=end
```
❾
```
   def maximum_representable()
      (@@roman_of.keys.max * 5) - 1
   end
```

❿
```
   def round_to_base(base)
      (self - (self % base)) / base
   end

end
```

How It Works

Since we only need to give Integers the ability to report their Roman numeral representation, we'll open up the Integer class and give it this new method. After defining some constants at ❶, let's skip down to ❷, where we define the public method to_roman that we've seen used in irb. In it, we define something called @@roman_of, and use the ||= operator to set its value to that of the output of a method called create_roman_of, unless @@roman_of already evaluates to true. Why does it have two @ signs at the front? We've already seen instance variables with a single @ sign and constants that must begin with an uppercase letter (and traditionally are entirely uppercase), but this is something new called a *class variable*.

Class Variables

Class variables are shared among every instance of a class but are able to change value. Let's verify in irb that several different instances of any given class variable have the same value.

```
irb(main):001:0> class String
irb(main):002:1> @@class_var = "I'm a Class Variable."
irb(main):003:1> def cv
irb(main):004:2> @@class_var
irb(main):005:2> end
irb(main):006:1> end
=> nil
irb(main):007:0> ''.cv
=> "I'm a Class Variable."
irb(main):008:0> 'Some other String'.cv
=> "I'm a Class Variable."
irb(main):009:0> 'Yet another String.'.cv
=> "I'm a Class Variable."
```

We define a new class variable called @@class_var for all Strings and also give all strings a new method called cv that returns @@class_var. We find that it has the same value for all Strings, including Strings that did not yet exist when we defined @@class_var.

We have a class variable called @@roman_of. What is it? To answer that, we need to look inside the private method create_roman_of at ❽. It returns a constant called ARABIC_TO_ROMAN, unless some other constant called SUBTRACTIVE is true. We can see from our constant definition section (❶) that we have set SUBTRACTIVE to true, so create_roman_of will not return ARABIC_TO_ROMAN with our current configuration settings. Instead, it will return the result of calling the method merge on ARABIC_TO_ROMAN, with SUBTRACTIVE_TO_ROMAN as its single argument.

Hash.merge

At this point we need to learn what ARABIC_TO_ROMAN is so we know what happens when merge is called on it. We can see from ❶ that both ARABIC_TO_ROMAN and SUBTRACTIVE_TO_ROMAN are Hashes. Their keys are Arabic numerals, and each key's value is the representation of the key as a Roman numeral. This script can only represent Roman numerals up to 4,999, so we could simply define a single Hash of ALL_ARABICS_TO_ROMAN with a key for every value from one to 4,999 and be done with it.

That would work, but it would be terribly inelegant. What we've done instead is define base cases from which we will extrapolate all cases between zero and 4,999. We also separate out cases of subtractive representation (such as *IV* for four) into a separate Hash, allowing us to easily turn that feature on or off, as we do with the SUBTRACTIVE constant and the create_roman_of method, which uses the merge method of Hashes. This merge method allows a Hash to incorporate the information from a second Hash into itself. Let's explore that in irb.

```
irb(main):001:0> hash1 = { 'key1' => 'value1', 'key2' => 'value2' }
=> {"key1"=>"value1", "key2"=>"value2"}
irb(main):002:0> hash2 = { 'key3' => 'value3', 'key4' => 'value4' }
=> {"key3"=>"value3", "key4"=>"value4"}
irb(main):003:0> hash1
=> {"key1"=>"value1", "key2"=>"value2"}
irb(main):004:0> hash2
=> {"key3"=>"value3", "key4"=>"value4"}
irb(main):005:0> hash1.merge(hash2)
=> {"key1"=>"value1", "key2"=>"value2", "key3"=>"value3", "key4"=>"value4"}
irb(main):006:0> hash3 = { 'key1' => nil }
=> {"key1"=>nil}
irb(main):007:0> hash1.merge(hash2).merge(hash3)
=> {"key1"=>nil, "key2"=>"value2", "key3"=>"value3", "key4"=>"value4"}
```

You can see not only that merge combines key/value pairs, but also that the incoming information (meaning the Hash argument to the merge method) overrides pre-existing pairs in the calling Hash. That's why the "key1"=>nil pair from hash3 overrides the "key1"=>"value1" pair from hash1. You'll also note that the returned value of the merge method is itself just another Hash, so we can call any Hash method on it, including merge again.

So the first time we call the to_roman method (❷), we create a class variable called @@roman_of that contains base cases for transliteration into Roman numerals. It either uses the subtractive approach or it doesn't, depending on our configuration options. It includes subtractive representation by default. After all that, we return an empty String at ❸ unless the Integer (self) is greater than zero.

You may remember that I said this script can handle Roman numerals for Integers up to 4,999. That's where line ❹ and the maximum_representable method (defined at ❾) come in. The largest value that Roman numerals can represent (without introducing vertical bars above letters that are not strictly part of the standard Roman alphabet) is 4,999, so I decided to stop there. If the Integer in question (self) is greater than the maximum value that can be shown, we simply return the result of the to_s method (❹). Let's see this in action in irb.

```
irb(main):001:0> digits = (0..9).to_a
=> [0, 1, 2, 3, 4, 5, 6, 7, 8, 9]
irb(main):002:0> digits.map { |d| (4995+d).to_roman }
=> ["MMMMCMXCV", "MMMMCMXCVI", "MMMMCMXCVII", "MMMMCMXCVIII", "MMMMCMXCIX",
"5000", "5001", "5002", "5003", "5004"]
```

Once we hit the upper limit, we still return a String representing a numeric value (which is all a Roman numeral is), we just use the familiar Arabic numeral symbols within our String.

More Recursion

If the lines from ❷ through ❹ remind you of the exit conditions in power_of.rb that prepared for a recursive call to the same method, you've been paying attention. That's exactly what we're about to do here. At ❺ we create a variable called base that is the value of a long chain of method calls starting on the @@roman_of class variable. The purpose of these method calls is to find the largest key of the @@roman_of Hash that is less than or equal to the self Integer.

We get the keys out with the keys method, which returns an Array of the Hash's keys. We then sort that Array in reverse order, meaning that we start from highest to lowest. We then call a new Array method called detect with the conditions of being less than or equal to self. I think a great alias for detect would be *find first*. Let's see it in irb.

```
irb(main):001:0> digits = (0..9).to_a
=> [0, 1, 2, 3, 4, 5, 6, 7, 8, 9]
irb(main):002:0> digits.detect { |d| d % 3 }
=> 0
irb(main):003:0> digits.reverse.detect { |d| d % 3 }
=> 9
irb(main):004:0> digits.detect { |d| d > 4 }
=> 5
irb(main):005:0> digits.reverse.detect { |d| d % 2 == 1 }
=> 9
```

The detect method cycles through each member of the Array and returns the first Array element that matches the conditions in the block. This is what allows us to find the highest value representable in terms of the `@@roman_of` Hash, which we put into the base variable at ❺. At ❻ we return the empty String, unless we both found a base and that base is greater than zero; without a base greater than zero, we can't return anything useful.

Multiples of Our Base

We now have a base that's an Integer greater than zero. If we're calling something like `1066.to_roman`, we have no problem, because our base value (1,000) is the entire thousands place portion of our Integer. But what if we want something like `2112.to_roman` instead? We need to be able to keep track of how many multiples of base can go into our Integer. That's what we do at ❼.

We use the method `round_to_base` (defined at ❿) to determine the number of multiples of base we need to deal with. Our call to `round_to_base` tells us how many multiples of base we need to handle. Calling `@@roman_of[base]` also finds the single letter used to represent the base.

Multiplying Strings by Integers

Multiplying a String by an Integer results in that String concatenated with itself as many times as the Integer. Let's see that in irb:

```
irb(main):006:0> 'M' * 2
=> "MM"
```

This is taken directly from our `2112.to_roman` example. The output of `"MM"` takes care of representing the 2,000 portion of 2,112, and at line ❼ we also make a recursive call to `to_roman`; this time, however, we call it on a smaller number, specifically 112. Because the number on which we call the `to_roman` method keeps getting smaller as we pull off multiples of base, we will eventually reach a point where we'll exit with the empty String at ❸, marking the end of all of our recursive calls to `to_roman`. That's when we get our final output.

Running the Script

This is easily demonstrated within irb.

```
$ irb -r roman_numeral.rb
irb(main):001:0> (0..9).to_a.map { |n| n.to_roman }
```

The Results

Here is the output:

```
=> ["", "I", "II", "III", "IV", "V", "VI", "VII", "VIII", "IX"]
```

Hacking the Script

There are other options you could take with this script. Instead of making SUBTRACTIVE a class constant, we could have made the to_roman method take an argument. If you do that, you would need to keep track of two separate [SOMETHING]_TO_ROMAN Hashes, one using the subtractive display method, and one not using it. I decided to assume that the subtractive approach would be used because it does seem to be very common for Roman numerals. However, I thought I would mention how you could customize this script to make it slightly more complicated—but also more flexible.

We'll revisit the idea of representing Integers as different sorts of Strings later when we create the to_lang method. For now, let's continue on to our first currency converter.

#18 Currency Conversion, Basic (currency_converter1.rb)

I mentioned earlier that the commify method needs to vary based on how each country treats the notation of numbers. The area where this issue comes up most often is with currency, of course. The actual conversion process consists of relatively straightforward math, but we'll use this script as a vehicle to set the stage for two important concepts introduced in our next script—notably the representation of data with either *XML* (eXtensible Markup Language, http://www.w3c.org/xml) or *YAML* (YAML Ain't Markup Language, http://www.yaml.org). We'll explore both XML and YAML further in the next script, but for now, let's try out our current script in irb with irb -r currency_converter.rb.

```
irb(main):001:0> cc = CurrencyConverter.new()
=> #<CurrencyConverter:0xb7c979f4 @name_of={"USD"=>"US Dollar"},
@base_currency="USD">
❶ irb(main):002:0> puts cc.output_rates(1)
1 US Dollar (USD) =
        46.540136 Indian Rupees(INR)
        0.781738 Euros(EUR)
        10.890852 Mexican Pesos(MXN)
        7.977233 Chinese Yuans(CNY)
        1.127004 Canadian Dollars(CAD)
=> nil
❷ irb(main):003:0> puts cc.output_rates(42)
42 US Dollars (USD) =
        1954.685712 Indian Rupees(INR)
        32.832996 Euros(EUR)
        457.415784 Mexican Pesos(MXN)
        335.043786 Chinese Yuans(CNY)
        47.334168 Canadian Dollars(CAD)
=> nil
```

We can see on our irb session's first response that our cc instance seems to have some fondness for the US dollar—but if you're in some other country, don't worry, you'll learn how to use different currencies in the improved version of the script. In ❶ you can see that our cc instance's `output_rates` method takes an argument and seems to output the equivalent of that many US dollars in a few other currencies. You can see in ❷ that the values shift as expected with a different number of US dollars. Let's see how this works by examining the source code.

The Code

Initializing Class Variables

```
#!/usr/bin/env ruby
# currency_converter1.rb
# Using fixed exchange rates

class CurrencyConverter

❶  BASE_ABBR_AND_NAME = { 'USD' => 'US Dollar' }

  FULLNAME_OF = {
    'EUR' => 'Euro',
    'CAD' => 'Canadian Dollar',
    'CNY' => 'Chinese Yuan',
    'INR' => 'Indian Rupee',
    'MXN' => 'Mexican Peso',
  }

  EXCHANGE_RATES = {
    'EUR' => 0.781738,
    'INR' => 46.540136,
    'CNY' => 7.977233,
    'MXN' => 10.890852,
    'CAD' => 1.127004,
  }

❷  def initialize()
    @base_currency = BASE_ABBR_AND_NAME.keys[0]
    @name          = BASE_ABBR_AND_NAME[@base_currency]
  end

❸  def output_rates(mult=1)
    get_value(mult, get_rates) + "\n"
  end

  private

❹  def get_rates()
    return EXCHANGE_RATES
  end

❺  def get_value(mult, rates)
❻    return pluralize(mult, @name) +
    " (#{@base_currency}) = \n" +
❼    rates.keys.map do |abbr|
❽      "\t" +
      pluralize(mult * rates[abbr], FULLNAME_OF[abbr]) +
```

```
        "(#{abbr})"
❾    end.join("\n")
    end


=begin rdoc
This assumes that all plurals will be formed by adding an 's'.
It could be made more flexible with a Hash of plural suffixes
(which could be the empty string) or explicit plural forms that
are simple replacements for the singular.

For convenience, this outputs a string with the number of items,
a space, and then the pluralized form of the currency unit.
That suited the needs of this particular script.
=end
❿    def pluralize(num, term)
      (num == 1) ? "#{num} #{term}" : "#{num} #{term}s"
    end


end
```

How It Works

At ❶, we define the "home" currency of the class, and immediately following, we define some handy codes for various other currencies via the FULLNAME_OF and EXCHANGE_RATES Hashes. The EXCHANGE_RATES Hash contains our preset exchange rate values. These were current at the time I created this object, but I'm sure they'll be at least slightly different by the time you read this.

The initialize method at ❷ gives us some handy instance variables related to the home currency, and our only public method output_rates (❸) is simply a wrapper for the private get_value method (❺) with a newline.[3] The get_value method also uses another private method called get_rates, the definition of which (❹) should be fairly clear to you at this point.

The get_value method also uses another private method called pluralize (❿), which returns a String in which the term for the currency is plural when appropriate. I've implemented this very simply, because English only requires an *s* at the end of a term to pluralize it. With a few changes, this method could handle other languages or terms with more complex pluralization needs, most likely a Hash with currency terms as keys and plural endings as values. For now, we just need to add an s to the end of currency amounts greater than one.

The get_value method returns (❻) a pluralized form of the base currency with an equals sign, followed by information about each of the currencies the class knows about. Starting at ❼, it maps an operation onto each currency type (represented by the keys of the rates Hash). The mapped operation (❽) is the outputting of a tab character, followed by properly pluralized output for that currency based on its relative value, full name, and abbreviation. Each currency's String output is then joined together with newline characters at ❾, concluding the return statement begun back at ❻.

---

[3] We defined initialize before the private keyword, but initialize is always a private method, so output_rates is the only public method of CurrencyConverter.

Running the Script

This is also easily demonstrated in irb with `irb -r currency_converter1.rb`.

The Results

```
$ irb -r currency_converter1.rb
irb(main):001:0> cc = CurrencyConverter.new()
=> #<CurrencyConverter:0xb7c94b4c @base_currency="USD", @name="US Dollar">
irb(main):002:0> cc.output_rates
=> "1 US Dollar (USD) = \n\t46.540136 Indian Rupees(INR)\n\t0.781738
Euros(EUR)\n\t10.890852 Mexican Pesos(MXN)\n\t7.977233 Chinese Yuans(CNY)\n\
t1.127004 Canadian Dollars(CAD)\n"
irb(main):003:0> puts cc.output_rates
1 US Dollar (USD) =
        46.540136 Indian Rupees(INR)
        0.781738 Euros(EUR)
        10.890852 Mexican Pesos(MXN)
        7.977233 Chinese Yuans(CNY)
        1.127004 Canadian Dollars(CAD)
=> nil
```

Notice how the prettier output comes from using `puts` and that the returned value from `output_rates` is `nil`, largely because it's intended to print results instead.

Hacking the Script

This is all fine when exchange rates are constant and can be stored in a constant Hash, as in this script. However, the main impetus of having a currency converter stems from the fact that exchange rates constantly change. We need a converter that can update itself with new information when that information becomes available and yet continue to work when such information is inaccessible, for whatever reason. That's our next script.

#19 Currency Conversion, Advanced (currency_converter2.rb)

This script builds on what we already know from the previous one and uses a similar approach for the actual conversion process. What we've added is the ability to store and retrieve external data in both YAML and XML formats. YAML is so readable that I will simply tell you what you need to know for this script, and I'm sure that you'll be inspired to learn more about how it works. XML is a bit more complicated, and it's beyond the scope of this book to teach it to you if you're not familiar with it, but you won't need to be an expert to follow along. I'll describe the relevant bits of XML for this script's operation, just as I'll do with YAML. If you find that the XML-related content of this chapter is going a bit too fast, please refer to the excellent online XML Tutorial at http://www.w3schools.com/xml.

This script differs from the previous in several ways. Let's see how.

The Code

```
#!/usr/bin/env ruby
# currency_converter2.rb

### RSS feeds for rates at
# http://www.currencysource.com/rss_currencyexchangerates.html

=begin rdoc
open-uri allows Kernel.open to read data using a URI, not just from
a local file.
=end
```
❶ `require 'open-uri'`
```
=begin rdoc
YAML[http://www.yaml.org] stands for "YAML Ain't Markup Language"
and is a simple human-readable data markup format.
=end
```
YAML   `require 'yaml'`
```

=begin rdoc
I also want to add a method to all <b>Hash</b>es.
=end
class Hash

=begin rdoc
Allow <b>Hash</b>es to be subtracted from each other.
=end
```
A Subtraction ❷   `def -(hash_with_pairs_to_remove_from_self)`
Method for
Hashes;
The delete
Method
```
    output = self.dup
    hash_with_pairs_to_remove_from_self.each_key do |k|
      output.delete(k)
    end
    output
  end

end
```
❸ `class CurrencyConverter`
```

  BASE_URL = 'http://currencysource.com/RSS'
  CURRENCY_CODES = {
    'EUR' => 'Euro',
    'CAD' => 'Canadian Dollar',
    'CNY' => 'Chinese Yuan',
    'INR' => 'Indian Rupee',
    'MXN' => 'Mexican Peso',
    'USD' => 'US Dollar',
  }
  RATES_DIRECTORY = 'extras/currency_exchange_rates'

  def initialize(code='USD')
```
The has_key? and
fail Methods
```
    unless CURRENCY_CODES.has_key?(code)
      fail "I know nothing about #{code}"
    end
```

```
        @base_currency = code
        @name          = CURRENCY_CODES[code]
      end

❹   def output_rates(mult=1, try_new_rates=true)
      rates = get_rates(try_new_rates)
      save_rates_in_local_file!(rates)
      return get_value(mult, rates) + "\n"
    end

    private

❺   def download_new_rates()
      puts 'Downloading new exchange rates...'
      begin
        raw_rate_lines = get_xml_lines()
      rescue
        puts 'Download failed. Falling back to local file.'
        return nil
      end
      rates = Hash.new('')
      comparison_codes = CURRENCY_CODES - { @base_currency => @name }
      comparison_codes.each_key do |abbr|
        rates[abbr] = get_rate_for_abbr_from_raw_rate_lines(
          abbr,
          raw_rate_lines
        )
      end
      return rates
    end

❻   def get_rates(try_new_rates)
      return load_old_rates unless try_new_rates
      return download_new_rates || load_old_rates
    end

    def get_rate_for_abbr_from_raw_rate_lines(abbr, raw_rate_lines)
      regex = {
        :open =>
          /^\<title\>1 #{@base_currency} = #{abbr} \(/,
        :close =>
          /\)\<\/title\>\r\n$/
      }
      line = raw_rate_lines.detect { |line| line =~ /#{abbr}/ }
      line.gsub(regex[:open], '').gsub(regex[:close], '').to_f
    end

    def get_value(mult, rates)
      return "#{pluralize(mult, @name)} (#{@base_currency}) = \n" +
        rates.keys.map do |abbr|
          "\t#{pluralize(mult * rates[abbr], CURRENCY_CODES[abbr])} (#{abbr})"
        end.join("\n")
    end
```

begin - rescue - end

```
      =begin rdoc
      get_xml_lines is able to read from a URI with the open-uri library.
      This also could have been implemented with the RSS library
      written by Kouhei Sutou <kou@cozmixng.org> and detailed at
      http://www.cozmixng.org/~rwiki/?cmd=view;name=RSS+Parser%3A%3ATutorial.en
      =end
```

XML ❼
```
      def get_xml_lines()
        open("#{BASE_URL}/#{@base_currency}.xml").readlines.find_all do |line|
          line =~ /1 #{@base_currency} =/
        end
      end
```

❽
```
      def load_old_rates()
        puts "Reading stored exchange rates from local file #{rates_filename()}"
```
YAML.load
```
        rates = YAML.load(File.open(rates_filename))
        fail 'no old rates' unless rates
        return rates
      end

      def pluralize(num, term)
        (num == 1) ? "#{num} #{term}" : "#{num} #{term}s"
      end
```

❾
```
      def rates_filename()
        "#{RATES_DIRECTORY}/#{@base_currency}.yaml"
      end
```

```
      =begin rdoc
      Store new rates in an external YAML file.
      This is a side-effect akin to memoization, hence the bang.
      =end
```
❿
```
      def save_rates_in_local_file!(rates)
        return unless rates
```
YAML.dump
```
        File.open(rates_filename, 'w') { |rf| YAML.dump(rates, rf) }
      end

    end
```

How It Works

How does this file differ from the previous one? The class definition of
CurrencyConverter is delayed until ❸, due to some more comments and
require statements at ❶. I also open the Hash class and give it a subtraction
method, identified by the minus sign at ❷. This new method takes another
Hash and returns the original Hash without any pairs found in the argument
Hash. Think of it this way: If merge is addition of Hashes, this method is the
subtraction of Hashes. I suppose a good alternative name would be either
demerge or unmerge.

Inside our CurrencyConverter class (❸), we have two new constants:
BASE_URL, which is used for downloading completely new exchange rates, and
RATES_DIRECTORY, which is used to store exchange rates once they have been

downloaded. The class's initialize method accepts a currency code, so folks from other countries can define their own native converters more easily. (It assumes US dollars with no argument.) If it gets a currency code that it doesn't understand, it shouldn't proceed, so we make it break out of the entire program with the command fail, which causes the program to stop running. The output_rates method (❹) also tries to get new rates when told to, saves rates in a local file, and performs the operations we already know about from the last script.

How does it get new rates? The get_rates method (❻) shows us that it either loads old rates or downloads new rates. If it tries to download_new_rates (❺) but fails to do so, it will fall back to its old rates again. It defaults to downloading new rates, so let's look at download_new_rates.

After some explanatory printing, we get a begin statement, which starts a block of code that means *Try something, and fall back to some other code if the attempt fails.* What we're trying to do is call the get_xml_lines method. If that fails, we'll explain to the user via puts that the download failed and return nil. The end statement tells us that the block of code pertaining to the begin has ended. The return nil is what allows us to fall back to old exchanges rates within get_rates if the get_xml_lines method failed.

So what does get_xml_lines do? It's defined at ❼, and it finds all lines from a given XML file in which one unit of the base currency appears with an equals sign. These lines tell us our exchange rates. Let's take a look at what one of those XML files looks like. Here are a few lines from a file I downloaded from http://www.currencysource.com/RSS/USD.xml.

```
<item>
<title>1 USD = ARS (3.017607)</title>
<link>http://www.currencysource.com/tables/USD/1X_USD.htm</link>
<description><![CDATA[As of Thursday, May 04, 2006...<br>1 U.S. Dollar (USD) =
3.017607 Argentine Peso (ARS)<br><br>Call 1-877-627-4817 for 'LIVE'
assistance.<br><br>Source: IMF<br><br>Aggregated and published by
CurrencySource.com<br>'Rated #1 in Currency Exchange']]></description>
<pubDate>Sun, 08 Oct 2006 06:00:04 CST</pubDate>
</item>
<item>
<title>1 USD = AUD (1.342818)</title>
<link>http://www.currencysource.com/tables/USD/1X_USD.htm</link>
<description><![CDATA[As of Sunday, October 08, 2006...<br>1 U.S. Dollar (USD)
= 1.342818 Australian Dollar (AUD)<br><br>Call 1-877-627-4817 for 'LIVE'
assistance.<br><br>Source: IMF<br><br>Aggregated and published by
CurrencySource.com<br>'Rated #1 in Currency Exchange']]></description>
<pubDate>Sun, 08 Oct 2006 06:00:04 CST</pubDate>
</item>
```

If you're not already familiar with XML, you can see here that it consists of text in which various content is enclosed by *tags*, which are those bits of text within the < and > characters. Newlines are not meaningful. We have two definitions of a type of thing called item, each of which has a title, a link, a description, and a pubDate. This is the content we're searching through. You'll notice that the `<title>` lines contain direct statements about exchange rates between the base currency and some other currency—in my example, the Argentinian peso and the Australian dollar.

The reason this operation might fail is that the file we're trying to open and call `readlines` on is not a local file, but a file retrieved from the Internet via a URL. The open-uri library that we required at ❶ modifies the `open` command to allow us to open URLs as well as local files. Without a functioning Internet connection, the `open` will fail, meaning that there will be no file on which to call the `readlines` method within `get_xml_lines`. However, if our download operation worked, we'll be able to assign content into the `raw_rate_lines` variable within `download_new_rates`. The rest of the `download_new_rates` method extracts the exchange rate content out of the raw lines.

Downloading Rates Information

The `download_new_rates` method extracts the exchange rate by first defining a variable for the rates, which is a Hash. We give `Hash.new` an argument halfway through `download_new_rates` so that when a given key is not found in the Hash, the returned value is no longer `nil`, but instead the argument that was passed to `Hash.new` (the empty String in our example). For our purposes, we want to find `comparison_codes`, which are all the pairs pertaining to currencies and their codes, without the `@base_currency`.[4] We then cycle through each key, which is the abbreviation or code associated with the matching currency, and call the `get_rate_for_abbr_from_raw_rate_lines` method, which gets the exchange rate for a given abbreviation from the `raw_rate_lines` variable.

The `get_rate_for_abbr_from_raw_rate_lines` method is defined immediately after the definition of `get_rates` at ❻. The `regex` variable is a Hash that stores some regular expressions that signify the opening and closing of the content we care about (the actual exchange rate value). We detect the first line containing the interpolated `abbr` value and then strip off the opening and closing `regex` values by substituting each of them with the empty string. We then `return` the floating-point version (via the `to_f` method) of what we have left. That's the exchange rate for the currency matching the `abbr` argument.

We've gotten our rates via downloading, which means that we're ready to save them into a local file within `initialize`. We immediately exit `save_rates_in_local_file!` (❿) and do nothing if we have no rates. The reason for this is that if there is some problem with getting rates, we don't want to overwrite our good stored data from a previous use of this script. Assuming that all is well, we open a new file for writing with the name `rates_filename`, which looks like a variable. It's actually a method, defined at ❾. It returns something like `"extras/currency_exchange_rates/USD.yaml"` or `"extras/currency_exchange_rates/CAD.yaml"`, depending on what your base currency is. It's a method because it's entirely dependent on the value of `@base_currency`.

---

[4] We remove the `@base_currency` since it's not useful to give the exchange rate between a given currency and itself—the rate would always be exactly one.

NOTE *Some schools of programming would have defined an instance variable @rates_filename within the initialize method, just as we did with @base_currency and @name. Conversely, we could have treated @name the same way we do rates_filename, defining a method called name that simply returns the value of CURRENCY_CODES[@base_currency]. Either approach is useful. Using an instance variable (the "eager" approach) is faster, but the different variables with a close relationship to each other could get out of sync, especially in a more complex program. Using a method (the "lazy" approach) is slower, because it has to recalculate its return value every time—but it also means that your variables won't get out of agreement with each other, at least in this case.*

Whether it's an instance variable or a method, our main concern regarding rates_filename is that it is a name of a file that can be written into. We do the writing using YAML.dump, which takes two arguments; the first is a data structure that will be converted into YAML and written into the second argument, which is a File object. Let's open extras/currency_exchange_rates/USD.yaml and see what we've written.

```
---
EUR: 0.789639
INR: 45.609987
CNY: 7.890017
MXN: 11.062366
CAD: 1.126398
```

That's the entire content of USD.yaml. It represents a single Hash whose keys are currency codes and whose values are floating-point numbers. You'll notice that newlines are significant, and while this example doesn't show it, so is indentation. There's a lot about YAML that you can learn at http://www.yaml.org, but I find that YAML.dump is a great way to learn how things are represented in YAML. If you pass a data structure that you understand into YAML.dump, you can read the resulting .yaml file to see what the proper representation is. You can then change the data structure in some specific way, rewrite using YAML.dump, and compare the results. It's very useful.

In any case, we have now stored our exchange rate data as YAML in an external file, using save_rates_in_local_file!. We still have the rates variable available, so we use it, calling the get_value method, which uses the same approach as in the previous script.

What If You Can't Download New Rates?

In a later call to the script, we might not be able to download new rates, as previously noted. Therefore, let's look at the get_rates method again and assume that we either told the script not to download new rates (using a false value for the try_new_rates argument) or that the download attempt failed. Either way, we'll need to get our rates from the stored YAML file.

The `load_old_rates` method is at ❽. It informs the user that there will be an attempt to read from the local file. Getting the real data out of a YAML file could hardly be easier: You just call `YAML.load`, and give it a File argument, which, in our case is the result of calling `File.open` on `rates_filename`. The result of `YAML.load` is whichever data structure was stored in the external file, so we simply assign it into a variable called `rates`. We then ensure that we were able to read data into `rates` before proceeding, and finally return `rates`.

Running the Script

After all this explanation, it's finally time to see the script in action in irb with `irb -r currency_converter2.rb`.

The Results

```
irb(main):001:0> usd = CurrencyConverter.new
=> #<CurrencyConverter:0xb7bfb498 @name="US Dollar", @base_currency="USD">
irb(main):002:0> inr = CurrencyConverter.new('INR')
=> #<CurrencyConverter:0xb7bef990 @name="Indian Rupee", @base_currency="INR">
irb(main):003:0> usd.output_rates(1)
Downloading new exchange rates...
=> "1 US Dollar (USD) = \n\t45.609987 Indian Rupees (INR)\n\t0.789639 Euros
(EUR)\n\t11.062366 Mexican Pesos (MXN)\n\t7.890017 Chinese Yuans (CNY)\n\
t1.126398 Canadian Dollars (CAD)\n"
irb(main):004:0> inr.output_rates(1)
Downloading new exchange rates...
=> "1 Indian Rupee (INR) = \n\t0.017313 Euros (EUR)\n\t0.242543 Mexican Pesos
(MXN)\n\t0.172989 Chinese Yuans (CNY)\n\t0.021925 US Dollars (USD)\n\t0.024696
Canadian Dollars (CAD)\n"
irb(main):005:0> usd.output_rates(1, false)
Reading stored exchange rates from local file extras/currency_exchange_rates/
USD.yaml
=> "1 US Dollar (USD) = \n\t0.789639 Euros (EUR)\n\t45.609987 Indian Rupees
(INR)\n\t7.890017 Chinese Yuans (CNY)\n\t11.062366 Mexican Pesos (MXN)\n\
t1.126398 Canadian Dollars (CAD)\n"
irb(main):006:0> inr.output_rates(100, false)
Reading stored exchange rates from local file extras/currency_exchange_rates/
INR.yaml
=> "100 Indian Rupees (INR) = \n\t1.7313 Euros (EUR)\n\t17.2989 Chinese Yuans
(CNY)\n\t24.2543 Mexican Pesos (MXN)\n\t2.4696 Canadian Dollars (CAD)\n\
t2.1925 US Dollars (USD)\n"
❶ irb(main):007:0> inr.output_rates(100, (not true))
Reading stored exchange rates from local file extras/currency_exchange_rates/
INR.yaml
=> "100 Indian Rupees (INR) = \n\t1.7313 Euros (EUR)\n\t24.2543 Mexican Pesos
(MXN)\n\t17.2989 Chinese Yuans (CNY)\n\t2.1925 US Dollars (USD)\n\t2.4696
Canadian Dollars (CAD)\n"
```

You can see that we can easily define converters for specific currencies; then we can tell the output_rates method to try to download new rates or not to download them, depending on whether or not the optional second argument evaluates to false. In line ❶, you see that I've passed in (not true) just to make that point. You'll also notice that the return values with special characters like newlines and tabs represent those characters the same way we do when we insert them, while printing those return values causes them to be interpreted, making the printing output prettier, or at least more easily readable.

Hacking the Script

This script depends on the directory hierarchy at BASE_URL staying the same. If it ever changes, you will need to update get_xml_lines() at ❼ accordingly. We're also about to get deeper into some functional programming topics. Once you're comfortable with lambda (introduced in the next chapter), you could replace the rates_filename method with a lambda that accepts RATES_DIRECTORY and @base_currency as arguments.

Chapter Recap

What was new in this chapter?

- Exponentiation in Ruby
- Returning nil when a method's operation is not possible
- More recursion and exit conditions
- Modules and Inheritance
- Hash.merge
- Class Variables
- Array.detect ("find first")
- Subtracting Hashes
- Exiting the entire script with fail
- begin—rescue—end
- Downloading with open-uri
- Parsing XML files with regular expressions
- Writing to YAML files with YAML.dump
- Reading from YAML files with YAML.load

It's almost as if this chapter weren't really about numbers—we covered a large amount of generically useful information, especially Modules, Class Variables, and external data storage and retrieval using either XML or YAML (or both). We've done a bit of functional programming already in the last two chapters, but we'll get into the deep lambda magic in Chapter 6.

6

FUNCTIONALISM WITH BLOCKS AND PROCS

Ruby has two main ancestors: Smalltalk and Lisp.[1] From Smalltalk, Ruby gets its heavy object orientation, which we've explored in some depth up to this point. From Lisp it derives several ideas from *functional programming*, which is a very mathematically inclined approach to programming with a few notable characteristics. First, variables tend to be defined once, without having their values changed later on. Additionally, functions tend to be simple, abstract, and used as building blocks for other functions; the line between *functions*, which perform operations, and *data*, on which functions operate, is often blurry, compared with non-functional approaches. Functions also tend to do their work by returning values, rather than having side effects—in Ruby terms, methods that end with an exclamation point are less common.

Ruby's support for functional programming is extensive and exciting. Let's dive in.

---

[1] This is a potentially contentious statement. At a RubyConf, I once asked Matz which other languages he thought were most influential on Ruby. His response was "Smalltalk and Common Lisp". Other folks in the Ruby community (many of them ex-Perl users) stress Ruby's clear similarity to Perl. Probably the safest statement is that Ruby descends from Smalltalk and Lisp, and while it's a lot like Perl, Perl is more like an aunt or uncle.

#20 Our First lambda (make_incrementer.rb)

This script explores how Ruby creates functions that should be treated as objects. Every "thing" in Ruby is an object, so the notion of treating functions as objects is not conceptually odd. In Ruby, we do this with the command lambda, which takes a block. Let's look at that in irb.

```
irb(main):001:0> double_me = lambda { |x| x * 2 }
=> #<Proc:0xb7d1f890@(irb):1>
irb(main):002:0> double_me.call(5)
=> 10
```

You can see by the return value of line one that the result of calling lambda is an instance of class Proc. *Proc* is short for *procedure*, and while most objects are defined by what they *are*, Procs can be thought of primarily as defined by what they *do*. Procs have a method called *call*, which tells that Proc instance to do whatever it does. In our irb example, we have a Proc instance called double_me that takes an argument and returns that argument, times two. On line two, we see that feeding the number *5* into double_me.call results in a return value of *10*, just as you would expect. It is easy to create other Procs that do other operations.

```
irb(main):003:0> triple_me = lambda { |x| x * 3 }
=> #<Proc:0xb7d105bc@(irb):3>
irb(main):004:0> triple_me.call(5)
=> 15
```

Since Procs are objects, just like everything else in Ruby, we can treat them like any other object. They can be the returned value of a method, either the key or value of a Hash, arguments to other methods, and whatever else any object can be. Let's look at the script that demonstrates this.

The Code

```
#!/usr/bin/env ruby
# make_incrementer.rb
```

Procs
```
❶ def make_incrementer(delta)
     return lambda { |x| x + delta }
   end

❷ incrementer_proc_of = Hash.new()
   [10, 20].each do |delta|
     incrementer_proc_of[delta] = make_incrementer(delta)
   end
```

Calling Procs
```
❸ incrementer_proc_of.each_pair do |delta,incrementer_proc|
     puts "#{delta} + 5 = #{incrementer_proc.call(5)}\n"
   end
```

```
❹ puts
```

The each_pair Method

```
❺ incrementer_proc_of.each_pair do |delta,incrementer_proc|
❻   (0..5).to_a.each do |other_addend|
      puts "#{delta} + #{other_addend} = " +
        incrementer_proc.call(other_addend) + "\n"
    end
  end
```

How It Works

At ❶ we define a method called make_incrementer. It takes a single argument called delta and returns a Proc (created via lambda) that adds delta to something else, represented by x. What is that something else? We don't know yet. That is precisely the point of this method—it allows us to define an operation that can be performed multiple times using different parameters, just like any other function.

We can see how this is useful in the rest of this script. At ❷ we define a new Hash called incrementer_proc_of. For each of the values 10 and 20, we make an incrementer (using either 10 or 20 for the value of delta in the make_incrementer method) and assign the resulting Proc into the incrementer_proc_of Hash. Starting at ❸, we read each delta and Proc pair out of the Hash using the each_pair method and then use puts to print a line describing that delta value and the result of calling its Proc with the argument of 5.

We ❹ print a spacer with puts (just for ease of reading the output), and finally ❺ output another set of data. This time we add another loop for a value called other_addend; this is a variable that serves a role analogous to our static value of 5 in the loop (❸). Let's run this program with ruby -w make_incrementer.rb and look at the output.

The Results

```
20 + 5 = 25
10 + 5 = 15

20 + 0 = 20
20 + 1 = 21
20 + 2 = 22
20 + 3 = 23
20 + 4 = 24
20 + 5 = 25
10 + 0 = 10
10 + 1 = 11
10 + 2 = 12
10 + 3 = 13
10 + 4 = 14
10 + 5 = 15
```

The first two lines before the empty line show the output of the first loop (with the static value of 5 for the addend), while the rest of the output shows the result of the second loop, which uses the other_addend variable. Notice also that each_pair does not order by key, which is why my output has the delta value of 20 appearing first. Depending on your implementation of Ruby, you might see a delta of 10 first.

Now you know how to create Procs. Let's learn how to use them for something more useful than just demonstrating themselves.

#21 Using Procs for Filtering (matching_members.rb)

So far, we've seen that to create a Proc, we call lambda with a block describing what that Proc should do. This would lead you to believe that there is a special relationship between Procs and blocks, which there is. Our next script demonstrates how to use Procs in place of blocks.

The Code

```ruby
#!/usr/bin/env ruby
# matching_members.rb

=begin rdoc
Extend the built-in <b>Array</b> class.
=end
class Array

=begin rdoc
Takes a <b>Proc</b> as an argument, and returns all members
matching the criteria defined by that <b>Proc</b>.
=end
```

Procs as
Arguments

❶
```ruby
  def matching_members(some_proc)
    find_all { |i| some_proc.call(i) }
  end

end
```

❷
```ruby
digits = (0..9).to_a
lambdas = Hash.new()
lambdas['five+']   = lambda { |i| i >= 5 }
lambdas['is_even'] = lambda { |i| (i % 2).zero? }
```

❸
❹
❺
❻
```ruby
lambdas.keys.sort.each do |lambda_name|
  lambda_proc  = lambdas[lambda_name]
  lambda_value = digits.matching_members(lambda_proc).join(',')
  puts "#{lambda_name}\t[#{lambda_value}]\n"
end
```

How It Works

In this script, we open the Array class in order to add a new method called matching_members (❶). It takes a Proc (creatively called some_proc—see the note below) as an argument and returns the result of calling find_all, which (as its name suggests) finds all members for which the block is true. In this case, the condition in the block is the result of calling the Proc argument on the Array with the Array member in question as the argument to `call`. After we finish defining our new method, we set up our `digits` Array and our Procs with appropriate names in the `lambdas` Hash at ❷.

NOTE   *Some of my co-workers make fun of the variable and method names I use—like* `some_proc`, *for example. I think names should either be very specific, like* `save_rates_to_local_file!`, *or explicitly generic, like* `some_proc`. *For truly generic operations, I often use variable names like* `any_proc` *or* `any_hash`, *which tell you explicitly that the operations being performed on them are meant to be useful for any Proc or Hash.*

At ❸, we loop through each sorted `lambda_name`, and at ❹ we extract each Proc out as a variable called `lambda_proc`. We then `find_all` members of the digits Array that match the condition described by that Proc at ❺ and `puts` an appropriate message at ❻.

Running the Script

Let's see it in action with `ruby -w matching_members.rb`.

The Results

```
five+    [5,6,7,8,9]
is_even  [0,2,4,6,8]
```

In each case, we filter the members of the `digits` Array based on some specific conditions. Hopefully, you'll find that the names I chose for each Proc match what that Proc does. The `five+` Proc returns `true` for any argument that is five or greater.[2] We see that the results of calling `five+` on each digit in turn returns the correct digits. Similarly, the `is_even` Proc filters its input, only returning `true` for arguments that are even, where *evenness* is defined as having a modulus two equal to zero. Again, we get the correct numbers.

What happens when we want to filter based on multiple criteria? We could filter once with one Proc, assign that result into an Array, and then filter that result by the second criterion. That's perfectly valid, but what if we have an unknown number of filtering conditions? We want a version of `matching_members` that can take an arbitrary number of Procs. That's our next script.

#22 Using Procs for Compounded Filtering (matching_compound_members.rb)

In this script, we'll filter Arrays using an arbitrary number of Procs. As before, we'll open up the Array class, this time adding two methods. Again, we'll filter digits based on simple mathematical tests. Let's take a look at the source code and see what's different.

---

[2] It does this by implicit Boolean evaluation of the expression `i >= 5`.

The Code

```ruby
#!/usr/bin/env ruby
# matching_compound_members.rb

=begin rdoc
Extend the built-in <b>Array</b> class.
=end
class Array

=begin rdoc
Takes a block as an argument and returns a list of
members matching the criteria defined by that block.
=end
```

Block Arguments ❶
```ruby
  def matching_members(&some_block)
    find_all(&some_block)
  end

=begin rdoc
Takes an <b>Array</b> of <b>Proc</b>s as an argument
and returns all members matching the criteria defined
by each <b>Proc</b> via <b>Array.matching_members</b>.
Note that it uses the ampersand to convert from
<b>Proc</b> to block.
=end
```
❷
```ruby
  def matching_compound_members(procs_array)
    procs_array.map do |some_proc|
      # collect each proc operation
```
❸
```ruby
      matching_members(&some_proc)
```
❹
```ruby
    end.inject(self) do |memo,matches|
      # find all the intersections, starting with self
      # and whittling down until we only have members
      # that have matched every proc
```

Array Intersections ❺
```ruby
      memo & matches
    end
```
❻
```ruby
  end

end

# Now use these methods in some operations.
```
❼
```ruby
digits = (0..9).to_a
lambdas = Hash.new()
lambdas['five+']   = lambda { |i| i if i >= 5 }
lambdas['is_even'] = lambda { |i| i if (i % 2).zero? }
lambdas['div_by3'] = lambda { |i| i if (i % 3).zero? }

lambdas.keys.sort.each do |lambda_name|
  lambda_proc   = lambdas[lambda_name]
  lambda_values = digits.matching_members(&lambda_proc).join(',')
```
❽
```ruby
  puts "#{lambda_name}\t[#{lambda_values}]\n"
end
```
❾
```ruby
puts "ALL\t[#{digits.matching_compound_members(lambdas.values).join(',')}]"
```

How It Works

We start by defining a method called matching_members (❶), just as before. However, this time our argument is called some_block instead of some_proc, and it is preceded by an ampersand. Why?

Blocks, Procs, and the Ampersand

The ampersand (&) is Ruby's way of expressing blocks and Procs in terms of each other. It's very useful for arguments to methods, as you might imagine. *Blocks*, you may remember, are simply bits of code between delimiters such as braces ({ "I'm a block!" }) or the do and end keywords (do "I'm also a block!" end). *Procs* are objects made from blocks via the lambda method. Either of them can be passed into methods, and the ampersand is the way to use one as the other. Let's test this in irb.

```
irb(main):001:0> class Array
irb(main):002:1> def matches_block( &some_block )
irb(main):003:2> find_all( &some_block )
irb(main):004:2> end
irb(main):005:1> def matches_proc( some_proc )
irb(main):006:2> find_all( &some_proc )
irb(main):007:2> end
irb(main):008:1> end
=> nil
```

We open the Array class and add a method called matches_block; this method takes a block (with an ampersand prefix), effectively duplicating the behavior of the existing find_all method, which it calls. We also add another method called matches_proc that calls find_all again, but takes a Proc this time. Then we try them out.

```
irb(main):009:0> digits = (0..9).to_a
=> [0, 1, 2, 3, 4, 5, 6, 7, 8, 9]
irb(main):010:0> digits.matches_block { |x| x > 5 }
=> [6, 7, 8, 9]
irb(main):011:0> digits.matches_proc( lambda { |x| x > 5 } )
=> [6, 7, 8, 9]
```

The matches_block method dutifully takes a block and passes it along to the find_all method, transforming it along the way with the ampersand—once on input and again when passed to find_all. The matches_proc method takes a Proc and passes that on to find_all, but it only needs to transform with the ampersand once.

You might think that we could omit the ampersand and just treat a block argument as a standard variable, like in irb below.

```
irb(main):001:0> class Array
irb(main):002:1> def matches_block( some_block )
irb(main):003:2> find_all( some_block )
irb(main):004:2> end
```

```
irb(main):005:1> end
=> nil
irb(main):006:0> digits = (0..9).to_a
=> [0, 1, 2, 3, 4, 5, 6, 7, 8, 9]
irb(main):007:0> digits.matches_block { |x| x > 5 }
ArgumentError: wrong number of arguments (0 for 1)
        from (irb):7:in `matches_block'
        from (irb):7
        from :0
```

That doesn't work, as you see. Ruby keeps track of the number of arguments that a given method, block, or Proc expects (a concept called *arity*) and complains when there is a mismatch. Our irb example expected a "real" argument, not just a block, and complained when it didn't get one.

NOTE   *The gist of the ArgumentError is that blocks are akin to "partial" or "unborn" blocks and need the lambda method to be made into full-fledged Procs, which can be used as real arguments to methods. Some methods, like find_all, can handle block arguments, but these block arguments are treated differently than regular arguments and don't count toward the number of "real" arguments. We'll cover this later when we discuss the willow_and_anya.rb script. For now, note that our new version of matching_members takes a block instead of a Proc.*

Filtering with Each Proc via map

We also define a new method called matching_compound_members at ❷. The matching_compound_members method takes an Array argument called procs_array and maps a call to matching_members onto each of procs_array's Proc elements; this transforms the elements into blocks with the ampersand at ❸ while doing the mapping. This results in an Array, each of whose members is an Array containing all members of the original Array that match the conditions defined by the Proc. Confused? Take a look in irb.

```
irb(main):001:1> class Array
irb(main):002:1> def matching_compound_members( procs_array )
irb(main):003:2> procs_array.map do |some_proc|
irb(main):004:3* find_all( &some_proc )
irb(main):005:3> end
irb(main):006:2> end
irb(main):007:1> end
=> nil
irb(main):008:0> digits.matching_compound_members( [ lambda { |x| x > 5 },
lambda { |x| (x % 2).zero? }])
=> [[6, 7, 8, 9], [0, 2, 4, 6, 8]]
```

On lines one through seven, we add a shortened version of matching_members to all Arrays. We call it on line eight, and find that the result is an Array of Arrays. The first sub-array is all digits greater than five—the result of the first Proc. The second sub-array is all even digits—the result of the second Proc. That's what we have at the end of the map (❹) inside matching_compound_members.

Finding the Intersections with inject

We don't stop there. Next we call our old friend the inject method on that Array of Arrays. You may remember that inject performs an operation successively and has a memory for intermediate results. That will be very useful for us. The inject method takes an optional non-block element for the initial state of its memory. In our script we use self (❹), meaning that the memory state will be the self Array as it exists prior to any filtering. We also say that each member of the Array resulting from the map operation will be called matches. This makes sense because the matches variable represents members of the initial Array that were found to match the Proc used for that particular stage of the map operation.

Array Intersections

At ❺, we call a method we haven't seen before on memo. This method happens to be expressed with the ampersand character, but it has nothing to do with converting blocks and Procs into each other; it has more to do with set math.

```
irb(main):001:0> digits = (0..9).to_a
=> [0, 1, 2, 3, 4, 5, 6, 7, 8, 9]
irb(main):002:0> evens = digits.find_all { |x| (x % 2).zero? }
=> [0, 2, 4, 6, 8]
irb(main):003:0> digits & evens
=> [0, 2, 4, 6, 8]
irb(main):004:0> half_digits = digits.find_all { |x| x < 5 }
=> [0, 1, 2, 3, 4]
irb(main):005:0> evens & half_digits
=> [0, 2, 4]
```

Can you guess what this ampersand means? It represents the intersection of two composite data sets. It basically means *Find all members of myself that also belong to this other thing*. When we call it within our inject, we ensure that once a given Array element fails one test, it no longer appears as a candidate for the next test. This happens because the memory of the inject method (represented by the variable called memo) is automatically set to the return value of each iteration of the inject method. At ❻, when we're done with all of our mapping and injecting, we're left with only those members of the original Array that pass the tests defined by every single Proc in the procs_array argument. Since Ruby returns the last expression evaluated in a method, matching_compound_members returns an Array of all members of self that pass every test represented by the members of procs_array.

After some setup at ❼ similar to that for the previous script, we output results using puts at both ❽ and ❾. Let's see it in action.

The Results

```
div_by3 [0,3,6,9]
five+   [5,6,7,8,9]
is_even [0,2,4,6,8]
ALL     [6]
```

We call each of these filtering Procs on the digits from zero to nine, getting the correct members each time. We finally output the prefix ALL followed by the members that pass all the tests. The number six is the only digit from zero to nine that is divisible by three, is greater than or equal to five, and is even. Therefore, it is the only member of the final output.

Hacking the Script

Try defining your own Procs using lambda. You can add them to the section at ❼ or replace some of the existing Procs. Feel free to alter the range used to create the digits Array as well. A larger range of values in digits could help demonstrate more complex relationships among a greater number of filtering Procs.

#23 Returning Procs as Values (return_proc.rb)

Let's look at a further demonstration of how to use Procs as data generated by another function. It's very similar to the make_incrementer.rb script.

The Code

```ruby
#!/usr/bin/env ruby
# return_proc.rb

❶ def return_proc(criterion, further_criterion=1)

    proc_of_criterion = {
      'div_by?' => lambda { |i| i if (i % further_criterion).zero? },
      'is?'     => lambda { |i| i == further_criterion }
    }

    # allow 'is_even' as an alias for divisible by 2
❷   return return_proc('div_by?', 2) if criterion == ('is_even')

❸   proc_to_return = proc_of_criterion[criterion]
    fail "I don't understand the criterion #{criterion}" unless proc_to_return
    return proc_to_return

  end

❹ require 'boolean_golf.rb'

  # Demonstrate calling the proc directly
❺ even_proc = return_proc('is_even') # could have been ('div_by', 2)
  div3_proc = return_proc('div_by?', 3)
  is10_proc = return_proc('is?', 10)
❻ [4, 5, 6].each do |num|
    puts %Q[Is #{num} even?: #{even_proc[num].true?}]
    puts %Q[Is #{num} divisible by 3?: #{div3_proc[num].true?}]
```

Procs as Hash Values (margin note)

Making Strings with %Q (margin note)

```
        puts %Q[Is #{num} 10?: #{is10_proc[num].true?}]
❼      printf("%d is %s.\n\n", num, even_proc[num].true? ? 'even' : 'not even')
       end

       # Demonstrate using the proc as a block for a method
❽      digits = (0..9).to_a
       even_results = digits.find_all(&(return_proc('is_even')))
       div3_results = digits.find_all(&(return_proc('div_by?', 3)))
❾      puts %Q[The even digits are #{even_results.inspect}.]
       puts %Q[The digits divisible by 3 are #{div3_results.inspect}.]
       puts
```

The inspect Method *(margin note)*

The Results

If we call this with the command ruby -w return_proc.rb, we get the following
output, all of which is true.

```
Is 4 even?: true
Is 4 divisible by 3?: false
Is 4 10?: false
4 is even.

Is 5 even?: false
Is 5 divisible by 3?: false
Is 5 10?: false
5 is not even.

Is 6 even?: true
Is 6 divisible by 3?: true
Is 6 10?: false
6 is even.

The even digits are [0, 2, 4, 6, 8].
The digits divisible by 3 are [0, 3, 6, 9].
```

How It Works

We define a method called return_proc starting at ❶ that takes a mandatory
criterion and an optional further_criterion, assumed to be one. It then defines
a Hash called proc_of_criterion with keys that match a specific criterion and
values that are Procs corresponding to each criterion. It then allows a caller
to use an alias is_even to mean *Divisible by two* at ❷. It does this by recursively
calling itself with the arguments div_by? and 2 when the alias is used.

Assuming that the is_even alias is not used, the method tries to read the
appropriate Proc to use at ❸; it fails if it gets a criterion it doesn't understand.[3]
If it gets past this point, we know that the method understands its criteria,
because it found a Proc to use. It then returns that Proc, appropriately called
proc_to_return.

---

[3] Were you to modify or extend this method, you could simply add more options to the
proc_of_criterion Hash.

We now know that return_proc lives up to its name and returns a Proc. Let's use it. At ❹, we require one of our first scripts, boolean_golf.rb. You may recall that that script adds the methods true? and false? to every object. This will come in handy for our next few lines. At ❺, we define three Procs that can test numbers for certain conditions. We then use those Procs within the each block starting at ❻. For each of the Integers 4, 5, and 6, we test for even-ness, being divisible by three, and being equal to ten. We also use both the printf command that we saw in the line_num.rb script and the main ternary operator, both of which happen at ❼.

Proc.call(args) vs. Proc[args]

Notice that we call our Procs with a different syntax here—we don't use the call method at all. We can simply put whatever arguments we would use inside square brackets, and it's just like using the call method. Let's verify this in irb.

```
irb(main):001:0> is_ten = lambda { |x| x == 10 }
=> #<Proc:0xb7d0c8a4@(irb):1>
irb(main):002:0> is_ten.call(10)
=> true
irb(main):003:0> is_ten[10]
=> true
irb(main):004:0> is_ten.call(9)
=> false
irb(main):005:0> is_ten[9]
=> false
```

I chose to use the bracket syntax in these examples for the sake of brevity. So far, I've shown how to use Procs that have been returned directly from the return_proc method. But we can also do other things, such as converting between blocks and Procs.

Using Procs as Blocks

From ❽ to the end of the script, we see how we can cast the output of return_proc (which we know to be a Proc) into a block with the ampersand without ever storing the Proc in a variable. After defining our usual digits Array, we call find_all twice, assigning the results into even_results and div3_results, respectively. Remember that find_all takes a block. The ampersand can convert any expression that evaluates to a Proc into a block, and (return_proc('is_even') is an expression that returns (evaluates to) a Proc. Therefore, we can coerce (or cast) the expression (return_proc('is_even') into a perfectly valid block for find_all. We do this, outputting the results via puts at ❾.

The inspect Method

Notice that we call a new method called inspect on each set of results to retain the brackets and commas that we normally associate with members of Arrays. The inspect method returns a String representation of whatever object it's called on. It is slightly different from the to_s method we've already seen. Let's check that out in irb.

```
irb(main):001:0> digits = (0..9).to_a
=> [0, 1, 2, 3, 4, 5, 6, 7, 8, 9]
irb(main):002:0> digits.to_s
=> "0123456789"
irb(main):003:0> digits.inspect
=> "[0, 1, 2, 3, 4, 5, 6, 7, 8, 9]"
```

You can see that the output of inspect is a bit prettier than the output of to_s. It also retains more information about what type of object it was called on.

You should now be pretty comfortable with calling Procs, passing them around, reading them out of Hashes, and converting them to and from blocks, whether with a lambda or when passing around to methods. Now let's look at nesting lambdas within other lambdas.

#24 Nesting lambdas

Let's review Procs for a bit. Procs are just functions that can be treated as data, what functional programming languages call *first-class functions*. Functions can create Procs; we saw that both make_incrementer and return_proc return Procs of different sorts. Given all that, what prevents us from making a Proc that returns another Proc when called? Nothing at all.

In the make_exp example below, we create specific versions of Procs that raise an argument to some specified power. That power is the exp argument taken by the outer lambda, which is described as a *free variable* because it is not an explicit argument to the inner lambda.

The inner lambda, which is returned, has a *bound variable* called x. It is bound because it is an explicit argument to that inner lambda. That variable x is the number that will be raised to the specified power. This example is short, and the returned value at each stage is very important, so we'll do this entirely in irb.

The Code

Nested Lambdas

```
irb(main):001:0> digits = (0..9).to_a
=> [0, 1, 2, 3, 4, 5, 6, 7, 8, 9]
irb(main):002:0> make_exp_proc = lambda { |exp| lambda { |x| x ** exp } }
=> #<Proc:0xb7c97adc@(irb):2>
irb(main):003:0> square_proc = make_exp_proc.call(2)
=> #<Proc:0xb7c97b18@(irb):2>
irb(main):004:0> square_proc.call(5)
=> 25
irb(main):005:0> squares = digits.map { |x| square_proc[x] }
=> [0, 1, 4, 9, 16, 25, 36, 49, 64, 81]
```

How It Works

We see up to this point that make_exp_proc is a Proc, which returns a Proc when called. That resulting Proc raises its argument to the exponent used in the initial call of make_exp_proc. Since in our example, we called make_exp_proc with 2, we created a Proc that squares its argument, appropriately calling it square_proc. We also see that the squaring Proc can be used in a mapping operation onto the digits Array, and that it returns the correct squared values.

```
irb(main):006:0> cube_proc = make_exp_proc.call(3)
=> #<Proc:0xb7c97b18@(irb):2>
irb(main):007:0> cube_proc.call(3)
=> 27
irb(main):008:0> cubes = digits.map { |x| cube_proc[x] }
=> [0, 1, 8, 27, 64, 125, 216, 343, 512, 729]
```

We also see in the rest of the example that make_exp_proc is flexible and can take arguments other than 2. It works perfectly well with an argument of 3, producing a cubing Proc, which we can use in the same ways as the squaring Proc.

Up to this point, our Procs have tended to implement simple mathematical operations, like addition, multiplication, or exponentiation. But Procs are functions like any other, and they can output any type of value. Let's move on to the next script, which uses Procs that manipulate Strings.

#25 Procs for Text (willow_and_anya.rb)

As I was planning the functional programming chapter of this book, I was watching DVDs of Joss Whedon's *Buffy the Vampire Slayer*. I mention this because I had Procs and blocks on my brain, and I happened to encounter two very good candidates for text-based examples of lambda operations. In an episode called "Him," there is discussion of a "love spell", an "anti-(love spell) spell", and an "anti-(anti-(love spell) spell) spell". That's a great example of successive modifications via a simple function. In another episode called "Same Time, Same Place," there is a conversation that demonstrates simple variable substitution. Both are great examples of simple functions and are good venues to explore how Procs in Ruby differ based on how we choose to create them. Here's the source code.

NOTE *You obviously don't need to like Buffy to benefit from reading about these examples. The specific content that the scripts modify is essentially arbitrary.*

The Code

This code consists of three distinct files: one each for the two necessary classes, and one separate script meant to be directly executed.

The Him Class

```
#!/usr/bin/env ruby -w
# him.rb
```

❶ `class Him`

```
    EPISODE_NAME = 'Him'
    BASE         = 'love spell'
```

Constant Procs
```
    ANTIDOTE_FOR = lambda { |input| "anti-(#{input}) spell" }
```

Class Methods ❷
```
    def Him.describe()
        return <<DONE_WITH_HEREDOC

In #{EPISODE_NAME},
  Willow refers to an "#{ANTIDOTE_FOR[BASE]}".
  Anya mentions an "#{ANTIDOTE_FOR[ANTIDOTE_FOR[BASE]]}".
  Xander mentioning an "#{ANTIDOTE_FOR[ANTIDOTE_FOR[ANTIDOTE_FOR[BASE]]]}"
might have been too much.

DONE_WITH_HEREDOC
    end

end
```

The SameTimeSamePlace Class

```
#!/usr/bin/env ruby -w
# same_time_same_place.rb
```

❸ `class SameTimeSamePlace`

```
    EPISODE_NAME = 'Same Time, Same Place'

=begin rdoc
This Hash holds various procedure objects. One is formed by the generally
preferred Kernel.lambda method. Others are created with the older Proc.new
method, which has the benefit of allowing more flexibility in its argument
stack.
=end
```

❹
```
    QUESTIONS = {

        :ternary => Proc.new do |args|
          state    = args ? args[0] : 'what'
          location = args ? args[1] : 'what'
          "Spike's #{state} in the #{location}ment?"
        end,

        :unless0th => Proc.new do |*args|
          args = %w/what what/ unless args[0]
```

```ruby
          "Spike's #{args[0]} in the #{args[1]}ment?"
        end,
```

Flexible Arity
with Proc.new

```ruby
        :nitems => Proc.new do |*args|
          args.nitems >= 2 || args.replace(['what', 'what'])
          "Spike's #{args[0]} in the #{args[1]}ment?"
        end,

        :second_or => Proc.new do |*args|
          args[0] || args.replace(['what', 'what'])
          "Spike's #{args[0]} in the #{args[1]}ment?"
        end,

        :needs_data => lambda do |args|
          "Spike's #{args[0]} in the #{args[1]}ment?"
        end

      }

❺  DATA_FROM_ANYA = ['insane', 'base']

❻  def SameTimeSamePlace.describe()

      same_as_procs = [
        SameTimeSamePlace.yield_block(&QUESTIONS[:nitems]),
        QUESTIONS[:second_or].call(),
        QUESTIONS[:unless0th].call(),
        SameTimeSamePlace.willow_ask,
      ]

          return <<DONE
In #{EPISODE_NAME},
  Willow asks "#{QUESTIONS[:ternary].call(nil)}",
  #{same_as_procs.map do |proc_output|
    'which is the same as "' + proc_output + '"'
    end.join("\n  ")
  }
  Anya provides "#{DATA_FROM_ANYA.join(', ')}", which forms the full question
  "#{SameTimeSamePlace.yield_block(DATA_FROM_ANYA, &QUESTIONS[:needs_data])}".

DONE
    end

    =begin rdoc
    Wrapping a lambda call within a function can provide
    default values for arguments.
    =end
❼  def SameTimeSamePlace.willow_ask(args = ['what', 'what'])
      QUESTIONS[:needs_data][args]
    end
```

```
                    =begin rdoc
                    Passing a block as an argument to a method
                    =end
      ❽    def SameTimeSamePlace.yield_block(*args, &block)
                        # yield with any necessary args is the same as calling block.call(*args)
The yield              yield(*args)
Method              end

                end
```

The willow_and_anya.rb Script

```
#!/usr/bin/env ruby -w
# willow_and_anya.rb

Arrays with %w    %w[him same_time_same_place].each do |lib_file|
                      require "#{lib_file}"
                  end

                  [Him, SameTimeSamePlace].each do |episode|
      ❾    puts episode.describe()
                  end
```

How It Works

This script performs some complex operations. Let's consider each class individually and then look at the separate script that uses them.

The Him Class: Creating Procs with lambda

We define a class called Him at ❶. It has three constants: its own EPISODE_NAME, a BASE item, and a lambda operation to create an ANTIDOTE_FOR something.[4] It has one class method called Him.describe (❷) that returns a long String constructed via a here doc. Remember that you can call a Proc with either some_proc.call(args) or some_proc[args]. In this case, we'll use the shorter bracket version again. We'll report that the character named Willow refers to the antidote for the base spell. Her associate Anya then mentions the antidote for that antidote. Whedon avoided yet another call to the antidote-creating Proc in his show, but our method will continue, outputting the antidote for the antidote for the antidote.

The SameTimeSamePlace Class: Alternatives to lambda for Creating Procs

Our next class explores more options. SameTimeSamePlace starts at ❸ and it defines a Hash constant called QUESTIONS right away at ❹. Its keys are Symbols, and its values are Procs. Up until now, we've always created Procs with the lambda method, but we know that Procs are instances of the class Proc. Traditionally, you can create an instance by calling the new method on a class. Let's try that in irb.

---

[4] I mentioned earlier in the book that lambdas can make excellent Class Constants. Now you can see that in action.

```
irb(main):001:0> is_even_proc1 = lambda { |x| (x % 2).zero? }
=> #<Proc:0xb7cb687c@(irb):1>
irb(main):002:0> is_even_proc2 = Proc.new { |x| (x % 2).zero? }
=> #<Proc:0xb7cacb4c@(irb):2>
irb(main):003:0> is_even_proc1.call(7)
=> false
irb(main):004:0> is_even_proc2.call(7)
=> false
irb(main):005:0> is_even_proc1.call(8)
=> true
irb(main):006:0> is_even_proc2.call(8)
=> true
```

That seems to work fine, and each Proc behaves as expected. In actual practice, there is little difference between Procs created via lambda and Procs created via Proc.new. Proc.new is a bit more flexible about how it handles arguments, which we'll soon see. For now, note that the value for the key :ternary in our QUESTIONS Hash at ❹ is a Proc that asks if someone named Spike has a certain state (which is neither already known nor static) in a certain location (which is also neither already known nor static).

NOTE *Don't be fooled by this script's surface-level silliness. It actually clarifies some very interesting behavior in Ruby's Procs with regard to arguments and arity. Later scripts that use these techniques for tasks that are more useful in the real world include scripts that convert temperatures and play audio files for a radio station.*

Flexible Arity for Proc.new

Next, we'll start exploring Proc.new more for the :unless0th Symbol key. You'll notice that the *args argument to this Proc has a preceding asterisk. This option is available to Procs created with Proc.new, but not to Procs created with lambda. It indicates that the argument with the asterisk is optional. Immediately inside the :unless0th Proc, we set the value of args if it has no value at the zeroth index; then we output the same question as the :ternary version. The only difference is that the args Array is optional for this version. Note also that we create our double "what" default Array with a %w with slash delimiters. This is a very handy way to create single-word Arrays.

For the :nitems Symbol key, we use an optional *args with Proc.new again. The only difference between this version and the :unless0th version is the way this tests args. In this version, we call the nitems method on the args Array, which returns the number of non-nil items. That number needs to be two or greater; if it isn't, that means we don't have enough elements, and so we will replace args with our default set of two "what"s, just as in the previous Procs.

For the :second_or Symbol key, we see yet another Proc within optional args created with Proc.new. This version simply tests whether or not the second item in the args Array can be read. If it cannot be read, we replace args just as in the :nitems version.

Finally, we create a Proc the way we always have, using lambda. Since arguments to lambda Procs are not optional, we identify this one with the Symbol :needs_data. Note that this makes the internals of the Proc simpler. It returns its output value, and we assume that it gets what it needs. After defining our Procs, the last of which needs data, we should probably have some data. Our source is Anya again, and we define her DATA_FROM_ANYA Array at ❺.

On to the method SameTimeSamePlace.describe at ❻. It takes no arguments and defines a local Array variable called same_as_procs. Its first element is the return value of calling SameTimeSamePlace.yield_block (defined at ❽) with an argument that is the Proc associated with the :nitems key in the QUESTIONS Hash. All of this is cast into a block with the ampersand. We haven't seen the yield_block method yet, but it takes two arguments: *args and &block. The first of these indicates *All of your regular arguments*, and the second means *Whatever block you got*.

Blocks, Arguments, and yield

Remember how I mentioned that blocks are not considered "real" arguments? Using an ampersand is the way to explicitly refer to the block used to call a method. Since we have the group of arguments, whatever they may be, and we have the block, we could call it via block.call(*args). That approach would work, but we have yet another alternative. Ruby has a method called yield that means *Call whichever block you received with whichever arguments are passed to yield*. When you get comfortable with this script, try replacing the yield line in yield_block with block.call(*args). It will not change the script's behavior at all. Let's verify some of this in irb.

```
irb(main):001:0> def yield_block(*args, &block)
irb(main):002:1> yield(*args)
irb(main):003:1> end
=> nil
irb(main):004:0> yield_block(0) { |x| x + 1 }
=> 1
irb(main):005:0> yield_block("I am a String") { |x| x.class }
=> String
irb(main):006:0> yield_block("How many words?") { |x| x.split(' ').nitems }
=> 3
irb(main):007:0> yield_block(0, 1) { |x,y| x == y }
=> false
irb(main):008:0> yield_block(0, 1) { |x,y| x < y }
=> true
```

Handy, isn't it? The yield_block method is completely generic, taking any number of regular arguments and any block and executing (or yielding) that block with those arguments. It's a very powerful technique.

Now we understand how our script is using the yield_block method within SameTimeSamePlace.describe (❻). The next two elements of same_as_procs are the return values of Procs pulled out of the QUESTIONS Hash with the call method. Our last element is the return value of SameTimeSamePlace.willow_ask (❼). This method provides a workaround for Procs created with lambda that need a specific number of arguments. willow_ask wraps a call to such a Proc within a traditional method that takes an optional argument. That argument is forcibly set to whatever the Proc expects before it ever gets to the Proc. This is another alternative for dealing with the arguments to a Proc.

That's it for the elements of our same_as_procs Array. Now let's use it. We return a long here doc String inside SameTimeSamePlace.describe (❻). This here doc String consists of several lines. The first calls the QUESTIONS[:ternary] Proc with one explicitly nil argument. This will cause our state and location variables to be set to their default values within the Proc. The next four lines of output are the result of mapping a String outputter onto the elements of same_as_procs. Remember that those elements are the return values of their respective Procs, not the Procs themselves. They have already been evaluated before being put into the Array.

The last few lines of the here doc report the data provided by Anya, which is defined as the constant Array DATA_FROM_ANYA (❺). We call the yield_block method, passing in DATA_FROM_ANYA as the "real" arguments and the value returned from QUESTIONS[:needs_data], cast from a Proc into a block. Then we close our here doc and end the SameTimeSamePlace.describe method.

Using Both Him and SameTimeSamePlace in willow_and_anya.rb

The first thing we do in the main running script, willow_and_anya.rb, is require each lib_file needed. Then we cycle through each class, referred to by the name episode, and describe that episode (❾), implemented in each specific case, as already discussed.

Running the Script

Let's look at the output returned by executing ruby -w willow_and_anya.rb.

The Results

```
In Him,
    Willow refers to an "anti-(love spell) spell".
    Anya mentions an "anti-(anti-(love spell) spell) spell".
    Xander mentioning an "anti-(anti-(anti-(love spell) spell) spell) spell"
    might have been too much.

In Same Time, Same Place,
    Willow asks "Spike's what in the whatment?",
    which is the same as "Spike's what in the whatment?"
    which is the same as "Spike's what in the whatment?"
    which is the same as "Spike's what in the whatment?"
    which is the same as "Spike's what in the whatment?"
    Anya provides "insane, base", which forms the full question
    "Spike's insane in the basement?".
```

That's a lot of data about some pretty esoteric programming topics. Congratulations for sticking with me this far. If you're genuinely curious about how this all works, I have some questions for you to ponder.

Hacking the Script

How would you duplicate just the successive `lambda` outputs of `Him.describe` using inject? Here's what I came up with. Maybe you can find a better alternative.

```
def Him.describe2(iterations=3)
  (1..iterations).to_a.inject(BASE) do |memo,output|
    ANTIDOTE_FOR[memo]
  end
end
```

Another question you may find interesting is why the `describe` methods are attached to classes, rather than instances. The reason is that the `episode` variable at ❾ represents a class, not an instance. If we wanted to use instance methods, we would need to create an instance of either `Him` or `SameTimeSamePlace`, rather than just calling the `describe` method on each class directly.

Chapter Recap

What was new in this chapter?

- Creating Procs with `lambda`
- Using Procs as arguments to methods
- Using blocks as arguments to methods, including your own new methods
- Using Procs as first-class functions
- The `inspect` method
- Nesting `lambdas` within other `lambdas`
- `Proc.new`
- The `yield` method

I have a confession to make. I love object orientation for many programming tasks, but this chapter about Ruby's functional heritage was the most fun to write so far. Functional programming has been respected in academia for decades, and it is starting to get some well-deserved attention from folks in the computer programming industry and others who are just curious about what it can do. Now that we know some functional programming techniques, let's put them to use and even try to optimize them, which is the subject of our next chapter.

7

USING, OPTIMIZING, AND TESTING FUNCTIONAL TECHNIQUES

This chapter shows some recursive and other functional solutions to simple problems, as well as some ways we can test and improve these solutions. Two very common programming topics that demonstrate functional programming are the factorial and Fibonacci mathematical series—largely because they're so easily described using recursive means.[1]

The *factorial* of a given positive number is the product of all the integers from 1 to that number, so factorial(3) = $3 \times 2 \times 1$, factorial(5) = $5 \times 4 \times 3 \times 2 \times 1$, and so on. This can be expressed generally as:

factorial$(x) = x \times (x - 1) \times (x - 2) \ldots 1$

The Fibonacci series is infinite, but you can look at a slice of it. The *Fibonacci* value for 0 is 0, and the value for 1 is 1. Subsequent values are calculated, rather than preset. The number in the Fibonacci series at a given index is the sum of the previous two numbers. Therefore, the Fibonacci series

---

[1] This is as good a place as any to mention tail recursion. A function or method is *tail recursive* if it can be easily converted from recursion (which is friendly to human readers at a high level of abstraction) to iteration (which is friendlier to computer hardware). The Ruby interpreter does not currently do such conversion. I mention this because we'll be doing a lot of recursing in this chapter.

starts like this: 0, 1, 1, 2, 3, 5, 8, 13, 21, 34, and so on. The formula for Fibonacci values for numbers greater than one can be expressed generally as Fibonacci(x) = Fibonacci(x-1) + Fibonacci(x-2).

If you think that the general definitions of both factorials and Fibonaccis look recursive, you're right. We'll look at Ruby code that generates both types of numbers using recursion.

#26 Basic Factorials and Fibonaccis (factorial1.rb through fibonacci5.rb)

The most common criticism of recursion and other functional techniques is that they are resource intensive. Each new version of these factorial or Fibonacci scripts adds some feature intended to *optimize* the code, or produce a speed improvement. In some cases, these features result in a very dramatic improvement, but in other cases, they either fail to improve the code or sometimes even make it worse. The places where these attempts fail to improve speed are often as interesting as where they succeed. There's an old adage among programmers: *Premature optimization is the root of all evil.*[2] Keep that in mind while reading these examples.

The Code

For this chapter, we'll be looking at some short scripts in pairs. Here's factorial1.rb:

```
#!/usr/bin/env ruby
# factorial1.rb

class Integer

  def fact()
❶    return 1 if (self.zero?) or (self == 1)
❷    return self * (self-1).fact
  end

end
```

And here's fibonacci1.rb:

```
#!/usr/bin/env ruby
# fibonacci1.rb

class Integer

  def fib()
❸    return 0 if (self.zero?)
```

---

[2] Commonly attributed to Donald Knuth, a computer programming genius if there ever was one.

```
❹        return 1 if self == 1
         return (self-1).fib + (self-2).fib
     end

end
```

How It Works

For factorial1.rb and fibonacci1.rb, we add a new method to all Integers: either fact or fib, respectively. In both cases, we have our exit conditions that return either zero or one. For factorials, we return 1 when self is either 0 or 1, testing for 0 with the predicate zero? (❶). For the Fibonacci series, we return either zero or one at ❸. At either ❷ or ❹, we return the appropriate calculated value: self times the factorial of one lower than self (❷), or the sum of the previous two Fibonaccis (❹), matching the definitions I gave for factorials and Fibonaccis, respectively. Both of these scripts are simple, accurate ways to produce the mathematical procedures we want. Let's look at the results using irb. Note that we can require more than one library file with multiple -r flags.[3]

The Results

```
$ irb -r factorial1.rb -r fibonacci1.rb
irb(main):001:0> 3.fact
=> 6
irb(main):002:0> 4.fact
=> 24
irb(main):003:0> 5.fact
=> 120
```

The factorial of 3 is $3 \times 2 \times 1$, which is 6, so that's fine. 6×4 is 24, and 24×5 is 120. So our fact method seems to work well. On to the fibonacci series.

```
irb(main):004:0> 3.fib
=> 2
irb(main):005:0> 4.fib
=> 3
irb(main):006:0> 5.fib
=> 5
```

The first seven values in the Fibonacci series are 0, 1, 1, 2, 3, 5, and 8. The *zeroth* number (the number at the 0 index) is 0, the first is 1, the second is also 1, the third is 2, the fourth is 3, and the fifth is 5. Our fib method also seems to work well.

---

[3] The integers resulting from factorial and Fibonacci operations can become rather large. Luckily, Ruby allows you to just treat them all as Integers, transparently doing whatever operations are needed with Bignums and Fixnums without making you worry about such things.

Hacking the Script

How could we improve the speed of this script? We have several options. I'll outline each of them in turn and discuss the possible motivations for each change, but we'll wait to test them (and therefore, to see the results of our assumptions) until the end.

NOTE   *Modifying a computer program to improve it without changing its external behavior is called* refactoring. *That's what we're doing with these scripts, because we're not changing the factorial or Fibonacci values for a given input—we're just changing how (and possibly how quickly) we return the same value. Refactoring is a fascinating topic; you can read more about it at http://refactoring.com or in Martin Fowler's* Refactoring: Improving the Design of Existing Code *(Addison-Wesley Professional, 1999). Unit testing, which we'll describe later in this chapter, is a critical tool to use when refactoring, as I'll explain in that section.*

Using include? (factorial2.rb and fibonacci2.rb)

Here's a variant that decides what to `return` via the `include?` method, which eliminates the need to run two separate tests to find out whether `self` is either zero or one. The motivation is that it could be faster to do a single test instead of two separate tests. Again, I'll show the alterations for both the factorial and Fibonacci scripts. Notice how both ❺ lines differ from either ❶ or ❸ in the initial scripts.

```ruby
#!/usr/bin/env ruby
# factorial2.rb

class Integer

  def fact()
    return 1 if [0, 1].include?(self)
    return self * (self-1).fact
  end

end
```
❺ (marks the line `return 1 if [0, 1].include?(self)`)

Here's the Fibonacci script:

```ruby
#!/usr/bin/env ruby
# fibonacci2.rb

class Integer

  def fib()
    return self if [0, 1].include?(self)
    return (self-1).fib + (self-2).fib
  end

end
```
❺ (marks the line `return self if [0, 1].include?(self)`)

Passing the returns1 or returns_self Array as an Argument (factorial3.rb and fibonacci3.rb)

In these variants we have an Array called either returns1 or returns_self that defines the return values for either a factorial or Fibonacci test. The Array is [0, 1] in both cases, because zero and one are the values we use in our rules to calculate other values in both tests. The motivation for this variant is the thought that it might be faster to create a data structure (such as returns1) once and pass it around, rather than re-creating our [0, 1] Array every time we make a new recursive call to either fact() or fib(). Notice how we define returns1 or returns_self as an argument to each of our methods at ❻ in each script and then use it subsequently for both our exit conditions testing and as an explicit argument to the recursive calls (❼).

```
#!/usr/bin/env ruby
# factorial3.rb

class Integer

❻   def fact(returns1 = [0, 1])
      return 1 if returns1.include?(self)
❼     return self * (self-1).fact(returns1)
    end

end
```

Here is the Fibonacci version:

```
#!/usr/bin/env ruby
# fibonacci3.rb

class Integer

❻   def fib(returns_self = [0, 1])
      return self if returns_self.include?(self)
❼     return (self-1).fib(returns_self) + (self-2).fib(returns_self)
    end

end
```

Making RETURNS1 or RETURNS_SELF a Class Constant (factorial4.rb and fibonacci4.rb)

Making returns1 or returns_self an argument seems silly for one reason: It's always the same value, [0, 1]. Things that don't change are ideal constants, so let's try that for both scripts. We'll define a constant with an appropriate name at ❽ in each script and then use it in our method's tests. Note that there is no longer any need to pass the constant as an argument to the recursive method calls, as we did in the previous variant at ❼.

```
#!/usr/bin/env ruby
# factorial4.rb

class Integer

❽   RETURNS_1_FOR_FACTORIAL = [0, 1]

    def fact()
      return 1 if RETURNS_1_FOR_FACTORIAL.include?(self)
      return self * (self-1).fact
    end

end
```

Here is the Fibonacci version:

```
#!/usr/bin/env ruby
# fibonacci4.rb

class Integer

❽   RETURNS_SELF = [0, 1]

    def fib()
      return self if RETURNS_SELF.include?(self)
      return (self-1).fib() + (self-2).fib()
    end

end
```

Memoization of Results (factorial5.rb and fibonacci5.rb)

One unexamined flaw in our scripts so far is that they're stupid. It sounds harsh, but it's fair.[4] They keep repeating the same calculations over and over again. For the sake of example, let's assume that we've called the fib() method on the Integer 5, and fib() is as defined in fibonacci4.rb, our most recent Fibonacci script variant. What happens?

The first thing of interest is that whenever our 5 is instantiated, it has a class constant called RETURNS_SELF, defined as an Array: [0, 1]. Next we call fib() on our 5. RETURNS_SELF does not include? 5, so we then call fib() on the expression (5-1), which is of course the Integer 4, and add its returned value to the result of calling fib() on the value (5-2), also known as the Integer 3. We then find that RETURNS_SELF does not include? 4, either, so we then call fib() on the expressions (4-1), which is the Integer 3, and add its returned value to the result of calling fib() on the value (4-2), also known as the Integer 2. We keep doing this recursively until we get a value of self that is found within the RETURNS_SELF Array.

---

[4] Maybe the criticism is more fair when directed at the author than the scripts. After all, the scripts only do what I tell them to. In fairness to me, I wrote them to demonstrate failed optimization attempts.

The main problem with doing this is that we keep re-calculating methods like 3.fib(). We had to calculate it in the guise of (self-2).fib() in our initial call to 5.fib(), and we had to calculate it in the guise of (self-1).fib() when our value for self was 4. The reason all this recalculation is a problem is that 3.fib() gives the same result, whether it is called as (5-2).fib() or as (4-1).fib()—it's the same thing under the hood. Wouldn't it be great if there were a way to call something like 3.fib() once and then remember its value for subsequent calls?

There is such a technique. It's called *memoization,* and it's a critical way to make recursive programs use processor time more efficiently. Take a look at our new script variants, which take advantage of memoization. In both variants, we define an appropriately named Array at ❾ that holds the memoized results so far. We already have starting results for both 0 and 1, which we defined in the returns1 Array in our earlier examples. We then use that memoized results Array (either @@factorial_results or @@fibonacci_results) at ❿, using the ||= operator to set a value for the self index within the Array, if there isn't a value already. Since Ruby methods always return the last evaluated expression, we don't need separate setting and returning operations. Now, whenever we need the fact or fib value for a lower self, we can just read it out. The ||= operator at ❿ evaluates the element from the Array as true and simply returns it without making a new assignment.[5]

A complement to memoization is lazy evaluation. Few languages implement this by default, Haskell being the most widely known exception. Most languages use *eager evaluation,* in which expressions are evaluated as early as possible, certainly on entry into a method or function. *Lazy evaluation* lets expressions be passed around unevaluated until their value is needed. The benefit for factorial and Fibonacci operations is that the operations on higher numbers can wait until the operations on lower numbers are already done, which speeds up the whole process. There's a library for lazy evaluation in Ruby at http://moonbase.rydia.net/software/lazy.rb.

```
#!/usr/bin/env ruby
# factorial5.rb

class Integer
```
❾
```
  @@factorial_results = [1, 1] # Both 0 and 1 have a value of 1
```

Memoization ❿
```
  def fact()
    @@factorial_results[self] ||= self * (self-1).fact
  end

  def show_mems()
    @@factorial_results.inspect
  end

end
```

[5] Our Perl friends do something similar to our use of ||= here that they call the *Orcish Maneuver.* Look it up at http://perl.plover.com/TPC/1998/Hardware-notes.html if you're curious. The name comes from both a pun and the prevalence of *The Lord of the Rings* fandom in the Perl community.

The Fibonacci version is:

```ruby
#!/usr/bin/env ruby
# fibonacci5.rb

class Integer

  @@fibonacci_results = [1, 1] # Both 0 and 1 have a value of 1

  def fib()
    @@fibonacci_results[self] ||= (self-1).fib + (self-2).fib
  end

end
```

❾ (marker next to `@@fibonacci_results = [1, 1]`)
❿ (marker next to `@@fibonacci_results[self] ||= ...`)

That should be enough variants to test. Note that this last factorial script also includes a method called show_mems that you can use to inspect the state of the memoization. If you'd like, you can add your own equivalent to fibonacci5.rb. On to the testing.

#27 Benchmarking and Profiling (tests/test_opts.rb)

Here we'll talk about two distinct ways to test the execution speed of code. *Benchmarking* measures the overall speed of the code, while *profiling* gives more detailed information about how long different parts of the code take to execute, relative to each other.

Benchmarking

The previous variants all showed ways to modify the base code in the hopes of making it faster. Here's where we test our assumptions and find out what really makes a difference. I store it in a directory called tests, meaning that I run it with ruby -w tests/test_opts.rb.

The Code

```ruby
#!/usr/bin/env ruby
# test_opts.rb

=begin comment
Run this without warnings to avoid messages about method redefinition,
which we are doing intentionally for this testing script.
=end
```

Benchmark Module

❶
```ruby
require 'benchmark'
include Benchmark
```

❷
```ruby
FUNC_OF_FILE = {
  'factorial' => 'fact',
  'fibonacci' => 'fib',
}
```

```
      UPPER_OF_FILE = {
        'factorial' => 200,
        'fibonacci' => 30,
      }

❸ ['factorial', 'fibonacci'].each do |file|

❹   (1..5).to_a.each do |num|
❺     require "#{file}#{num}"
      upper = UPPER_OF_FILE[file]

❻     bm do |test|

❼       test.report("#{file}#{num}") do
❽         upper.send(FUNC_OF_FILE[file])
        end

      end

    end

end
```

How It Works

First, I require a file called 'benchmark' (❶); the include command that immediately follows it mixes in a Module called Benchmark. This is the workhorse
of our script. It provides a facility for testing how long specific operations take
within a program. In order to do those tests, we need to set up a few Constants,
which we do at ❷. The FUNC_OF_FILE constant contains the name of the method
(or function) we want to call in each file, and UPPER_OF_FILE determines
the largest Integer on which to call that function (the upper limit, in
other words).

At ❸, we loop through each file, and at ❹, we loop through each num,
which is the filename suffix. Then we require a specific, dynamically generated filename at ❺. Note that this will override any previous definitions of
methods with the same name. (This is why we will run this script without
warnings, as the RDoc at the beginning of the file indicates.) We then set the
value of the upper local variable. At ❻, we call the method bm, provided by the
Benchmark module. It takes a block whose local variable is the test to be
run. That test has a method called report, which (as the name suggests)
generates a report of the test's findings. The report method also takes a
block that contains the code comprising the test. That block consists of
only one line at ❽. We haven't seen the send method yet, but calling
some_object.send(some_func_name, some_arg) is the same as calling
some_object.some_func_name(some_arg). I'll describe send in greater detail
in the to_lang.rb script in Chapter 10. For now, just understand that
it calls the desired method (either fact or fib) for each file.

Running the Script

You'll want to run this with the command ruby tests/test_opts.rb. Notice that we eschew the -w flag in this particular case. The reason is that we are redefining methods, which triggers a warning. Since we are doing this intentionally and are aware of the situation, the warning is merely an annoyance in this particular case.

The Results

Here are my results. Your results may vary considerably, depending on how fast your machine is.

	user	system	total	real
factorial1	0.016667	0.000000	0.016667 (	0.002705)
	user	system	total	real
factorial2	0.000000	0.000000	0.000000 (	0.001517)
	user	system	total	real
factorial3	0.000000	0.000000	0.000000 (	0.001532)
	user	system	total	real
factorial4	0.000000	0.000000	0.000000 (	0.001491)
	user	system	total	real
factorial5	0.000000	0.000000	0.000000 (	0.001508)
	user	system	total	real
fibonacci1	8.416667	1.900000	10.316667 (	6.207565)
	user	system	total	real
fibonacci2	11.316667	1.866667	13.183333 (	8.567413)
	user	system	total	real
fibonacci3	9.066667	1.816667	10.883333 (	6.809812)
	user	system	total	real
fibonacci4	9.233333	1.533333	10.766667 (	6.520220)
	user	system	total	real
fibonacci5	0.000000	0.000000	0.000000 (	0.000166)

The benchmarking output shows seconds used from the perspective of the user, system, total, and real labels. You can read more about the specific meanings of these labels via the command man time on a Unix-like system. For now, keep in mind that they are useful for measuring the time one process takes, relative to another process. I'll be referring to the real time in my discussion. You can see that there is very little variation among the factorial scripts. The main reason for this is that the factorial operation is comparatively simple, since it is a single, recursive multiplication. We see more striking data for the Fibonacci scripts because each recursive Fibonacci operation spawns two additional Fibonacci operations, unless it uses memoization. This double spawning is why I set the upper limit of Fibonacci operations at the much lower value of 30, compared with the factorial's upper limit of 200.

Our tests showed that the simple fibonacci1.rb took about 6.20 seconds to run 30 consecutive operations of calling fib on the numbers from one to five. Things actually get worse when we try the include? optimization in fibonacci2.rb (it takes about 8.56 seconds), and improve only slightly for the argument optimization in fibonacci3.rb (which takes about 6.81 seconds).

The run time doesn't significantly change until we introduce memoization in `fibonacci5.rb`, where the time spent drops so much that it's no longer significant.

The moral of the story is twofold. First, we've learned that it's better to base code optimization for speed on tests, rather than intuitions. By trying to squeeze some faster performance out of a piece of code, you can waste time in an area that isn't even your speed bottleneck, and it will only make your code harder to read. The second moral is that memoization (as used in `factorial5.rb` and `fibonacci5.rb`) is a crucial addition to any recursive operations that are likely to be repeated.

Profiling

Of course, benchmarking is only part of the story. If you're worried about the speed of your code, knowing only the total time it takes to run is not especially useful. What's more useful is the information provided by *profiling*, which breaks down the parts of your code and gives speed reports at a finer level of detail.

Ruby has a profiling library called `profile`. It can be required, just like benchmark, but it doesn't demand specific testing code like the `bm` method and its block. The library can be automatically applied to an execution of code simply by including `profile` via the `-r` flag. Let's do so with a command-line execution of the first script we wrote:

```
ruby -r profile -r 99bottles.rb -e 'wall = Wall.new(99); wall.sing_one_verse!
until wall.empty?'.
```

Notice how all we have to do is require `profile` with the `-r` flag; our `-e` flag contains code to be executed that works just like the irb session we used with `99bottles.rb` when we wrote it in Chapter 2. Here is an extremely truncated version of its results:

```
2 bottles of beer on the wall, 2 bottles of beer
take one down, pass it around, 1 bottle of beer on the wall.

1 bottle of beer on the wall, 1 bottle of beer
take one down, pass it around, no more bottles of beer on the wall.
```

% time	cumulative seconds	self seconds	calls	self ms/call	total ms/call	name
31.25	0.08	0.08	297	0.28	0.45	Wall#sing
18.75	0.13	0.05	99	0.51	2.53	Wall#sing_one_verse!
18.75	0.18	0.05	99	0.51	0.51	Wall#take_one_down!
12.50	0.22	0.03	297	0.11	0.11	Fixnum#==
6.25	0.23	0.02	100	0.17	0.17	Wall#empty?
6.25	0.25	0.02	297	0.06	0.06	Fixnum#>
6.25	0.27	0.02	99	0.17	0.17	Kernel.puts
0.00	0.27	0.00	1	0.00	0.00	Wall#initialize
0.00	0.27	0.00	5	0.00	0.00	Module#method_added

0.00	0.27	0.00	1	0.00	0.00	Class#inherited
0.00	0.27	0.00	99	0.00	0.00	IO#write
0.00	0.27	0.00	594	0.00	0.00	String#+
0.00	0.27	0.00	99	0.00	0.00	Fixnum#-
0.00	0.27	0.00	100	0.00	0.00	Fixnum#zero?
0.00	0.27	0.00	1	0.00	0.00	Class#new
0.00	0.27	0.00	296	0.00	0.00	Fixnum#to_s
0.00	0.27	0.00	1	0.00	0.00	Module#private
0.00	0.27	0.00	1	0.00	266.67	#toplevel

This report provides a great deal of interesting information, including the percentage of total time that a given method takes, the raw seconds used by that method call, the number of calls to each method, and the number of milliseconds taken per call. This data gives you something to use when you're trying to improve execution speed. If the number of calls to a given method is high, perhaps the method is being called multiple times in a loop. You can increase speed by pre-running that method only once and passing its value into the loop for use. You can also try different ways of implementing the same operation to see which way runs faster, and so on.

Hacking the Script

There are several variations you could try with these scripts. The simplest code modifications involve changing the upper limit values in upper_of_file for each file. You can also try operations other than factorial or Fibonacci ones. You can also run any of the scripts in this book with -r profile. When writing them, I focused on pedagogy rather than speed, so you can probably make some speed improvements to these stock scripts. Now let's move on to a practical application of functional programming that should remind you of some earlier scripts.

#28 Converting Temperatures (temperature_converter.rb)

For this example, we'll write a converter script. This time, instead of converting currencies, we'll convert units for other real-world factors like length, mass, temperature, and so on. The version that I show here only handles temperatures, but you can download units_converter.rb at this book's companion website; it is a more comprehensive script that also handles length, volume, and mass. We'll concentrate on converting to and from English and metric units, but we'll also support kelvins. Let's take a look.

The Code

```ruby
#!/usr/bin/env ruby
# temperature_converter.rb
# See also GNU units at http://www.gnu.org/software/units/units.html
```

```
# Converts Metric/SI <-> English units.

=begin rdoc
Converts to and from various units of temperature.
=end
class Temperature_Converter

  # every factor has some base unit for multi-stage conversion
  # I allow either full or shortened name as the key
❶   BASE_UNIT_OF = {
    'temperature' => 'K',
    'temp'        => 'K',
  }

❷   C_TO_F_ADD       = 32.0
    F_TO_C_RATIO     = 5.0/9.0
    C_TO_K_ADD       = 273.15

❸   C2K = lambda { |c| c + C_TO_K_ADD }
    F2C = lambda { |f| (f - C_TO_F_ADD ) * F_TO_C_RATIO }
    K2C = lambda { |k| k - C_TO_K_ADD }
    C2F = lambda { |c| (c / F_TO_C_RATIO) + C_TO_F_ADD }
    F2K = lambda { |f| C2K.call( F2C.call(f) ) }
    K2F = lambda { |k| C2F.call( K2C.call(k) ) }

❹   CONVERSIONS = {
    # most units just need to get to the base unit
    # have => {want => how_many_wants_per_have},
    'C'    => { 'K' => C2K },
    'F'    => { 'K' => F2K },

❺   # The base unit requires more conversion targets
    'K'    => {
      'F'    => K2F,
      'C'    => K2C,
    },

  }

  OUTPUT_FORMAT = "%.2f"

❻   def convert(params)
    conversion_proc =
      CONVERSIONS[params[:have_unit]][params[:want_unit]] ||
      get_proc_via_base_unit(params)

    return "#{params[:have_num]} #{params[:have_unit]} = " +
      "#{sprintf( OUTPUT_FORMAT, conversion_proc[params[:have_num]] )} " +
      "#{params[:want_unit]}"
  end

  private
```

Composition of Functions

```ruby
=begin rdoc
If there is no direct link between the known unit and the desired unit,
we must do a two-stage conversion, using the base unit for that factor
as a "Rosetta Stone."
=end
  def get_proc_via_base_unit(params)
❼    base_unit        = BASE_UNIT_OF['temperature']
❽    have_to_base_proc = CONVERSIONS[params[:have_unit]][base_unit]
❾    base_to_want_proc = CONVERSIONS[base_unit][params[:want_unit]]
❿    return lambda do |have|
       base_to_want_proc.call( have_to_base_proc.call( have ) )
     end
   end

end
```

How It Works

This script uses a few functional techniques that we haven't covered yet. Let's step through the code. At ❶, we define a BASE_UNIT_OF Hash that holds the base unit. Note that *temperature* and *temp* are both acceptable, and that the script uses kelvins, the scientific unit of absolute temperature, as its internal temperature unit. Next, we define some helpful conversion constants. I've broken these up into paragraphs: The first paragraph of definitions (❷) holds simple addition and multiplication constants, while the second paragraph (❸) uses lambda to define Procs that will use the values from the first paragraph. Temperature conversion is a bit more complicated than conversion of length or mass.

Most unit conversions consist of a simple multiplication operation. If you have 100 pounds and you want to know how many kilograms that is, you simply multiply 100 by 0.45. But to convert temperature between Fahrenheit and Celsius, you must multiply *and* add. The general formula is F = (C × 9/5) + 32. Conversely, C = (F − 32) × 5/9. Note also that one degree Celsius and one kelvin are the same size (meaning there is no multiplication needed to convert between them), but they are offset by 273.15, so 0 degrees Celsius = 273.15 kelvins, and 0 kelvins (absolute zero) = -273.15 degrees Celsius. That's cold.

At ❸, we define constants with three-character names that suggest the type of temperature conversion they do; for example, the K2C conversion Proc accepts kelvins and returns the Celsius equivalent. Most of these are pretty straightforward and implement the temperature relationships I described in the paragraph of declarations (❷).

However, the F2K and K2F Procs are more interesting. They use previously defined Procs inside themselves and then use the call method successively to perform two-stage conversions. F2K accepts some Fahrenheit value f, converts that to Celsius via F2C.call(f), and then uses that Celsius value as the argument to C2F.call(). This general operation of performing successive function calls is called *composition*. F2K composes C2K and F2C, and K2F composes C2F and K2C. This has the same benefits as breaking operations up into functions or methods: You only need to have a single, definitive place where any given operation is defined, and you can just call that operation as you build more complicated operations that depend on earlier definitions.

We have some useful constants, including temperature-related Procs. Next is our CONVERSIONS Hash at ❹. This is a doubly nested Hash, and the outermost keys are the units we have. Each of those keys points to yet another Hash, with a key representing the units we want to convert to and a value that is the necessary conversion Proc. If we have degrees Celsius and we want kelvins, our conversion operation is CONVERSIONS['C']['K'], which is the C2K Proc constant.

NOTE *The purpose of the CONVERSIONS Hash is to pass in some identifier(s) and get something useful out, specifically the Proc needed to do the requested unit conversion. This is very similar to a* Factory *in object orientation, which is an object that creates other objects based on the parameters it receives. Our CONVERSIONS Hash is an example of the same concept applied to Procs.*

The first paragraph of data in CONVERSIONS converts to our base unit for each factor—kelvins, in our case. But what if someone asks for a final output that isn't our base unit? We need to be able to convert from the base unit to all the other units, which is what the next paragraph of code at ❺ is for. It's still part of the CONVERSIONS Hash, and it still follows the same structure of { have => { want => some_conversion_proc } }, but it has two conversion targets instead of one. We close the constants with OUTPUT_FORMAT, which restricts our reported values to two decimal places.

At ❻ we define our main method, called convert. It takes a mandatory argument called params and defines a local variable called conversion_proc that has the value of either CONVERSIONS[params[:have_unit]][params[:want_unit]] or, failing that, the output of get_proc_via_base_unit(params). We already know that the value of CONVERSIONS['C']['K'] is the Celsius-to-kelvins Proc. Let's verify that in irb:

```
$ irb -r temperature_converter.rb
irb(main):001:0> tc = Temperature_Converter.new
=> #<Temperature_Converter:0xb7ccdb04>
irb(main):002:0> tc.convert( {:have_unit => 'C', :want_unit => 'K', :have_num
=> 15} )
=> "15 C = 288.15 K"
```

There is another key to params here other than :have_units and :want_units, but it should be fairly clear. We also need to tell the converter how many units we have, which is what :have_num does. These results look good; they are examples in which there is a value available for CONVERSIONS[params[:have_unit]][params[:want_unit]] inside the convert method, meaning that it doesn't need to use get_proc_via_base_unit(params). After it's got the conversion_proc, it returns the output you already saw in irb, which shows the number and unit already known, and what it converts into.

This is straightforward enough. But what happens when there isn't a value for CONVERSIONS[params[:have_unit]][params[:want_unit]] available? This would be true in cases such as converting degrees Celsius to degrees Fahrenheit. There is no Proc at CONVERIONS['C']['F']. Does this mean that our base unit needs to be either the known or desired value? Yes and no. Yes in only the most pedantic sense. No in any practical sense, because we can use the get_proc_via_base_unit method to create our own conversion_proc by composing two other known conversion_procs, just like the ones we hard-coded into the temperature converters.

If the unit our params asks for doesn't have a built-in conversion Proc, we can use get_proc_via_base_unit, as noted. Inside get_proc_via_base_unit, we first get the base_unit (❼). We then create the have_to_base_proc by getting the Proc out of CONVERIONS that would be used to convert from the known unit to the base_unit (❽). Then we get the base_to_want_proc by getting the Proc out of CONVERIONS that would be used to convert from the base_unit to the unit we want (❾). Then at ❿, we compose base_to_want_proc and have_to_base_proc, just as we did in the ❸ section for F2K and K2F. We could have called our new Proc have_to_want_proc, but we just return it, and it becomes conversion_proc inside the convert method at ❻.

The Results

Let's try it out in irb. It was 65 degrees Fahrenheit in Buffalo, New York in November today (yes, really), and I was talking with a Canadian coworker about this temperature conversion script. Let's start with that.

```
$ irb -r temperature_converter.rb
irb(main):001:0> tc = Temperature_Converter.new
=> #<Temperature_Converter:0xb7c75b5c>
irb(main):002:0> tc.convert( { :have_num => 65.0, :have_unit => 'F', :want_unit => 'C' } )
=> "65.0 F = 18.33 C"
irb(main):003:0> tc.convert( { :have_num => 0, :have_unit => 'K', :want_unit => 'F' } )
=> "0 K = -459.67 F"
```

These examples should give you an idea of this program's interface. You can also call it with other conversions that are of interest to you.

Hacking the Script

As I already noted, there is a more complex version of this script available for download at the book's website. If you find that you want to convert to or from units that I don't have built in, just create a key/value pair in CONVERSIONS that converts from your new unit to the appropriate base unit and another that converts from the base unit to your new unit. That should give you the ability to convert to and from any unit relative to your new unit.

We also use implicit composition in `temperature_converter.rb`—at ❸ for definition and at ❿ for use. You could modify the script to have an explicit compose method that takes two Procs and returns a new Proc that performs each operation in order. Here's an example in irb:

```
irb(main):001:0> def compose(inner_proc, outer_proc, *args)
irb(main):002:1> return lambda { |*args| outer_proc.call(inner_proc[*args]) }
irb(main):003:1> end
=> nil
irb(main):004:0> square = lambda { |x| x ** 2 }
=> #<Proc:0xb7cda048@(irb):4>
irb(main):005:0> inc = lambda { |x| x + 1 }
=> #<Proc:0xb7ccb8f4@(irb):5>
irb(main):006:0> square_then_inc = compose( square, inc )
=> #<Proc:0xb7ce5204@(irb):2>
irb(main):007:0> inc_then_square = compose( inc, square )
=> #<Proc:0xb7ce5204@(irb):2>
irb(main):008:0> square_then_inc.call(1)
=> 2
irb(main):009:0> square_then_inc.call(2)
=> 5
irb(main):010:0> inc_then_square.call(2)
=> 9
```

Line 8 gives us 2, because (1 ** 1) + 1 = 2. Line 9 gives us 5, because (2 ** 2) + 1 = 5. Line 10 gives us 9, because (2 + 1) ** 2 = 9. Once you have this compose method, you can even use it on Procs that are the returned value from a previous call to compose, allowing you to stack successive operations as much as you like.

#29 Testing temperature_converter.rb (tests/ test_temp_converter.rb)

Up until this point, our testing scripts have been relatively primitive, and to a very large degree, we have rolled our own testing solutions. It's silly to do that repeatedly, especially in computer programs, because good programming languages allow you to express abstract concepts abstractly, as well as to adapt general-purpose tools in code libraries to your specific needs.

Ruby has a general-purpose testing library called Test::Unit. Here is code that allows you to use its power to test the script temperature_converter.rb.

The Code

```
#!/usr/bin/env ruby
# test_temp_converter.rb

require 'temperature_converter'
require 'test/unit'
```
❶

Unit Testing

❷ `class Tester < Test::Unit::TestCase`

```ruby
  def setup
    @converter = Temperature_Converter.new()
  end

  def test_temps()

    tests = {
      '100.0 C = 212.00 F' => {
        :have_num  => 100.0,
        :have_unit => 'C',
        :want_unit => 'F',
      },
      '212.0 F = 100.00 C' => {
        :have_num  => 212.0,
        :have_unit => 'F',
        :want_unit => 'C',
      },
      '70.0 F = 294.26 K' => {
        :have_num  => 70.0,
        :have_unit => 'F',
        :want_unit => 'K',
      },
      '25.0 C = 298.15 K' => {
        :have_num  => 25.0,
        :have_unit => 'C',
        :want_unit => 'K',
      },
    }
    general_tester( tests )

  end

  private

  def general_tester(tests)
    tests.each_pair do |result,test_args|
      assert_equal( result, @converter.convert( test_args ) )
    end
  end

end
```

The markers ❸ appears next to `tests = {`, ❹ next to `def general_tester(tests)`, ❺ next to `tests.each_pair do |result,test_args|`, and ❻ next to the `assert_equal` line.

The Results

Let's run it and see what happens.

```
$ ruby -w tests/test_temp_converter.rb
Loaded suite tests/test_temp_converter
Started
.
```

```
Finished in 0.001094 seconds.

1 tests, 4 assertions, 0 failures, 0 errors
```

All four of our assertions passed with no failures or errors. That's wonderful news. Now let's look at what it means.

NOTE *One term you may hear in reference to testing is* code coverage, *which is the degree to which the tests adequately examine the pertinent code. This can be defined in terms of the percentage of total code lines that are tested, the percentage of Boolean evaluations that are tested, and other similar metrics.*

Earlier in this chapter, I mentioned refactoring, the practice of cleaning up code implementation while leaving its behavior unchanged. Unit testing is very useful when refactoring, especially if you use tests that have high *entry/exit coverage*, meaning they try to ensure that all outputs from functions stay the same as long as those functions get the same inputs. This type of testing keeps your refactoring honest.

How It Works

First, we need access to the code that we'll be testing. Luckily, we've followed good design practice and defined our code in a library called temperature_converter.rb, so we require both it and the test/unit library at ❶. Then we define a new class called Tester; as you can see at ❷, this class is a child of Test::Unit::TestCase, meaning that it inherits all of the methods and characteristics of Test::Unit::TestCase.

We then define a testing method called test_temps. It's just a wrapper for a multi-level Hash called tests, defined at ❸ inside test_temps. You'll notice that each key of tests is a String that looks like the output of Units_Converter.convert; that key's value is a Hash that you use as the argument into Units_Converter.convert in order to get output that matches that key. Inside test_temps, we then pass tests as an argument into a private method called general_tester, which we define at ❹.

The general_tester method loops through each_pair in the tests Hash at ❺, calling the expected result result and the argument Hash needed to produce that result, test_args. For each of those pairs, we assert that result and @converter.convert(test_args) are equal, using the appropriately named assert_equal method (❻). That's all there is to it.

Hacking the Script

Try making a change in one of the tests Hashes. If you either change only the key (which becomes result in general_tester) or only the value (which becomes test_args in general_tester), the call to assert_equal will fail, because the two items passed as arguments to be compared will no longer be equal. You can also add entirely new elements to the tests Hash, with new values you want to verify.

This script only scratches the surface of how to use `Test::Unit`. Type `ri Test::Unit` at the command line for more information. You can also browse to http://www.ruby-doc.org/stdlib/libdoc/test/unit/rdoc within the Ruby Standard Library Documentation site. Note that the HTML generated for that documentation came from RDoc.

I already mentioned that testing can be useful during refactoring. A good place to start with testing is what I've done here, pre-figuring expected values from a method based on a set of known input parameters. The `assert_equal` method is very useful for such testing. There are other methods available, which you can read about by typing `ri Test::Unit::Assertions` at the command line. Notables include `assert_instance_of`, which checks whether its argument belongs to a specified class; `assert_nil`, which checks whether its argument is `nil`; `assert_raise`, which you can use to intentionally raise an Exception (i.e., break something); and `assert_respond_to`, which checks whether a given argument knows how to respond to a given specified method.

Chapter Recap

What was new in this chapter?

- Recursive factorials and Fibonaccis as good profiling candidates
- Refactoring
- Memoization
- Testing with Benchmark
- Profiling
- Converting temperatures
- Hashes with Proc values as Proc Factories
- Composition of Procs
- Testing with `Test::Unit`

Again, that's a lot to take in. This list is deceptively short, because some of these concepts require more contemplation than those we've considered in previous chapters. Let's move on to the next chapter, in which we'll write some tools for processing HTML and XML.

8

HTML AND XML TOOLS

Text runs the Web. This is especially true of text that is encoded within some sort of markup, such as HyperText Markup Language (HTML) or eXtensible Markup Language (XML). Even non-programmers know that HTML is the markup generally used by websites, even if they've never heard the term markup before. XML is becoming increasingly important for both data transfer and data storage. As I work on the chapters of this book, I save them as a filetype that consists of a compressed collection of XML files. I also used a type of XML called DocBook (http://docbook.org) for my Doctoral dissertation. The bottom line is, XML-based markup is everywhere. Luckily, Ruby can understand, output, and manipulate XML (and HTML).

#30 Cleaning Up HTML (html_tidy.rb)

Let's start with HTML. This markup language has had several numbered releases, similar to different versions of software, and it's come a long way since Tim Berners-Lee made the first web page at CERN in the mid '90s.

Recent versions of HTML are subsets of XML and are called XHTML as a result. However, the earlier versions of HTML were not as disciplined; they allowed very liberal interpretations of HTML. Especially when people were first learning how to use HTML, they would often throw together pages that were not very well designed, either aesthetically or technically. But browser manufacturers didn't want to take the blame for rendering content badly, so they made their browsers very forgiving.

In the short term, the practice of allowing non-compliant HTML was great, because it meant that more people could view more content. In the long term, however, that liberality had some negative consequences because it allowed web designers to continue using some uncorrected bad techniques. There's a lot of sloppy HTML out there, and there's little reason to add to the mess. We want a tool that helps us make sure that our own HTML is up to spec.

NOTE *I'm assuming that you have a basic familiarity with HTML. If not, there's a good guide at http://w3schools.com/html/default.asp. If you're curious about the various versions of HTML and its relationship to XML, browse to the World Wide Web Consortium (W3C) MarkUp page at http://www.w3.org/MarkUp. This page also has a link to the HTML Tidy program that the html_tidy.rb script depends on.*

There's an excellent program that does most of this clean-up work already. It's called HTML Tidy, and it was written by Dave Raggett. It's available at http://tidy.sourceforge.net, but it also comes prepackaged within many GNU/Linux distributions. Seeing no need to reinvent the wheel, I wrote html_tidy.rb to use Raggett's program and add some specific features that I wanted. Let's take a look at the code.

The Code

```ruby
#!/usr/bin/env ruby
# html_tidy.rb
# cleans up html files

❶ EMPTY_STRING = ''

SIMPLE_TAG_REPLACEMENTS = {

    #closers
    /\<\/b\>/i              => '</strong>',
    /\<\/i\>/i              => '</em>',
    /\<\/strong\>\<\/td\>/i => '</th>',
    /\<\/u\>/i              => '</div>',

    #openers
    /\<b\>/i                => '<strong>',
    /\<i\>/i                => '<em>',
    /\<td\>\<strong\>/i     => '<th>',
    /\<u\>/i                => '<div style="text-decoration: underline;">',
    # again, more as appropriate

}
```

=> Operator

```
      TIDY_EXTENSION = '.tidy'

      TIDY_OPTIONS = '-asxml -bc' # possible add -access 3

❷ UNWANTED_REGEXES = [
      /^<meta name=\"GENERATOR\" content=\"Microsoft FrontPage 5.0\">$/,
      /^ *$/,
      /^\n$/,
      # more as appropriate
    ]

❸ def declare_regexes_and_replacements()
      replacement_of = Hash.new()
      UNWANTED_REGEXES.each do |discard|
        replacement_of[discard] = EMPTY_STRING
      end
      return replacement_of.merge(SIMPLE_TAG_REPLACEMENTS)
    end

    =begin rdoc
    This lacks a ! suffix because it duplicates the argument and
    returns the changes made to that duplicate, rather than overwriting.
    =end
❹ def perform_replacements_on_contents(contents)
      output = contents.dup
      replacement_of = declare_regexes_and_replacements()
❺    replacement_of.keys.sort_by { |r| r.to_s }.each do |regex|
        replace = replacement_of[regex]
❻      output.each { |line| line.gsub!(regex, replace) }
      end
      return output
    end

    =begin rdoc
    This has the ! suffix because it destructively writes
    into the filename argument provided.
    =end
❼ def perform_replacements_on_filename!(filename)
❽    if (system('which tidy > /dev/null'))
        new_filename = filename + TIDY_EXTENSION
        system("tidy #{TIDY_OPTIONS} #{filename} > #{new_filename} 2> /dev/null")
❾      contents = File.open(new_filename, 'r').readlines()
        new_contents = perform_replacements_on_contents(contents)
        File.open(new_filename, 'w') { |f| f.puts(new_contents) }
      else
        puts "Please install tidy.\n"
      end
    end

❿ ARGV.each do |filename|
      perform_replacements_on_filename!(filename)
    end
```

Standard Error

How It Works

We start by defining some constants at ❶. EMPTY_STRING should be obvious, and SIMPLE_TAG_REPLACEMENTS is a Hash whose keys are regular expressions and whose values are whatever the corresponding key should be replaced with. You'll notice that you need to mark certain characters within a regular expression with a backslash (\)—that's because some characters have special meanings within regular expressions. You've already seen examples of that, where ? means *Zero or one of whatever preceded me* and * means *Zero or more of whatever preceded me*. Similarly, \ means *Treat whatever follows me as a literal character, not a special regex character*.

Why do I make these particular replacements? The <b> and <i> tags are still commonly used, but they are not compliant with the Web Accessibility Initiative (WAI). I've set up this script to replace them with appropriate tags that accomplish the same goal but don't discriminate against the visually impaired. I also replace /\<td\>\<\strong\>/ with <th> because I find that people often make "almost" table headers by putting formatting within a table cell, rather than making the cell a real header. Finally, I've taken out the <u> tag because it doesn't mean anything, even if it creates an underline. It's just a visual formatting tag with no semantic meaning, which is a no-no. Formatting is what stylesheets are for—the markup itself should just have content. Therefore, I replace <u> with a <div> that has an underline style attached to it. I make all these replacements both for the opening tags and the closing tags.

NOTE *Web accessibility is important: These fixes help people who are visually impaired surf the Web. The* html_tidy.rb *script fixes my mistakes, at least for these particular cases. If you're curious, read more about accessibility and its importance at the W3C's Web Accessibility Commission page (http://www.w3c.org/WAI).*

We continue with more constants, including some TIDY_OPTIONS. Execute man tidy at the command line to see what these do. These options reflect my preferences, but you can certainly make some changes to the constant once you're comfortable with operating the script. At ❷, we have an Array constant called UNWANTED_REGEXES. It sounds harsh, but there are some things I just don't want in my HTML. One of these is a <meta> tag, which Microsoft's FrontPage sometimes adds to files. I also don't want either lines with only whitespace (which /^ *$/ matches) or completely empty lines (which /^\n$/ matches). As the comment suggests, you can add to this Hash.

The first method, declare_regexes_and_replacements, is at ❸. It combines SIMPLE_TAG_REPLACEMENTS with UNWANTED_REGEXES by looping through UNWANTED_REGEXES and making a Hash called replacement_of, whose keys are the elements of UNWANTED_REGEXES and whose values are all the EMPTY_STRING. This makes sense—if a regex is unwanted, we want to replace it with the empty string. The declare_regexes_and_replacements method then returns the merged Hash, which is made up of both SIMPLE_TAG_REPLACEMENTS, which was already a Hash in the first place, and our new replacement_of Hash.[1]

---

[1] I generally find Perl rather sloppy, but one benefit of its policy of storing Hashes as even-length Arrays is that you can make Hashes out of Arrays very easily. The Perl equivalent of our UNWANTED_REGEXES.each loop would be something like this: my %replacement_of = map { $_ => EMPTY_STRING } @unwanted_regexes;. Of course, it's more trouble to merge Hashes in Perl, so I still like Ruby better. Don't worry about any of this if you don't know Perl.

On to ❹ and the `perform_replacements_on_contents` method. It takes an argument, unsurprisingly called `contents`, immediately duplicates it with the `dup` method, and calls the result `output`. It then calls `declare_regexes_and_replacements` (defined at ❸), getting the return value which we already know is a Hash that is called `replacement_of`. For simplicity, we'll keep the same name for that Hash inside `perform_replacements_on_contents`. At ❺, we sort the keys of `replacement_of` with the `sort_by` method, which takes a block. Strings know how to compare themselves to other Strings for sorting purposes, whereas regular expressions don't. Therefore, we convert each of our regular expression keys into a String for sorting purposes.

NOTE   *Strings know how to compare themselves to other Strings because* `String` *has a* `<=>` *method, and one of* `String`'s *ancestors is the Comparable module.*[2] *Comparable uses the* `<=>` *method to implement the other comparison operators, such as* `==`, `<=`, `>=`, *and so on. If you create a new class and want it to be sortable, give it a method called* `<=>`, *figure out how to implement it in a way that makes sense, and then mix in Comparable. You'll get lots of sorting value for a minimal amount of effort, and you'll make your objects more useful.*

In an earlier version of `html_tidy.rb`, I didn't include the sorting at ❺, and I would occasionally miss replacements described in `SIMPLE_TAG_REPLACEMENTS`. The reason was that Hash keys do not have a deterministic order, so sometimes my program would replace `<b>` with `<strong>` before getting to replacing `</strong></td>` with `</th>`, but sometimes it wouldn't. To make my program more robust, I'd either need to add a Hash pair that replaced `</b></td>` with `</th>` or enforce a specific order on how I used `replacement_of` at ❺. I chose to enforce order, not just because it makes the program more dependable, and not just because I'm a petty tyrant at heart, but also because it makes the program simpler.

We sort the keys of `replacement_of` and loop through each of them at ❺, calling them `regex` in turn. We also want the replacement value, so we read that out of the Hash as `replace`. Then at ❻, we loop through each `line` of the eventual `output`, destructively `gsub!`ing `regex` with `replace`. The `output` variable is now ready to be returned. That's how we `perform_replacements_on_contents`. Where do we get the `contents`?

The `perform_replacements_on_filename!` method is at ❼. At ❿, we call it on each element of the `ARGV` Array, which we call `filename` as we pass it into `perform_replacements_on_filename!` as the single argument. We first attempt a system call of `'which tidy > /dev/null'` (❽). Without getting too deep into Unix black magic, I'll tell you that when executed, this command determines whether there is a version of `tidy` installed on the machine.

If the test succeeds, we know we can use `tidy`. First, we define a `new_filename`, which is just the old `filename` with the `TIDY_EXTENSION` appended to it. We then make a call to `tidy` itself, passing it its own `TIDY_OPTIONS` (as an interpolated String) and calling it on `filename`. We pass its output into the `new_filename`, discarding any error messages. The `new_filename` file now contains all of the tidying done by `tidy` itself but none of our add-on changes.

---

[2] Since Comparable is a module, rather than a class, it is an ancestor of String via mixing in, rather than straightforward inheritance. However, `String.ancestors` includes Comparable, so I've referred to it as an ancestor here.

NOTE *The > character in the Unix shell just means* Send my output into the following filename, *so* some_command > some_file *takes the output of* some_command *and writes it into a
file called* some_file. *Putting a 2 in front of* > *makes it apply to error messages, instead
of regular output. Unix calls the output of error messages* Standard Error. *The file
called* /dev/null *just means* nowhere, *so* some_command > some_file 2> /dev/null
means Send some_command's *output into* some_file, *and I don't care about any
error messages.*

We then read new_filename's contents using File.open and the readlines
method at ❾. That contents variable is ready for perform_replacements_on_contents,
which we call on it, assigning the results into new_contents. We then open the
new_filename file again, this time for writing, and replace its contents with
new_contents.

If the which tidy test fails, we know that our beloved tidy is not present,
so there's little point in proceeding. We simply ask the user to install tidy.

Running the Script

I have a sample file at extras/eh.html, so we can call this script with the
command ruby -w html_tidy.rb extras/eh.html. Here's the original version,
extras/eh.html:

```
<!DOCTYPE html PUBLIC "-//W3C//DTD XHTML 1.0 Strict//EN"
"http://www.w3.org/TR/xhtml1/DTD/xhtml1-strict.dtd">
<html
    lang="en"
    xml:lang="en"
    xmlns="http://www.w3.org/1999/xhtml">

<head>
<meta http-equiv="refresh" content="10" />
<title>English Horn for No Clergy</title>
<style>
@import url('../css/noclergy.css');
h1, h2 { display: none; }
</style>
</head>

<body>

<div id="notation">
<h1>No Clergy:</h1>
<p style="text-align:center;">
<img src="../../png/eh-page1.png" />
</p>
</div>

<table>
<tr>
<td><b>I'm a header, but I don't know it.</b></td>
```

```
<td><u>I'm some underlined content.</u></td>
<td><i>I'm some italicized content.</i></td>
</tr>
</table>

<p>I'm an unclosed paragraph. The horrors.

</body>
</html>
```

The Results

And here's the new version, extras/eh.html.tidy:

```
<!DOCTYPE html PUBLIC "-//W3C//DTD XHTML 1.0 Transitional//EN"
    "http://www.w3.org/TR/xhtml1/DTD/xhtml1-transitional.dtd">
<html lang="en" xml:lang="en" xmlns="http://www.w3.org/1999/xhtml">
<head>
<meta name="generator" content=
"HTML Tidy for Linux/x86 (vers 1 September 2005), see www.w3.org" />
<meta http-equiv="refresh" content="10" />
<title>English Horn for No Clergy</title>

<style type="text/css">
/*<![CDATA[*/
@import url('../css/noclergy.css');
h1, h2 { display: none; }
/*]]>*/
</style>

<style type="text/css">
/*<![CDATA[*/
 p.c1 {text-align:center;}
/*]]>*/
</style>
</head>
<body>
<div id="notation">
<h1>No Clergy:</h1>
<p class="c1"><img src="../../png/eh-page1.png" /></p>
</div>
<table>
<tr>
<th>I'm a header, but I don't know it.</th>
<td><div style="text-decoration: underline;">I'm some underlined content.
</div></td>
<td><em>I'm some italicized content.</em></td>
</tr>
</table>
<p>I'm an unclosed paragraph. The horrors.</p>
</body>
</html>
```

Notice how tidy added a <meta> tag for itself and wrapped the style information inside CDATA markers. It also defined a paragraph class called c1 for our text-align:center; style that is attached to the free-floating <p> tag. In addition to everything that tidy does, our script does what I've described above. It replaced the tags for our "almost" header with a <th>, converted the underlining from a bad <u> tag to a style declaration, and changed the <i> tag to an <em> tag, making this content a little friendlier to an audio browser, such as a blind person might use.

Hacking the Script

Could we use inject, rather than each, to modify declare_regexes_and_replacements at ❸ and make it more functional? Here's one way:

```
def declare_regexes_and_replacements()
  return UNWANTED_REGEXES.inject({}) do |h,discard|
    h.merge( { discard => EMPTY_STRING } )
  end.merge(SIMPLE_TAG_REPLACEMENTS)
end
```

In this variant, h takes the place of replacement_of, and it is the memoized Hash that persists from one iteration of inject to the next. Each time, we merge it with the new pair (consisting of discard as a key pointing to the EMPTY_STRING), so we end up with a Hash of things to replace, all of whose replacements are the EMPTY_STRING—just like in the original version. This time, however, our temporary variables are confined entirely within the inject loop.

Could we have simply altered contents in place with a method called perform_replacements_on_contents!? Of course. I just wanted to show both a destructive method (perform_replacements_on_filename!) and a regular method (perform_replacements_on_contents) whose output we would then use for demonstration purposes. Both could have been either destructive or non-destructive. Change the script as you like if you'd prefer these to use the same approach.

#31 Counting Tags (xml_tag_counter.rb)

XML is strict about its internal structure. It can only have a single top-level element (called the *root element*), but that root element can have any number of elements within itself, and each of those elements can have any number of other elements within itself, continuing on recursively. We want a script that we can run on an XML file that will output how many times each tag (or element) occurs within that document, no matter how many layers deep it appears—for example, we want to find all <p> tags regardless of whether or not those tags are immediately within the top-level <html> element, or within some other element, such as a <blockquote> or <div>. Let's take a look.

The Code

```ruby
#!/usr/bin/env ruby
# xml_tag_counter.rb

=begin rdoc
This script uses the Rexml parser, which is written in Ruby itself.
Find out more at http://www.germane-software.com/software/rexml.
=end
```

REXML ❶ require 'rexml/document'

```ruby
class Hash
```

❷
```ruby
=begin rdoc
Given that <b>self</b> is a <b>Hash</b> with keys of
XML tags and values of their respective counts in an
XML source file, sort by the tag count, descending.
Fall back to an ascending sort of the tag itself,
weighted half as strongly.
=end
  def sort_by_tag_count()
    self.sort do |a, b|
```
❸
```ruby
      ( (b[1] <=> a[1]) * 2 ) + (a[0] <=> b[0])
    end
  end
```

❹
```ruby
=begin rdoc
Merge with another <b>Hash</b>, but add values rather
than simply overwriting duplicate keys.
=end
```
Hashes as Histograms
```ruby
  def merge_totals(other_hash)
    other_hash.keys.each do |key|
      self[key] += other_hash[key]
    end
  end
```

❺
```ruby
=begin rdoc
Your basic pretty formatter, returns a <b>String</b>.
=end
  def pretty_report()
    output = ''
    sort_by_tag_count.each do |pair|
      tag, count = pair
      output += "#{tag}: #{count}\n"
    end
    return output
  end

end # Hash
```

```
❻ =begin rdoc
   Returns DOM elements of a given filename.
   =end
   def get_elements_from_filename(filename)
     REXML::Document.new(File.open(filename)).elements()
   end

❼ =begin rdoc
   Returns a <b>Hash</b> with keys of XML tags and values
   of those tags' counts within a given XML document.
   Calls itself recursively on each tag's elements.
   =end
   def tag_count(elements)
❽   count_of = Hash.new(0) # note the default value of 0
     elements.to_a.each do |tag|
       count_of[tag.name()] += 1
❾     count_of.merge_totals(tag_count(tag.elements))
     end
     return count_of
   end

❿ puts tag_count(get_elements_from_file(ARGV[0])).pretty_report()
```

How It Works

Most of the work in this script comes from adding new methods to the Hash class. First, at ❶, we require the rexml/document library, an XML processing library. Then at ❷, we start the RDoc explaining the sort_by_tag_count method. The RDoc explains the method's goals, but let's look at each step. First, self.sort converts a Hash into an Array of Arrays. Each element of the main Array is another Array with the structure *[key, value]*. Let's show this in irb:

```
irb(main):001:0> h = { 0 => 1, 1 => 2 }
=> {0=>1, 1=>2}
irb(main):002:0> h.sort
=> [[0, 1], [1, 2]]
```

Since this in the context of a method called sort, the Array of Arrays is sorted. The sort method takes a block, which allows us to specify how we'd like it to be sorted. We do this at ❸ with the expression ((b[1] <=> a[1]) * 2) + (a[0] <=> b[0]). What does this expression mean?

First, we need to talk a bit about sorting. You see in the line before ❸ that we identify the variables within the sort loop as a and b. Those names are traditional for sorts, although Ruby allows you to pick other names if you like. Our expression calls the <=> method on whatever b[1] is, with a[1] as the argument. It then multiplies this by two and adds the result of calling <=> on a[0], with b[0] as an argument. That should clear everything up, right?

The <=> method returns 1 when self is greater then the argument, however it is defined; -1 when self is less than the argument, hopefully according to the same criteria; and 0 when they are equal. Keep this in mind when you create your own classes that implement the <=> method. Our project specifications from "#31 Counting Tags (xml_tag_counter.rb)" on page 148 says that the pairs of our Array of Arrays from sort_by_tag_count will have keys that are the names of XML tags and values that are the number of times that the tag appears in the document being analyzed. The first part of our expression (the part that is doubled) is just a sort on the tag count, as the name suggests. We put b[1] before a[1] because we want to sort in descending order, so the most common tags come first.

What happens when two different tags occur the same number of times in the document? That's what the second part of the expression is for. When the tag count is tied, we want to then sort on the name of the tag, which is either a[0] or b[0]. We put these in regular order, where a comes before b, because we want to sort in ascending order. Our output is sorted by descending tag count first, and ascending tag name within a given tag count. Why do we double the value of <=> for the tag counts?

Since <=> always returns -1, 0, or 1, and this is true for either sorting by tag count or tag name, we need to give tag count sorting greater weight somehow. Doubling does this very well, because it increases the magnitude of either 1 or -1 for the tag count sort relative to the tag name sort, but does nothing for tag count ties, because zero doubled is still zero. Our tag name sort still counts for something, just less than the sort_by_tag_count.[3]

We now know how to sort_by_tag_count, but we also want to be able to merge Hashes together, take another Hash as an argument, add their tag counts together, and have that new pair be the pair in the result. Hashes already have a method called merge, which takes a Hash argument. That should take care of everything, right? Sadly, no. The preexisting merge method *replaces* any existing key => value pair with whatever is in the hash taken as an argument. We don't want that—we want to keep the key that they share, but add the values together. How do we do that?

As is often true in Ruby, the answer is, *Write your own method and add it to an existing class*. The RDoc for merge_totals starts at ❹ and explains what we want to happen. All we do is loop through each key of the other_hash (the one taken as an argument) and add its value for that key to self[key]. Simple. There's a problem, though. What's the value of some_hash[some_key] when some_key isn't one of some_hash's keys? The value is nil, and nil doesn't like to be added. Let's see what happens in irb:

```
irb(main):001:0> h = { 0 => 1 }
=> {0=>1}
irb(main):002:0> h[1]
=> nil
irb(main):003:0> h[1] + 0
```

---

[3] To paraphrase George Orwell's *Animal Farm*, "All sorts are equal, but some are more equal than others."

```
NoMethodError: undefined method '+' for nil:NilClass
        from (irb):3
        from :0
```

That's not good. We'll need to find a way around that problem—but we'll do that later in the script. For now, know that `merge_totals` will properly add the counts for tags in Hashes that follow the format { tag => tag_count } when that tag is present.

We have one more method called `pretty_report` to add to all Hashes (❺). This method outputs a String showing each tag and its count within the document. It accomplishes that by sorting through each pair in the Array of Arrays returned by `sort_by_tag_count` from ❷, and creating an output String to which it adds a line with the tag, a colon, a space, the tag count, and a new-line character. Then it returns that String. That's it for the new methods in Hash.

This script also has two functions not attached as methods to the Hash: `get_elements_from_filename` (❻) and `tag_count` (❼). The `get_elements_from_filename` method takes one argument called `filename` and instantiates a new `REXML::Document`, which takes an instance of File as its argument. We provide that File via `File.open(filename)`. Instances of `REXML::Document` have a method called `elements`, which does much of our script's work for us, returning all the XML elements from the File.

The `tag_count` method takes those `elements` as an argument, it instantiates a new Hash called `count_of` at (❽), and passes 0 into the new method. This 0 argument sets the default value for this Hash, which is the value returned by `count_of` when it lacks the key it is asked for. This default of 0 is how we deal with the problem of adding tag counts that don't yet exist in the `merge_totals` method. The `self` Hash has a default of zero, so when a new tag comes in to `merge_totals` (which we call at ❾), it is assumed to have a `count_of` 0 for that tag. Unlike `nil`, a 0 is happy to have another Integer added to it, so our addition problem is solved. We continue recursively, calling `tag_counts` on the `elements` found within each tag, which then calls `tag_counts` as needed on its own `elements`, if there are any. It all continues, aggregating tag counts with `merge_totals`.

NOTE *Hashes similar to count_of often benefit from having default values of either 0 or the empty string. Hashes serving as histograms, like count_of, count occurrences of something, and should have a default of 0. Other hashes, which accumulate Strings for whatever reason, could have a default of the empty string. Since Strings know to concatenate with other objects, the script could accumulate Strings with +=, just as in our example, which uses Integers as Hash values.*

At ❿, we get the output of `tag_count`, which expects `elements`. We get those `elements` by calling `get_elements_from_filename` on the first command-line argument. Since `tag_count` returns a Hash, that return value has the method `pretty_report`, which provides the argument to the `puts` method and provides information to the user.

Running the Script

Let's use the file extras/eh.html.tidy, the corrected output provided by the html_tidy.rb script. Let's try ruby -w xml_tag_counter.rb extras/eh.html.tidy:

The Results

Here's the output:

```
div: 2
meta: 2
p: 2
style: 2
td: 2
body: 1
em: 1
h1: 1
head: 1
html: 1
img: 1
table: 1
th: 1
title: 1
tr: 1
```

Hacking the Script

What if we wanted sort_by_tag_count to return a Hash, rather than an Array? We could theoretically make a method like this:

```
def sorted_by_tag_count()
  # sort_by_tag_count returns an Array of Arrays...
  sort_by_tag_count.inject({}) do |memo,pair|
    tag, count = pair
    memo.merge( { tag => count } )
  end
  # so we can re-Hash it with inject
end
```

The problem is all Hash pairs are unordered. Our new sorted_by_tag_count goes to all the trouble of calling sort_by_tag_count but then rehashes it, losing the ordering.

What if we wanted to implement pretty_report with inject? Here's one way to do it. Notice how the method becomes a bit shorter, and the output variable becomes internal to inject.

```
def pretty_report()
  sort_by_tag_count.inject('') do |output,pair|
    tag, count = pair
    output += "#{tag}: #{count}\n"
  end
end
```

Finally, instead of calling get_elements_from_filename only on the first command-line argument, we could have used ARGV.each to allow the script to analyze multiple files in succession.

#32 Extracting Text from XML (xml_text_extractor.rb)

Counting occurrences of tags is fine, but XML is designed to hold text wrapped in tags, providing some organization beyond what's available simply from the content. That said, though, sometimes having just the text content is handy. When I was preparing a document using DocBook, I found myself wanting to use a spell checker on it. There are spell checkers that are XML-aware, but another approach would be to run a text extractor on XML and pass that output into a spell checker that expects plain text. This xml_text_extractor.rb is just such a script.

The Code

```
#!/usr/bin/env ruby
# xml_text_extractor.rb

❶ CHOMP_TAG = lambda { |tag| tag.to_s.chomp }

=begin rdoc
This script uses the Rexml parser, which is written in Ruby itself.
Find out more at http://www.germane-software.com/software/rexml
=end
❷ require 'rexml/document'

=begin rdoc
Returns DOM elements of a given filename.
=end
❸ def get_elements_from_filename(filename)
    REXML::Document.new(File.open(filename)).elements()
  end

=begin rdoc
Returns a <b>String</b> consisting of the text of a given XML document
with the tags stripped.
=end
❹ def strip_tags(elements)
❺   return '' unless (elements.size > 0)
❻   return elements.to_a.map do |tag|
❼     tag.texts.map(&CHOMP_TAG).join('') + strip_tags(tag.elements)
❽   end.join(' ')
  end

❾ puts strip_tags(get_elements_from_filename(ARGV[0]))
```

Mapping Procs onto Arrays

How It Works

This `xml_text_extractor.rb` script is similar to `xml_tag_counter.rb`, although it is simpler—ironic, since its output is arguably more complex. It starts out at ❶ by defining a Proc Constant called `CHOMP_TAG`, which accepts a single argument and returns the chomped version of that argument's rendition as a String. Following that, it requires the REXML library at ❷, just as in `xml_tag_counter.rb`. At ❸, it defines its own version of `get_elements_by_filename`, identical to the one in `xml_tag_counter.rb`.

NOTE *These scripts are designed to demonstrate techniques, rather than to function as production code. For production code, the definition of a method that will be used in multiple places should reside in a single library file that is required by any other file that needs access to that method. Please forgive the duplication in this case for the sake of simplicity.*

Next, we have `strip_tags` at ❹. Contrast the design of this function with `pretty_report` in `xml_tag_counter.rb`. Rather than a more iterative approach of (for example) defining an output variable looping through an Array with the each method and appending results onto the output variable), this uses a more functional approach. It maps an action onto each member of elements (which it calls `tag`) at ❻. That action is itself a mapping of the `CHOMP_TAG` Proc onto each member of `tag.texts` (❼). Then it joins the resulting Array with an empty String separator between each element, and appends the results of a recursive call to `strip_tags` onto the elements of tag. The result of a map is an Array, so it joins the elements of that Array with a space character before returning (❽). It also has an exit condition, which returns the empty String if there are no elements (❺).

Running the Script

Since `strip_tags` returns either the elements of a map joined on a space (which is a String) or the empty String, that String can easily be printed with puts at ❾. Let's look at the output returned by `ruby -w xml_text_extracter.rb extras/eh.html.tidy`.

The Results

```
  English Horn for No Clergy
/**/
@import url('../css/noclergy.css');
h1, h2 { display: none; }
/**/
/**/
 p.c1 {text-align:center;}
/**/ No Clergy:  I'm a header, but I don't know it. I'm some underlined
content I'm some italicized content I'm an unclosed paragraph. The horrors.
```

Hacking the Script

As I mentioned, one change that could be done on both xml_text_extractor.rb and xml_tag_counter.rb would be to take the common get_elements_by_filename method and place it in a single library file that both xml_text_extractor.rb and xml_tag_counter.rb access via require. This operation has a name in the refactoring community: *Pull Up Method*. The xml_text_extractor.rb script could also massage the output of strip_tags, stripping out empty lines and/or lines consisting entirely of whitespace, as html_tidy.rb does with UNWANTED_REGEXES.

#33 Validating XML (xml_well_formedness_checker.rb)

All the XML processing in the world won't do any good if your XML file is not well-formed. Since an XML document either is or is not well-formed, a well-formedness checker that will return either true or false seems like an ideal predicate method. Since XML documents are Files with Strings as their contents, we'll add a well_formed_xml? method to both the File class and the String class.

The Code

```ruby
#!/usr/bin/env ruby
# xml_well_formedness_checker.rb

=begin rdoc
This script uses the xml/dom/builder, written by YoshidaM.
=end
require 'xml/dom/builder'

class File

  def well_formed_xml?()
    read.well_formed_xml?
  end

end

class String

  def well_formed_xml?()
    builder = XML::DOM::Builder.new(0)
    builder.setBase("./")

    begin
      builder.parse(self, true)
    rescue XMLParserError
      return false
    end
```

The DOM ❶

❷

Root Element

❸

❹

❺

```
❻      return true
     end

   end

❼ def well_formed?(filename)
❽   return unless filename
❾   return File.open(filename, 'r').well_formed_xml?
   end

❿ puts well_formed?(ARGV[0])
```

How It Works

At ❶, we require the `XML::DOM::Builder` library file, which is available as part of
Ruby's standard library. DOM stands for *Document Object Model*, and it's a way
to express an XML document as a object with methods like `elements`, which
returns the elements found within whatever `self` is at the time—it could be
the entire document, or it could be a sub-element within the document. We've
used `elements` already in our previous scripts with the REXML library.

NOTE *Programmers that do a lot of Ajax or other JavaScript are intimately familiar with the
DOM. Because JavaScript's most common use is as a client-side scripting language
within web browsers, JavaScript programs often find themselves dealing with XML
(especially XHTML) data. JavaScript is an excellent language with a terribly misleading
name and some poor implementations. It shares a similar fused OO/functional heritage
with Ruby.*

We said that we'd be adding a `well_formed_xml?` predicate to File, which is
what we do at ❷. The read method of a File returns the contents of that File as
a String. We know that we want to add `well_formed_xml?` to all Strings as well as
all Files, so we just call `read.well_formed_xml?` within File's `well_formed_xml?`
method and assume that String will do its job and provide its own version of
`well_formed_xml?` for us.

We don't want to make Strings out to be liars, so we provide String with
its own `well_formed_xml?` predicate at ❸. This delegates some of its work to the
`XML::DOM::Builder` library, instantiating a Builder and setting its base to `'./'`,
which stands for the root element of an XML document.

NOTE *The 0 argument to XML::DOM::Builder.new tells it to ignore default events, which has no
impact our script. You can read more about XML::DOM::Builder at http://raa.ruby-lang.org/
gonzui/markup/xmlparser/lib/xml/dom/builder.rb?q=moduledef:XML.*

We then start a block at ❹ with the `begin` keyword, which indicates a
block that may fail so disastrously to do what's asked of it that it could exit the
program entirely. The `begin` keyword allows you to trap that error and deal
with it in some intelligent way, without causing the program to crash. We ask
our builder instance to `parse` the XML content represented by `self`, which is
of course a String within a String instance.

This parse operation is the one that might fail. The potentially disastrous error has a type called XMLParserError, so at ❺ we use the rescue keyword to trap that particular error type and prevent it from killing the entire program. Since our predicate tests for XML well-formedness, an XMLParserError indicates that the document is not well-formed. Therefore, we should return false in the event of an XMLParserError. If we get out of the begin block without entering the rescue section, that means there was no error, so we can safely return true at ❻.

We'll finish the xml_wellformedness_checker.rb script with a well_formed? function that accepts a filename argument, created at ❼. It returns an implicit nil for a nil filename at ❽. We then return a call to well_formed_xml? on the File instance created by opening filename at ❾. Finally, ❿ prints the result of calling well_formed? to the user via puts.

Running the Script

We know that we have a well-formed XML file in extras/eh.html.tidy because we ran html_tidy.rb on it to fix it. We also know that extras/eh.html had an unclosed paragraph tag, which would make it not well-formed. Let's see how xml_wellformedness_checker.rb performs.

The Results

```
ruby -w xml_well_formedness_checker.rb extras/eh.html.tidy
true
$ ruby -w xml_well_formedness_checker.rb extras/eh.html
false
$ ruby -w xml_well_formedness_checker.rb xml_well_formedness_checker.rb
false
$ ruby -w xml_well_formedness_checker.rb
nil
```

The extras/eh.html.tidy file is well-formed XML, so it properly reports true. The extras/eh.html and xml_wellformedness_checker.rb files are either not well-formed XML or not XML at all, so they properly report false. If we call xml_wellformedness_checker.rb with no filename, it returns nil, as we expect from ❽.

Hacking the Script

Calling a separate function called well_formed? on a filename argument is really just for demonstration purposes. In production code, a more likely use for this script would be to add another method to String called well_formed_xml_filename?, implemented as well_formed?, except that it would use self in place of filename. Or, in whatever code opens a given XML file, that file could be checked using File's well_formed_xml? method before performing any operations that depend on the file's contents being well-formed XML.

Chapter Recap

What was new in this chapter?

- Tidying HTML/XML markup
- Piping output to standard error with 2>
- The Web Accessibility Initiative
- The <=> method and the Comparable module
- Processing XML with REXML and XML::DOM::Builder
- Manipulating XML documents with regular expressions
- Making Hashes out of Arrays with inject
- Hashes serving as histograms
- Mapping Procs onto Arrays
- The Document Object Model
- The begin and rescue keywords

That's it for our XML-processing scripts. I hope these example scripts are not only useful in and of themselves but that they also might give you ideas about how you could modify or extend them to suit new tasks other than those presented here. For now, we'll proceed to our next chapter, "More Complex Utilities and Tricks, Part I." As the name suggests, its scripts are more detailed, and they will continue to introduce some new functional techniques, as well.

9

MORE COMPLEX UTILITIES
AND TRICKS, PART I

This chapter is the first of two that explore more complex operations in Ruby. This one deals extensively with text manipulations and larger-scale searches, while the next details an important functional technique that expands your options for abstraction in a very powerful way. For now, let's dive right in to learn some text processing techniques.

#34 Finding Codes in the Bible or *Moby-Dick* (els_parser.rb)

This script analyzes a phenomenon in large texts called equidistant letter sequences (ELSes). These sequences are popularly known as *Bible Codes* or *Torah Codes*, largely due to their description in Michael Drosnin's book *The Bible Code* (Simon & Schuster, 1997), in which he examined the Hebrew Bible. An *ELS* is a collection of letters (what Ruby would call a String) with a known starting point within the source text, a known length, and a known *ship value*, which is the distance between the letters comprising that ELS. You could construct an ELS by saying, "Start with the 23rd letter in this newspaper article and add every 8th letter until you have 11 letters." That String of 11 letters would be an ELS. Drosnin's work suggests that ELSes of particular significance (generally due to relevance to the text they're drawn from or due to accurate prediction of future events, such as assassinations) appear at a rate greater than chance within certain religious texts.

My els_parser.rb script also uses the work of Professor Brendan McKay of The Australian National University. McKay has done his own research (available at http://cs.anu.edu.au/~bdm/dilugim/torah.html) to find ELSes in texts like *War and Peace* and *Moby-Dick*, thus concluding that the ELSes that Drosnin refers to as the Bible Codes do not occur more often in the Hebrew Bible than can be expected due to chance. I can't read Hebrew, so for this script I've chosen to analyze Herman Melville's *Moby-Dick* in English instead of the Hebrew Bible. I downloaded the text from Project Gutenberg (http://www.gutenberg.org) into extras/moby_dick.txt. The els_parser.rb script allows you to choose a text and a set of input parameters that describe a potential set of ELSes; then els_parser.rb will report whether any ELSes that match the description exist within the source text.

The Code

ELS

```ruby
#!/usr/bin/env ruby
# els_parser.rb

require 'palindrome2.rb'
# I want all Strings to have the private letters_only
# method from this file.

class String

=begin rdoc
This provides a public method to access the private letters_only
method we required from palindrome2.rb.
=end
  def just_letters(case_matters)
    letters_only(case_matters)
  end

end

=begin rdoc
A text-processing parser that does ASCII-only
Equidistant Letter Sequence analyses similar to that described
at http://en.wikipedia.org/wiki/Equidistant_letter_sequencing

For my example, I use Moby Dick taken from
Project Gutenberg, http://www.gutenberg.org.
=end
class ELS_Parser
```

❶

```ruby
❷    DEFAULT_SEARCH_PARAMS = {
       :start_pt => 4500,
       :end_pt   => nil, # assumes the end of the String to search when nil
       :min_skip => 126995,
       :max_skip => 127005,
       :term     => 'ssirhan',
     }

     def initialize(filename, search_params=nil)
       @contents = prepare(filename)
       @filename = filename
       reset_params(search_params || DEFAULT_SEARCH_PARAMS)
     end

     def reset_params(search_params)
       @search_params           = search_params
       @search_params[:end_pt] ||= (@contents.size-1)
       # ||= for :end_pt allows nil for 'end of file'
       return self # return self so we can chain methods
     end

=begin rdoc
Performs an ELS analysis on the <i>filename</i> argument, searching for
the term argument, falling back to the default.
=end
❸    def search(term=@search_params[:term])
       @search_params[:term] = term
       reversed_term = term.reverse
       warn "Starting search within #{@filename} " +
         "using #{@search_params.inspect}" if ($DEBUG)
❹     final_start_pt = @search_params[:end_pt] - @search_params[:term].size
       @search_params[:start_pt].upto(final_start_pt) do |index|
         @search_params[:min_skip].upto(@search_params[:max_skip]) do |skip|
❺          candidate = construct_candidate(index, skip)

❻          if (candidate == @search_params[:term])
             return report_match(skip, index)
           end

           if (candidate == reversed_term)
             return report_match(skip, index, 'reversed ')
           end

         end
       end
❼     return report_match(false, false)
     end

     private

❽    def construct_candidate(index, skip)
       output = ''
       0.upto(@search_params[:term].size-1) do |char_index|
         new_index = (index + (char_index * (skip + 1)))
```

$DEBUG

```
       return '' if (new_index >= @contents.size)
      output += @contents[new_index].chr
    end
    return output
  end

=begin rdoc
Creates a 'letters only' version of the contents of a <i>filename</i>
argument in preparation for ELS analysis. Assumes case-insensitivity.
=end
  def prepare(filename, case_matters=false)
    File.open(filename, 'r').readlines.to_s.just_letters(case_matters)
  end

=begin
Either report the variables at which a match was found, or report
failure for this set of search params.
=end
  def report_match(skip, index, reversed='')
    return "No match within #{@filename} using " +
      @search_params.inspect unless index
    return "Match for #{@search_params[:term]} " +
      "#{reversed}within #{@filename} " +
      "at index #{index}, using skip #{skip}"
  end

end # ELS_Parser
```

How It Works

The els_parser.rb script only processes letters, ignoring whitespace and punctuation. We know that Strings can also have non-letter characters, such a whitespace, numbers, punctuation, and so on; therefore, we need a method that strips all non-letters out of a String. Fortunately, we already have such a method—letters_only, defined in palindrome2.rb. It is easy to take advantage of letters_only with a require at the top of els_parser.rb. However, palindrome2.rb defined letters_only as a private method, and (as will become clear), we want it available as a public method. What can we do? One approach, which is what els_parser.rb does at ❶, is to define a new public method, just_letters, that exists merely to call the pre-existing private method letters_only.

The just_letters method is for Strings, but we want a new class called ELS_Parser to do the overall management of the searching. ELS_Parser has a Hash Constant called DEFAULT_SEARCH_PARAMS at ❷. The values for the :start_pt and :end_pt Symbol keys represent the earliest and latest character index for the search, respectively. The value for :term is the text to be searched for. Finally, the values for :min_skip and :max_skip are the minimum and maximum number of letters to jump past (i.e., skip) during the search. Why these particular default values? They could have been any values, but I took a shortcut and started with values from McKay's web page (http://cs.anu.edu.au/~bdm/dilugim/moby.html) that are known to correspond to a particular match within the text of *Moby-Dick*.

Note some subtle differences—my values are 0-based (where a skip of 0 means *Go to the next letter*), whereas McKay defines moving to the next letter as a skip of 1. There is a similar difference with regard to starting points. He also accomplishes searches for backward terms using a negative skip value, while els_parser.rb uses a positive skip search on a reversed term.

For example, in the String 'abcdefgh', which we'll call contents, searching for an ELS with a :start_pt of 0, a :term of 'abc', and a :min_skip of 0 would find a match, because the String 'abc' exists within contents starting at 0 (right at the beginning) with a skip value of 0. Similarly, 'ceg' would be found within contents starting at 2 with a skip value of 1, and 'heb' would be found starting at 1 with a skip value of 2, but as a reversed String. If you expand these concepts greatly, use longer search terms, much larger contents (such as the Bible or *Moby Dick*), and much larger starting, ending, and skip values, you will begin to understand the basics of ELS analysis.

After defining DEFAULT_SEARCH_PARAMS, our ELS_Parser needs an initialize method, in which it will define the instance variables @contents, to hold the text being searched, and @filename, to store the name of the file it read @contents from.

The @contents variable is the result of calling the prepare method (defined at ❾) on the filename. The prepare method takes in a mandatory filename argument and an optional case_matters argument. All it does is open a new file, extract its contents into a String with readlines.to_s, and call just_letters on that String. This ensures that we strip out inappropriate characters from our String before storing it in @contents. Note that just_letters takes an optional argument for case sensitivity. If you're curious about how this works, remember that just_letters just calls the letters_only method defined in palindrome2.rb, so you can refer to that script for further study.

The initialize method also calls the reset_params method, defined right below initialize, which simply sets the instance variable @search_params to the search_params argument passed into initialize, falling back to the DEFAULT_SEARCH_PARAMS. It also sets the :end_pt value to fall back to the last index of @contents if the :end_pt value would otherwise be nil. This gives ELS_Parser a handy shortcut: leaving out the :end_pt automatically means *Search to the end of @contents*.

Next is search at ❸. It allows an optional term argument, which automatically updates @search_params[:term] as needed. Since search is set up to find reversed terms as well as normal-order terms, we define reversed_term right away. We also report that the search is starting if $DEBUG is true using the method warn, which writes out to *standard error*, instead of *standard out*. $DEBUG is generally set as a command-line option to ruby, such that $DEBUG is true when you execute ruby with either the -d or --debug flag. You may remember standard error from html_tidy.rb. In that script, we sent standard error to /dev/null, meaning we didn't care about it. Here, we have a special message designed specifically to go to standard error.

After the standard error warning, we define final_start_pt at ❹. To understand what final_start_pt is for, let's go back to our contents = 'abcdefgh' search example. What if we search for 'hiccup' with a :start_pt of 100? There aren't even 100 letters in our contents, so a search with that :start_pt value would automatically fail. Instead of letting that happen, we want to figure out the maximum starting index that could conceivably work, and make sure :start_pt is not larger than that value.

It's even more complicated than that. Our search terms will always have letters, and those letters take up space. If we start too close to the end of @contents, we could run out of room even with relatively low skip values. We need to keep enough room for the term being searched for, which we store in @search_params[:term], so we set final_start_pt accordingly.

After setting final_start_pt, we enter two nested loops—one on index from the lowest to highest starting points and one using skip to refer to each number from the lowest to highest skip values. The first thing we do within those loops is use index and skip at ❺ to assign the expression returned from construct_candidate, defined at ❽, into candidate. The construct_candidate method takes the existing index and skip values and makes a String of the same length as the term being searched for. For a @contents of 'abcdefgh', construct_candidate(2, 1) produces 'ceg' where @search_params[:term] has three characters in it. The construct_candidate method returns the empty String if the new_index being asked for ever goes beyond the @contents String. Our final_start_pt limits should prevent this from ever being needed, but it's an additional safety check.

NOTE   *The* construct_candidate *method also uses the* chr *method, because extracting a single character out of a String gives you that character's ASCII value.*

You can test this in irb:

```
irb(main):001:0> s = 'abcde'
=> "abcde"
irb(main):002:0> s[0]
=> 97
irb(main):003:0> s[0].chr
=> "a"
```

After establishing our candidate, we want to see if it is a successful match, which we start to do at ❻. If it does match, we return the result of calling report_match with skip and index as arguments. However, we also want to know whether our candidate matches the reversed_term instead of the term in regular order, so we call report_match, again with skip and index as arguments, but we also add the String 'reversed '. Finally, at ❼ we return the result of calling report_match with two explicit false arguments if we've looped through all of the appropriate skip and index loops without already returning something. This just means that we never found a match, either forward or reversed.

We need to know how report_match works. It's defined at ❿, and it takes arguments for skip, index, and an optional reversed String, as already shown. If index is false, report_match returns a String informing the user that there was no match found. Otherwise, It returns the details of the successful match. Note that reversed adds the String 'reversed ' (including the trailing space) as needed.

Running the Script

We can test this with another script called demo_els_parser.rb. Here is its code:

```ruby
#!/usr/bin/env ruby
# demo_els_parser.rb

require 'els_parser.rb'

moby_dick = ELS_Parser.new('extras/moby_dick.txt')
puts moby_dick.search() # assumes 'ssirhan'
puts moby_dick.reset_params( {
  :start_pt => 93060,
  :end_pt   => nil, # assumes 'to the end'
  :min_skip => 13790,
  :max_skip => 13800,
  :term     => 'kennedy'
} ).search()
puts moby_dick.reset_params( {
  :start_pt => 327400,
  :end_pt   => nil, # 'to the end' again
  :min_skip => 0,
  :max_skip => 5,
  :term     => 'rabin'
} ).search()
puts moby_dick.reset_params( {
  :start_pt => 104620,
  :end_pt   => 200000, # not to the end
  :min_skip => 26020,
  :max_skip => 26030,
  :term     => 'mlking'
} ).search()
```

The Results

Here is the result of calling this script:

```
ruby -w --debug demo_els_parser.rb
Starting search within extras/moby_dick.txt using {:end_pt=>924955,
:min_skip=>126995, :max_skip=>127005, :term=>"ssirhan", :start_pt=>4500}
Match for ssirhan within extras/moby_dick.txt at index 4546, using skip 126999
Starting search within extras/moby_dick.txt using {:end_pt=>924955,
:min_skip=>13790, :max_skip=>13800, :term=>"kennedy", :start_pt=>93060}
Match for kennedy within extras/moby_dick.txt at index 93062, using skip 13797
Starting search within extras/moby_dick.txt using {:end_pt=>924955,
:min_skip=>0, :max_skip=>5, :term=>"rabin", :start_pt=>327400}
Match for rabin reversed within extras/moby_dick.txt at index 327500, using
skip 3
Starting search within extras/moby_dick.txt using {:end_pt=>200000,
:min_skip=>26020, :max_skip=>26030, :term=>"mlking", :start_pt=>104620}
Match for mlking reversed within extras/moby_dick.txt at index 104629, using
skip 26025
```

Hacking the Script

We could significantly increase the speed of `construct_candidate` by checking against the search terms as we go and returning the empty string whenever it fails to match—an application of the return guard notion within the construction of the candidate. Where we define `final_start_pt`, we could also either limit `:max_skip` in a similar way or report an error if impossible search parameters were asked for.

NOTE *There's also a better way to include the `letters_only` method than the way I've done it here, using a concept called a mixin. Jump ahead to the `to_lang.rb` script in Chapter 10 to see mixins in action.*

#35 Mutating Strings into Weasels (methinks.rb)

This script is based on a program from Richard Dawkins' *The Blind Watchmaker* (W.W. Norton, 1996). The program demonstrates a simplified model of asexual natural selection, starting with a String consisting of random characters and successively mutating it to produce "children" that differ from the parent. The program then selects the "best" child String (meaning the one that most closely matches the target String `methinksitislikeaweasel`, a reference from *Hamlet*) to be the next generation's parent. This process continues until the parent String matches the target String.

Let's implement Dawkins' process in Ruby.

NOTE *Dawkins wrote his program to demonstrate a version of cumulative selection over time that was intentionally simpler than real-world neo-Darwinian natural selection. Critics contend that the program is a suboptimal model, with the most prominent criticisms being that it is overly simplified, it is unable to fail, and it has a preset target, making it a better model of artificial selection than natural selection. See "Hacking the Script" on page 175 for general suggestions for modifying this version of the program to be a better model of real-world Darwinian selection.*

The Code

```ruby
#!/usr/bin/env ruby
# methinks.rb

=begin rdoc
Recreate Richard Dawkins' Blind Watchmaker program, in which a purely
random string is mutated and filtered until it matches the target string.
=end
```

Inheritance ❶
```ruby
class Children < Array

  def select_fittest(target)
    inject(self[0]) do |fittest,child|
      child.fitter_than?(fittest, target) ? child : fittest
    end
  end
```

```
            end

❷   class String

          ALPHABET = ('a'..'z').to_a

          LETTER_OFFSET = 'a'[0]

          PARAMS = {
            :generation_size => 20,
            :mutation_rate   => 10,
            :display_filter  => 5,
            :mutation_amp    => 6
          }

          TARGET = 'methinksitislikeaweasel'

          @mutation_attempts ||= 0
```

Differences
between Strings

❸
```
          def deviance_from(target)
            deviance = 0
            split('').each_index do |index|
              deviance += (self[index] - target[index]).abs
            end
            return deviance
          end

          def fitter_than?(other, target)
            deviance_from(target) < other.deviance_from(target)
          end
```

❹
```
          def mutate(params)
            split('').map do |char|
              mutate_char(char, params)
            end.join('')
          end
```

❺
```
          def mutate_until_matches!(target=TARGET, params=PARAMS)
            return report_success if (self == target)
            report_progress(params)
            @mutation_attempts += 1
            children = propagate(params)
            fittest  = children.select_fittest(target)
            replace(fittest)
            mutate_until_matches!(target, params)
          end
```

❻
```
          def propagate(params)
            children = Children.new()
            children << self
            params[:generation_size].times do |generation|
              children << self.mutate(params)
            end
            return children
          end
```

```ruby
❼    def report_progress(params)
        return unless (@mutation_attempts % params[:display_filter] == 0)
        puts "string ##{@mutation_attempts} = #{self}"
      end

      def report_success()
        puts <<END_OF_HERE_DOC
I match after #{@mutation_attempts} mutations
END_OF_HERE_DOC
        return @mutation_attempts
      end

      =begin rdoc
      Replace self with a <b>String</b> the same length as the
      <i>target</i> argument, consisting entirely of lowercase
      letters.
      =end
❽    def scramble!(target=TARGET)
        @mutation_attempts = 0
        replace( scramble(target) )
      end

      def scramble(target=TARGET)
        target.split('').map do |char|
          ALPHABET[rand(ALPHABET.size)]
        end.join('')
      end

      private

      =begin rdoc
      Limit 'out of bounds' indices at end points of the ALPHABET.
      =end
❾    def limit_index(alphabet_index)
        alphabet_index = [ALPHABET.size-1,  alphabet_index].min
        alphabet_index = [alphabet_index, 0].max
        return alphabet_index
      end

❿    def mutate_char(original_char, params)
        return original_char if rand(100) > params[:mutation_rate]
        variance = rand(params[:mutation_amp]) - (params[:mutation_amp] / 2)
        # variance with amp of 6 now ranges from -3 to 2,
        variance += 1 if variance.zero? # therefore move (0..2) up to (1..3)
        alphabet_index = (original_char[0] + variance - LETTER_OFFSET)
        alphabet_index = limit_index(alphabet_index)
        mutated_char = ALPHABET[alphabet_index]
        return mutated_char
      end

    end
```

How It Works

We start by defining a new class called Children at ❶. You'll notice the peculiar `Children < Array` within the class definition, which suggests a relationship between Children and Arrays. That relationship is *inheritance*. Children inherits from Array, meaning that it behaves as an Array in every way, while also adding whatever new characteristics we give it. In our case, the only new characteristic is a new method called `select_fittest`, which uses inject to find the fittest child within Children, defined by the `fitter_than?` method.

CHILDREN DON'T LIE

There's one other way in which a child class (or subclass) differs from its parent, and that's the expression returned by the class method. It returns the name of the subclass when called on an instance of the subclass:

```
$ irb -r methinks.rb
irb(main):001:0> a = Array.new
=> []
irb(main):002:0> c = Children.new
=> []
irb(main):003:0> a.class
=> Array
irb(main):004:0> c.class
=> Children
```

Some people may think that's obvious, but it's worth noting.

After defining Children, we open the String class at ❷. We add several Constants, including an Array of letters that we'll call the ALPHABET, and LETTER_OFFSET. The LETTER_OFFSET Constant requires some explanation. It represents characters as ASCII values to determine how closely certain Strings match each other. Converting letters to numerical value is convenient, as it allows us to use basic mathematical operations to find the "most fit" child string. Ruby converts characters to numerical values by treating a String as an Array and reading values out with indices. Let's demonstrate in irb (the chr method converts from ASCII values back to a String):

```
irb(main):001:0> s = 'abcde'
=> "abcde"
irb(main):002:0> s[0]
=> 97
irb(main):003:0> s[0].chr
=> "a"
irb(main):004:0> 'a'[0]
=> 97
irb(main):005:0> s[1]
=> 98
```

You can see that the ASCII value for the String 'a' (the character at index 0 in String s) is 97, that the chr method converts that ASCII value back to 'a', and that the ASCII value for 'b' is 98. The number 97 is our LETTER_OFFSET. Astute readers will notice that LETTER_OFFSET is the index at which 'a' appears in our ALPHABET, as well. Observe the following in irb:

```
irb(main):001:0> letters = ('a'..'z').to_a
=> ["a", "b", "c", "d", "e", "f", "g", "h", "i", "j", "k", "l", "m", "n", "o",
"p", "q", "r", "s", "t", "u", "v", "w", "x", "y", "z"]
irb(main):002:0> 's'[0]
=> 115
irb(main):003:0> 's'[0] - 'a'[0]
=> 18
irb(main):004:0> letters[18]
=> "s"
```

Calling [0] on a character and subtracting LETTER_OFFSET ('a'[0], or 97) gives us the index of that character within our ALPHABET Array. This will be very handy in the mutate_char method at ❿, which we'll discuss when we get there.

Our next two Constants are PARAMS and TARGET. Both of these establish defaults for items that might be overridden by optional arguments. PARAMS is a now-familiar Hash with Symbol keys, each value of which determines the specific behavior of our mutations. The value for :generation_size is the number of children, :mutation_rate's is the percentage chance that a mutation will occur at all, :display_filter just sets how often our program will give updates while it's running, and :mutation_amp determines how strong or divergent a given mutation can be—basically a numeric measure of how different children can be from their parents.

TARGET is our default final goal: methinksitislikeaweasel. Finally, after the Constants, we have a single class variable called @mutation_attempts, which is just a counter that increments every time we mutate. We're ready to start defining some methods.

Our first new method to add to String is deviance_from (❸). It takes a mandatory target argument (the default fallback to the TARGET Constant occurs in mutate_until_matches! at ❺, which is later in the code but is called earlier). The deviance_from method returns an Integer (deviance) which is a numeric measure of how different two Strings are. Each character of difference at each point within the String increments deviance by one. Here are some irb examples:

```
irb -r methinks.rb
irb(main):001:0> 'aaa'.deviance_from('aaa')
=> 0
irb(main):002:0> 'aaa'.deviance_from('aab')
=> 1
irb(main):003:0> 'aaa'.deviance_from('aac')
=> 2
irb(main):004:0> 'aaa'.deviance_from('bac')
=> 3
irb(main):005:0> 'aaa'.deviance_from('baq')
=> 17
```

This method is useful for our script, because if we are trying to model the survival of the fittest, we need to be able to measure fitness. A low `deviance_from` the target represents fitness. Just below `deviance_from` is `fitter_than?`, a simple predicate that compares the `deviance_from` value for `self` and the `deviance_from` value for the other String, both relative to the same target. It only returns `true` when `self`'s `deviance_from` value is lower, making `self` fitter. Take a look at "Hacking the Script" on page 175 for a way to eliminate this method entirely.

Next up is `mutate` (❹). It takes a mandatory `params` argument, which falls back to the default `PARAMS` Constant in `mutate_until_matches!` (❺) earlier within the script's operation, if necessary. The `mutate` method is remarkably lazy, in that it `splits` its calling object into individual characters, and calls `mutate_char` (❿) on each of those characters via map.

The `mutate_char` method is a bit more complicated. It takes mandatory arguments for the `original_char` and `params`, and it exits immediately if `params` says that it should not mutate, which is determined by a random percentage being higher than `params[:mutation_rate]`. Assuming it passed `params`' test, `mutate_char` will mutate the character. First, it declares a variance, which is just the amount and direction of change based on the `:mutation_amp`. The values for variance range from `+(:mutation_amp / 2)` to `-(:mutation_amp / 2)`, excluding zero. They initially vary from `-(:mutation_amp / 2)` to one less than `+(:mutation_amp / 2)`, including zero, but the line that executes `variance +=1 if variance.zero?` ensures that values of zero or higher are bumped up by one.

It then creates an `alphabet_index` variable, which uses `LETTER_OFFSET` as previously discussed to find that index within `ALPHABET` for our `original_char`, plus any appropriate variance. It then limits `alphabet_index` with the `limit_index` method (❾), which clips or truncates `alphabet_index` to a maximum of the last index within `ALPHABET` and minimum of 0, which is the first index within `ALPHABET`. Since it then has a dependable index to read from `ALPHABET`, it does so, placing that value within a variable called `mutated_char`, which it then returns.

Following `mutate` is `mutate_until_matches!` (❺), which is the public-facing workhorse of the script. It takes optional arguments for target and `params`, falling back to String's `TARGET` and `PARAMS` Constants, as mentioned in earlier discussions of other methods. If `self` matches the target exactly, we want to `report_success`. Failing that, we want to `report_progress`. We can look at both of those methods, which start at ❼. The `report_success` method uses `puts` to show that it matches exactly after a certain number of attempts, and it returns `@mutation_attempts` without incrementing it. (There's no need to increment it, since no new mutation occurred.) The `report_progress` method returns with no value unless `@mutation_attempts` is a multiple of (i.e., has a modulus of 0 relative to) `params[:display_filter]`. If we set a lower display filter, we have a chattier mutation process. Assuming that it should output, it uses `puts` to show what `self` is after however many `@mutation_attempts`.

After reporting its progress, `mutate_until_matches!` should then actually do some mutating. It increments `@mutation_attempts` and then creates a new variable called `children`, which is the output of `propagate` (❻). The `propagate` method takes some `params` and instantiates a new instance of Children (❶), meaning that it has access to `select_fittest`, which is not available to Arrays. It appends itself onto children, the effect of which is that if the parent (self) is fitter than all of the children, the parent will again be the source of the generation of children after this one. The propagate method then appends a child (a mutated version of itself) onto children, doing so a number of times equal to params[:generation_size]. Finally, it returns the children, who will then try to make their way in the cruel world.

The effect of the cruel world is accomplished via Children's select_fittest method. The world is cruel indeed, because only one child survives, as discussed already. We call the fittest child fittest, appropriately, and replace the parent with this fittest child. Then mutate_until_matches! recursively calls itself, mutating until it finally matches the target.

Two methods remain undescribed: scramble and scramble! (❽). Both of these methods take an optional target argument that defaults to TARGET. Since scramble! is destructive, it sets self's @mutation_attempts to 0 and replaces itself with the value returned by the non-destructive scramble. The scramble method splits the target at each char and creates a new Array via map; each member of the new Array is a random element from ALPHABET. Note that we don't even make any use of char—we just use map to make sure that the scrambled String is the same size as the target. The scramble method then joins that Array of random characters with the empty String and returns the resulting String: a String of the same length as the target, consisting entirely of random letters.

Running the Script

Let's try it out in irb.

```
irb -r methinks.rb
irb(main):001:0> candidate = String.new.scramble!()
=> "rnvrtdldcgaxlsleyrmzych"
irb(main):002:0> candidate.mutate_until_matches!()
```

The Results

```
string #0 = rnvrtdldcgaxlsleyrmzych
string #5 = okvpqekfcicsnsleysmzsci
string #10 = pkvnnekhdkdslrjeztmvseh
string #15 = pkvjnekjfmgslrjeytjrsei
string #20 = plvflekjhmislljettjosel
string #25 = oisfmejkimisllkeqtjlsel
string #30 = mfsgmgjnimislkkeotgjsel
string #35 = mfsglgjqimislkkeivfhsel
string #40 = mesgigkqiriskhleivffsel
string #45 = mesgikkqirislhleivfasel
string #50 = mesgikkqirislhkegvfasel
string #55 = metiilksitislhkegvfasem
string #60 = metiilksitislhkefvfasem
string #65 = meshinlsitislhkeaweweasel
string #70 = methinlsitislhkeaweweasel
string #75 = methinlsitislhkeaweweasel
string #80 = methinlsitislikeaweweasel
string #85 = methinlsitislikeaweweasel
```

```
string #90 = methinlsitislikeaweasel
string #95 = methinlsitislikeaweasel
string #100 = methinlsitislikeaweasel
string #105 = methinlsitislikeaweasel
string #110 = methinlsitislikeaweasel
string #115 = methinlsitislikeaweasel
string #120 = methinlsitislikeaweasel
string #125 = methinlsitislikeaweasel
string #130 = methinlsitislikeaweasel
string #135 = methinlsitislikeaweasel
string #140 = methinlsitislikeaweasel
string #145 = methinlsitislikeaweasel
string #150 = methinlsitislikeaweasel
I match after 152 mutations
=> 152
```

Try it on your own machine, and notice that the results are random—sometimes the script takes more generations, sometimes fewer. If you pass in different values, you can get dramatically different results:

```
irb(main):005:0> candidate = String.new.scramble!('hello')
=> "wnwdi"
irb(main):006:0> candidate.mutate_until_matches!('hello')
string #0 = wnwdi
string #5 = onsdj
string #10 = lnpgj
string #15 = ijlkj
string #20 = hemlj
string #25 = hemll
string #30 = hemlo
I match after 34 mutations
=> 34
```

We'll explore this program further in our next script, `methinks_meta.rb`.

Hacking the Script

The `select_fittest` method could be expressed as follows in terms of `sort_by`, rather than `inject`. The returned value is exactly the same, whether it's the memoization within `inject` or the member of the sorted `Children` at the zeroth index. Using `sort_by` would also allow us to eliminate the `fitter_than?` method entirely.

```
return sort_by do |child|
  child.deviance_from(target)
end[0]
```

The `replace` in `mutate_until_matches!` is what makes it destructive, making it appropriate for its name to end with a bang. The `mutate_until_matches!` method could easily have been purely functional by replacing the last two lines of the method with return `fittest.mutate_until_matches(target, params)`, although the name would then have been misleading, even without the bang—

perhaps simply get_match would be a better name in this case. In addition, the @mutation_attempts variable would not be retained from mutation to mutation. We would have to alter mutate_until_matches! (or get_match, or whatever other new name it would have) to accept mutation_attempts as an optional argument, defaulting to zero for the first call. Its treatment would be very similar to how els_parser.rb updates @search_params[:term] with the optional term argument.

What would stop us from implementing the propagate method (❻) with something like the following code?

```
return [self] +
  (1..params[:generation_size]).to_a.map do |gen|
    self.mutate(params)
  end
```

The main problem is that the returned value from propagate would be an Array, not a Children, meaning that it would not have access to the select_fittest method that we added to Children, our subclass of Array. We could use our new definition of propagate by eliminating the subclassing of Children < Array (❶) and simply adding the select_fittest method to all Arrays.

You could also modify this program to be a more accurate model of a more complex type of cumulative selection, such as real-world Darwinian selection. Such a program would have multiple competing "species" of Strings, something to represent food supplies (which would be in finite supply and be consumed by the reproduction process), multiple potentially-successful targets not preset by the programmer, and so on. The changes would allow some Strings' descendants to be unable to produce competitive children (and thus become extinct), while other Strings' descendants would flourish, just like organisms in the real world.

#36 Mutating the Mutation of Strings into Weasels (methinks_meta.rb)

This script uses the previous one, methinks.rb, so make sure you understand how that one works before trying this one, methinks_meta.rb. This script uses techniques similar to those used in methinks.rb to find the "best" input parameters for methinks.rb.

The previous script's performance (the number of generations it takes to match the target) can vary greatly from one run to the next. Two major factors affect that variation in our results: The first factor is the set of arbitrary starting parameters. We saw that a target of hello was much easier to reach quickly than a target of methinksitislikeaweasel. Using other values for :mutation_rate or the other parameters also has an impact. The second factor is the unpredictable nature of the random variations while the program runs. Over time, after many runs, the laws of probability will cause this second factor to be less and less important—and in any case, randomness is part of the given problem. Our arbitrary starting parameters are crucial. How do we decide what they should be?

NOTE *Varying the :display_filter has no impact on how many generations it takes to reach the target, only how often the program reports on its own progress. Also, genuine random number generation is possible with computers—often by measuring the decay of radioactive elements or listening to noise from a microphone—but our "random" number generation is actually only pseudo-random. Pseudo-random numbers come from a process that has a pattern, making them unsuitable for use in heavy-duty applications like stress testing or cryptography. They're random enough for our script's purposes, though. This pseudo-random caveat applies to all random numbers in this book.*

The arbitrary set of input parameters is the major problem facing the efficiency of our string's mutations. Luckily, we'd recognize an ideal set of parameters if we saw them, and we can easily rate parameter sets as better or worse in relation to each other, because we have an easy way to measure success: A low number of generations needed to reach the target String. We already have a way to process candidates repeatedly to reach a given target—it's called methinks.rb.

Just as we can create a Proc that returns another Proc (as shown in "#24 Nesting lambdas" on page 111), we can create a mutator that operates at a higher level of mutation—mutating not just Strings, but the mutation of those Strings. We can define fitter as *requiring a lower number of generations to reach the target*, plug in some parameters, and go. Our new script, methinks_meta.rb, will (pseudo-)randomly vary arbitrary input parameters and filter them by this fitness criterion to find ever-better input parameters for us. Let's see the code.

The Code

```ruby
#!/usr/bin/env ruby
# methinks_meta.rb

❶ require 'methinks'

class Hash

❷   def get_child()
    new_hash = {}
    each_pair do |k,v|
      new_hash[k] = (rand(v) + (v/2))
    end
    new_hash[:display_filter] = 5
    return new_hash
  end

end # Hash
```

```
###

❸ class Meta_Mutator

  NEW_TARGET   = 'ruby'
  MAX_ATTEMPTS = 2
  TARGET = NEW_TARGET || String::TARGET

  def initialize()
    @params_by_number_of_mutations = {}
  end

❹ def mutate_mutations!(params, did_no_better_count=0)
    return if did_no_better_count > MAX_ATTEMPTS

    num = update_params_by_number_of_mutations!(params)

    return mutate_mutations!(
      @params_by_number_of_mutations[best_num],
      get_no_better_count(num, did_no_better_count)
    )

  end

❺ def report()
    @params_by_number_of_mutations.sort.each do |pair|
      num, params = pair
      puts sprintf("%0#{digits_needed}d", num) +
        " generations with #{params.inspect}"
    end
  end

  private

❻ def best_num()
    @params_by_number_of_mutations.keys.sort[0] || nil
  end

❼ def digits_needed()
    @params_by_number_of_mutations.keys.max.to_s.size
  end

❽ def get_children(params, number_of_children = 10)
    (0..number_of_children).to_a.map do |i|
      params.get_child()
    end
  end

❾ def get_no_better_count(num, did_no_better_count)
    return did_no_better_count if (num == best_num)
    did_no_better_count + 1
  end
```

```
❿   def update_params_by_number_of_mutations!(params)
       children = get_children(params)
       number_of_mutations = nil
       children.each do |params|
         candidate = String.new.scramble!(TARGET)
         number_of_mutations = candidate.mutate_until_matches!(TARGET, params)
         @params_by_number_of_mutations[number_of_mutations] = params.dup
       end
       return number_of_mutations
     end

   end # Meta_Mutator

   ###

   params = {
     :generation_size => 200,
     :mutation_rate   => 30,
     :display_filter  => 5,
     :mutation_amp    => 7
   }

   mm = Meta_Mutator.new()
   mm.mutate_mutations!(params)
   mm.report()
```

How It Works

Since we're performing operations that use methinks.rb, we require that file at ❶.
We then immediately open the Hash class, adding a new method called
get_child at ❷. The get_child method, which could also have been named
mutate or *reproduce*, performs random variations on all of the values for the given
Hash. It assumes that those values are Integers, and can thereby be varied
with the rand method—in this case, from half the given value to 1.5 times the
given value. Since the :display_filter value has no impact on fitness, we just
forcibly set that to 5. We accomplish the mutation through the construction
of a new_hash by iterating over self with the each_pair method and making the
necessary changes before writing to new_hash, which we then return.

NOTE   *We already noted how get_child makes the assumption that all of its Hash's values are
           Integers. It also assumes that the Hash has a key called :display_filter. This assumption
           works fine for our script, but if the get_child method were to become part of a commonly-
           used library, we would have to make it play nicely with other programs. A programmer
           can avoid this method for inappropriate Hashes, but a better solution would be for the
           programmer to take responsibility for making new methods more robust when he or she
           opens an existing class and adds a new method. A production-ready version of get_child
           would check that the Hash's values can implement numeric addition and also check for the
           presence of a :display_filter key before performing the operations laid out in our example.*

Next, we create our Meta_Mutator class at ❸. It has several Constants. The NEW_TARGET Constant defines a different target String. This was mainly for the convenience of having a shorter target, so that runs of the program would take a shorter time. The MAX_ATTEMPTS Constant defines the maximum number of attempts we should make to beat our previously fittest mutation attempt before giving up and trying a new set of parameters. TARGET is either our NEW_TARGET or the familiar String::TARGET from methinks.rb. This definition allows us to override the TARGET easily while still having a default value, and not having to constantly change code later when we want different targets—we just always use TARGET. The Meta_Mutator class also has the expected initialize method, which takes no arguments and defines an empty Hash for @params_by_number_of_mutations. We'll see this instance variable in action later.

Next comes the public method mutate_mutations! at ❹. Note that it is destructive, and it takes two arguments: a required params Hash, and an optional Integer for the did_no_better_count, assumed to be zero, which makes sense for an initial run. It has a return guard, which allows it to exit early if the did_no_better_count is greater than the MAX_ATTEMPTS allowed. Assuming it should continue, it calls update_params_by_number_of_mutations! (defined at ❿), passes in the params argument, and places its returned value into the local num variable.

Let's jump down to ❿ to see what update_params_by_number_of_mutations! does. It creates some children, using get_children, defined at ❽. Then get_children creates an Array to be returned by mapping the operation of calling get_child on the params Hash onto an Array with as many members as the requested number_of_children (assumed to be 10). The update_params_by_number_of_mutations! method then loops through each of those children, calling each one params. It constructs a new candidate and determines the number_of_mutations needed to reach the TARGET by calling mutate_until_matches! (from methinks.rb) on that candidate. We now have our measure of fitness and the params used to achieve that level of fitness. We update @params_by_number_of_mutations, setting the value at the number_of_mutations key to be params, as the name @params_by_number_of_mutations suggests. It then returns the number_of_mutations required by this pass through mutate_until_matches!.

Back in mutate_mutations! (❹), we recursively call mutate_mutations! again, this time with the "fittest" result in @params_by_number_of_mutations as the first argument and the result of calling get_no_better_count(num, did_no_better_count) as the second argument.

The best_num method is defined at ❻, and it is straightforward. The keys of @params_by_number_of_mutations are the number of mutations needed to reach the target. Since they're Integers, the lowest (and therefore "fittest") value will be the first element of the resulting Array when we sort them. We can get that easily with [0]. The get_no_better_count method is defined at ❾; it takes the existing num and did_no_better_count as its only arguments. It returns 0 if this pass' num is the best_num, resetting the did_no_better_count. Otherwise, it returns did_no_better_count + 1.

That's it for `mutate_mutations!`. There's one other public method, `report`, defined at ❺. It sorts through each pair within `@params_by_number_of_mutations`, outputting results via `puts`, `inspect`, String interpolation, and the `digits_needed` method, defined at ❼. It simply takes all the keys of `@params_by_number_of_mutations`, finds the `max`, and converts that highest Integer to a String with `to_s`. That String's `size` method returns the number of characters, which is our desired number of `digits_needed` for display purposes.

We can compute values as well as report them. We establish default `params` near the bottom of `methinks_meta.rb`, instantiate a `Meta_Mutator`, and call its `mutate_mutations!` and `report` methods. Let's see the results.

NOTE   *This script is not meant to demonstrate proper statistical analysis. Your results could be highly variable based on initial conditions. To accurately measure the improvement (or lack thereof) between variations, you should perform multiple runs of each version and verify that the differences you're seeing are statistically significant. That's beyond the scope of this book though. If this program inspires you to write programs that manipulate other programs, it's done its job.*

Running the Script

```
$ ruby -w methinks_meta.rb
```

The Results

```
string #0 = onti
string #5 = ppbm
string #10 = rtbq
string #15 = rubv
I match after 18 mutations
string #0 = tfjc
string #5 = uuar
I match after 9 mutations
string #0 = qmsi
string #5 = rqln
string #10 = rugv
I match after 13 mutations
string #0 = yuqa
string #5 = uupf
... (several lines removed)...
string #0 = umsv
string #5 = rupy
I match after 10 mutations
string #0 = vclv
string #5 = rlay
I match after 8 mutations
04 generations with {:generation_size=>243, :mutation_rate=>25,
:mutation_amp=>11, :display_filter=>5}
```

```
08 generations with {:generation_size=>251, :mutation_rate=>28,
:mutation_amp=>7, :display_filter=>5}
09 generations with {:generation_size=>234, :mutation_rate=>31,
:mutation_amp=>10, :display_filter=>5}
10 generations with {:generation_size=>112, :mutation_rate=>15,
:mutation_amp=>7, :display_filter=>5}
11 generations with {:generation_size=>162, :mutation_rate=>26,
:mutation_amp=>7, :display_filter=>5}
12 generations with {:generation_size=>118, :mutation_rate=>30,
:mutation_amp=>5, :display_filter=>5}
13 generations with {:generation_size=>100, :mutation_rate=>24,
:mutation_amp=>3, :display_filter=>5}
14 generations with {:generation_size=>191, :mutation_rate=>29,
:mutation_amp=>5, :display_filter=>5}
15 generations with {:generation_size=>146, :mutation_rate=>22,
:mutation_amp=>8, :display_filter=>5}
17 generations with {:generation_size=>161, :mutation_rate=>14,
:mutation_amp=>7, :display_filter=>5}
18 generations with {:generation_size=>112, :mutation_rate=>18,
:mutation_amp=>3, :display_filter=>5}
22 generations with {:generation_size=>277, :mutation_rate=>40,
:mutation_amp=>4, :display_filter=>5}
24 generations with {:generation_size=>112, :mutation_rate=>41,
:mutation_amp=>4, :display_filter=>5}
27 generations with {:generation_size=>120, :mutation_rate=>24,
:mutation_amp=>3, :display_filter=>5}
36 generations with {:generation_size=>140, :mutation_rate=>17,
:mutation_amp=>4, :display_filter=>5}
```

Our winner is {:generation_size=>243, :mutation_rate=>25, :mutation_amp=>11, :display_filter=>5}, with a match after only four generations. Again, the :display_filter doesn't matter, it's the other three parameters that really make a difference. You can rerun methinks_meta.rb as many times as you like, seeing if your winning values seem to hover around a given range of values for each important parameter. You can then reset the default params at the bottom of methinks_meta.rb and keep going as long as you want.

Hacking the Script

If we want the results to always show the params keys in alphabetical order, we could override the built-in inspect method of all Hashes with the following code:

```
def inspect()
  '{' + keys.sort_by do |k|
    k.inspect
  end.map do |k|
    "#{k.inspect} => #{self[k].inspect}"
  end.join(', ') + '}'
end
```

Chapter Recap

This chapter's mandate was to use techniques you've already learned at some broader levels. However, there were still a few new concepts or approaches.

- Equidistant Letter Sequences and larger-scale text searches
- Extracting single characters from Strings
- The `chr` method
- Modeling natural selection with `methinks.rb`
- Subclassing (`Children < Array`) and inheritance
- Calculating differences between Strings
- `select_fittest` : `inject` versus `sort_by`
- Genuine random versus pseudo-random
- Meta-mutation with `methinks_meta.rb`
- Alphabetizing `inspect` through overriding

Our next chapter is the second of two chapters that consider more complex programs. While this chapter mainly expanded upon concepts we've already learned, the next one uses an exciting new type of abstraction, known as a *callback*. Let's get to it.

10

MORE COMPLEX UTILITIES AND TRICKS, PART II

In this chapter, I'll describe an important functional technique called the *callback*, in which a general-purpose method uses a Proc to determine its specific result. We've actually seen this plenty of times before, because it's built right into many Ruby methods. Let's say we want to double every number in a list. That's easy. We just use [0, 1, 2].map { |x| x * 2 } and get [0, 2, 4] as the result. If we want to find all numbers greater than 1, we use [0, 1, 2].find_all { |x| x > 1 } and get [2] instead.

All we're doing in either case is using a general purpose method like map or find_all that takes a block, like { |x| x * 2 } or { |x| x > 1 }, and bases its output on the results of that block. The map method performs the block's operation on every member of its calling object, while find_all returns a collection that only contains members that passed the test that the block describes. In both cases, the specifics are completely determined by the block. Conceptually, that's all a callback is. Let's see a specific useful example that uses Procs instead of blocks to describe callbacks.

#37 Overnight DJ (radio_player1.rb)

One of my friends has had a very colorful employment history. He's been a DJ and general manager of a radio station, a union organizer, a journalist and translator in Japan, and a professional nightclub musician.[1] Back when he was running a jazz radio station, he had a problem: His station relied heavily on volunteers and automation, as many jazz stations do, and the station operators would set up an automated computer system to play sound files overnight. The drawback was that the system had no logging, so if a listener heard something he or she liked at 2:47 AM, the operators couldn't find out what the specific tune was. No one was at the station to take a phone call, and the next morning, there was no log of what sound file was played when, so no one could track down what was playing at a specific time that morning before anyone came in.

Enter radio_player1.rb and radio_player2.rb. These programs demonstrate a solution to this type of problem. The radio_player1.rb script gets us started with the basics, including an explanation of how Ruby uses callbacks, and radio_player2.rb does the real heavy lifting, including logging. Note that radio_player1.rb doesn't really do any playback, it just demonstrates the techniques.

The Code

```
#a/usr/bin/env ruby
# radio_player1.rb
```

Callbacks

```
❶ PLAY_FILE_PROC = lambda do |filename|
     puts "I'm playing #{filename}."
   end

❷ DONT_PLAY_FILE_PROC = lambda do |filename|
     puts "I'm not playing #{filename}. So there."
   end

❸ class RadioPlayer
```

CVS

```
❹   DIRS_TO_IGNORE = ['.', '..', 'CVS']

❺   PICK_FROM_DIR_PROC = lambda do |dir, callback_proc, dir_filter|

       puts "I'm inside #{dir}" if $DEBUG
❻       (Dir.open(dir).entries - DIRS_TO_IGNORE).sort.each do |filename|

❼         if ((filename =~ dir_filter) or not dir_filter)
             item = "#{dir}/#{filename}"
             puts "#{item} passes the filter" if $DEBUG

❽           if File.directory?(item)
               puts "#{item} is a directory" if $DEBUG
```

---

[1] Now he blogs and podcasts at http://thejasoncraneshow.com.

```
                PICK_FROM_DIR_PROC.call(
                  item, callback_proc, dir_filter
                )
            else
              puts "#{item} is a file" if $DEBUG
              callback_proc.call(item)
            end

        end

      end

    end

❾  def self.walk(dir, callback_proc, dir_filter=nil)
      puts
      puts "I'm walking #{dir} using filter #{dir_filter.inspect}" if $DEBUG
      PICK_FROM_DIR_PROC.call(dir, callback_proc, dir_filter)
    end

  end

❿ dir = 'extras/soundfiles'
   callback  = (ARGV[0] == 'play') ? PLAY_FILE_PROC : DONT_PLAY_FILE_PROC
   dir_filter = ARGV[1] ? Regexp.new(ARGV[1]) : nil
   RadioPlayer.walk(dir, callback, dir_filter)
   puts
```

How It Works

First, we define our callbacks as Proc Constants. At ❶, we have the PLAY_FILE_PROC, and at ❷, we have the DONT_PLAY_FILE_PROC. Since radio_player1.rb is just a demonstration script, both of these Procs merely report what they would do instead of actually doing anything. Think of them as "dry run" testing examples. At ❸ we define a new class called RadioPlayer. We'll detail that class soon, but for now, it'll be easier to understand how this script works if we skip down to ❿, where we see how the class is used.

We define a variable called dir, with the value 'extras/soundfiles'. That's where I stored the audio files used by this example; it's analogous to the directory that contains the radio station's songs, sound bites, station identification, and so forth. We then set the value of a variable called callback. It stores the appropriate Proc, either PLAY_FILE_PROC or DONT_PLAY_FILE_PROC. If the first argument to the script (ARGV[0]) is 'play', it uses PLAY_FILE_PROC. Otherwise, it uses DONT_PLAY_FILE_PROC. Next, we define a variable called dir_filter, which is either a defined RegExp instance or nil. As the name suggests, this filters directories within the main dir soundfile directory. If dir_filter is nil, it does no filtering, and it assumes the entire contents of dir are available for playing. We then call the walk (❾) class method of RadioPlayer with the arguments dir, callback, and dir_filter.

The self.walk method takes three arguments: dir, callback_proc, and dir_filter. The first two are mandatory, while dir_filter is optional, defaulting to nil. It prints an empty line with puts, and if the script is called with the -d flag (which sets $DEBUG to true), self.walk also prints some boilerplate indicating what it's doing. It then executes a call to a Proc Constant called PICK_FROM_DIR_PROC, using the same three arguments—dir, callback_proc, and dir_filter.

Now, to understand what that means, we'll describe the RadioPlayer class at ❸. It has two Constants: DIRS_TO_IGNORE and PICK_FROM_DIR_PROC. DIRS_TO_IGNORE (❹) lists the directories that the script should not care about. It includes the current directory ('.'), the directory up a level ('..'), and the directory used by CVS.

NOTE   *Concurrent Versions System (CVS) is a program that keeps track of different versions of files. It's most often used for software development. You can read more about it at http://www.nongnu.org/cvs.*

The second Constant within RadioPlayer is PICK_FROM_DIR_PROC (❺), which is a Proc that picks from directories. We create it in the usual way with lambda and define it to take three arguments: dir, callback_proc, and dir_filter. These correspond to the three arguments to walk (❾) that we described at the bottom of this script at ❿.

Now we get to see what these arguments end up being used for. The PICK_FROM_DIR_PROC Constant has several debugging lines that puts a given message if $DEBUG is set to true. I won't detail each of them, as they should be fairly self explanatory. We start by looping through each sorted filename, based on the entries within dir, minus the DIRS_TO_IGNORE (❻). Next, we verify that either the filename matches the dir_filter with a regular expression test, or there is no dir_filter in place (❼). Assuming we should proceed, we assign the interpolated String "#{dir}/#{filename}" into a local variable called item. We'll be using item frequently enough that it's worthwhile to set it once and reuse it, rather than recalculate it every time.

Next, we use the File.directory? predicate (❽) to determine whether or not item is a directory. If it is a directory, we need to pick from that directory as well, so we recursively call PICK_FROM_DIR_PROC, with the arguments item, callback_proc, and dir_filter. The current value of item now becomes the value of dir in the new recursive call, so when we get to the assignment into item within the recursive call, that item consists of a String like the following: "#{top_dir}/{next_dir}/#{filename}", and so on. This keeps happening until we reach a non-directory filename. What happens then?

In this case we consult the else clause within the if block at ❽. Here, we finally call the callback_proc, with item as the argument. Let's assume that we are using PLAY_FILE_PROC as the callback_proc. We'll therefore puts a message saying that we're playing filename. This happens for every terminal (non-directory) filename within the execution of self.walk (❾). Let's see it in action. First let's see the contents of extras/soundfiles:

```
$ ls -R extras/soundfiles/
extras/soundfiles/:
01-Neal_And_Jack_And_Me.ogg  CVS  legal  promo
```

```
extras/soundfiles/CVS:
Entries  Repository  Root

extras/soundfiles/legal:
CVS  legal1  legal2

extras/soundfiles/legal/CVS:
CVS  Entries  Repository  Root

extras/soundfiles/legal/CVS/CVS:
Entries  Repository  Root

extras/soundfiles/promo:
CVS  promo1  promo2

extras/soundfiles/promo/CVS:
CVS  Entries  Repository  Root

extras/soundfiles/promo/CVS/CVS:
Entries  Repository  Root
```

Other than those CVS directories I mentioned, we have a file called 01-Neal_And_Jack_And_Me.ogg at the top level, a directory called legal with the files legal1 and legal2, and a directory called promo with the files promo1 and promo2. Now, let's run radio_player1.rb with various arguments.

The Results

```
$ ruby -w radio_player1.rb

I'm not playing extras/soundfiles/01-Neal_And_Jack_And_Me.ogg. So there.
I'm not playing extras/soundfiles/legal/legal1. So there.
I'm not playing extras/soundfiles/legal/legal2. So there.
I'm not playing extras/soundfiles/promo/promo1. So there.
I'm not playing extras/soundfiles/promo/promo2. So there.
```

We provided no ARGV[0], so it assumed DONT_PLAY_FILE_PROC for the callback. It also had no dir_filter, so it "not played" every file within extras/soundfiles, except within the directories we told it to ignore—maybe it's silly to explicitly "not play" sound files, but I just wanted a callback that could show in an obvious fashion that it was being called. Let's see some more.

```
$ ruby -w radio_player1.rb play legal

I'm playing extras/soundfiles/legal/legal1.
I'm playing extras/soundfiles/legal/legal2.
```

Here, ARGV[0] is 'play', and ARGV[1] limits available files to those matching /legal/. It worked.

```
$ ruby -w radio_player1.rb play

I'm playing extras/soundfiles/01-Neal_And_Jack_And_Me.ogg.
I'm playing extras/soundfiles/legal/legal1.
I'm playing extras/soundfiles/legal/legal2.
I'm playing extras/soundfiles/promo/promo1.
I'm playing extras/soundfiles/promo/promo2.
```

It worked again.

Hacking the Script

The most basic hack of this script is to call it with the -d command-line option. That tells you where the script is at any given point, and it may reveal some useful information as you try different arguments, create your own files and directories with extras/soundfiles, or do whatever other customization you think is appropriate.

The beauty of callbacks is that you can hack your program by simply using a different one. The overall structure of the manner in which you do some particular operation stays the same, while the specific operation being done can change, often quite drastically. We'll see an example of that in the next script.

#38 Better Overnight DJ (radio_player2.rb)

This script, radio_player2.rb, is an improvement on radio_player1.rb. Instead of placeholder Procs, it will actually play sound files, as well as log playback with specific times.

The Code

```
#a/usr/bin/env ruby
# radio_player2.rb

❶ LOG_FILE = '/tmp/radio_player2.log'

❷ PLAYERS = {
    '.mp3' => 'mpg321',
    '.ogg' => 'ogg123',
    ''     => 'ls'
}

❸ # these are variables, local to Kernel.
  # They work just as well as constants.
  play_file_proc = lambda do |filename|
❹   ext = File.extname(filename)
❺   system("#{PLAYERS[ext]} #{filename}") if PLAYERS[ext]
❻   File.open(LOG_FILE, 'a') do |log|
      log.puts([Time.now, filename].join("\t") + "\n")
    end
```

Callbacks

```
end

dont_play_file_proc = lambda do |filename|
  puts "I'm not playing #{filename}. So there."
end

class RadioPlayer

  DIRS_TO_IGNORE = ['.', '..', 'CVS']

  PICK_FROM_DIR_PROC = lambda do |dir, callback_proc, dir_filter|

    (Dir.open(dir).entries - DIRS_TO_IGNORE).sort.each do |filename|

      if ((filename =~ dir_filter) or not dir_filter)
        item = "#{dir}/#{filename}"

        if File.directory?(item)
          PICK_FROM_DIR_PROC.call(
            item, callback_proc, dir_filter
          )
        else
          callback_proc.call(item)
        end

      end

    end

  end

  def self.walk(dir, callback_proc, dir_filter=nil)
    puts
    PICK_FROM_DIR_PROC.call(dir, callback_proc, dir_filter)
  end

end

dir = 'extras/soundfiles'
callback   = (ARGV[0] == 'play') ? play_file_proc : dont_play_file_proc
dir_filter = ARGV[1] ? Regexp.new(ARGV[1]) : nil
RadioPlayer.walk(dir, callback, dir_filter)
puts
```

How It Works

For this section, I'll merely detail the changes between radio_player1.rb and
radio_player2.rb. The first change is the definition of the LOG_FILE Constant
at ❶. As you might expect, this is the filename into which radio_player2.rb
writes logging messages. Next, we declare a Hash Constant called PLAYERS at ❷,
with keys of file extensions for particular types of soundfiles and values of the
names of programs that one might use to play those types of files on a Unix
system.

Next, we define our Procs at ❸, this time as variables rather than Constants. There's no particular reason to use variables instead of Constants, as the comment notes. I just wanted to show that either approach works well for our purposes. Aside from being variables rather than Constants, the playing Proc is substantively different.

The play_file_proc acts as a closure, binding the PLAYERS Hash inside itself. It establishes the extension (and therefore, type) of its filename argument as ext at ❹. It then tries to play that filename using system at ❺, but only if the PLAYERS Hash has an appropriate player for that file extension. I made sure that PLAYERS had an entry for no file extension at all, so radio_player2.rb could still demonstrate that it was either playing or not playing the dummy files like legal1 and promo2 that have no file extension. Since I just wanted to show the dummy files, I decided that the Unix command ls, which just lists files, was the appropriate value to use in PLAYERS.

The radio_player2.rb script also logs playback within the play_file_proc. At ❻, it opens a new file for appending, using 'a' as the second argument to File.open. It then refers to that log file as log, and uses log's puts method to append the current Time and the filename being played, separated by tabs, all followed by a carriage return. Whenever we use radio_player2.rb, we can check the contents of LOG_FILE to see what's been played.

The only other differences are the removal of the debugging messages and referring to the Procs by the lowercase variable names rather than the all-caps Constant names. Let's see this version in action.

The Results

Let's try a basic playback of everything.

```
$ ruby -w radio_player2.rb play


Audio Device:   OSS audio driver output

Playing: extras/soundfiles/01-Neal_And_Jack_And_Me.ogg
Ogg Vorbis stream: 2 channel, 44100 Hz
Title: Neal and Jack and Me
Artist: King Crimson
Album: Beat
Date: 1982
Track number: 01
Tracktotal: 08
Genre: Prog Rock
Composer: Belew, Bruford, Fripp, Levin
Musicbrainz_albumid: 5ddbe867-ebce-445d-a175-d90516e426da
Musicbrainz_albumartistid: b38225b8-8e5f-42aa-bcdc-7bae5b5bdab3
Musicbrainz_artistid: b38225b8-8e5f-42aa-bcdc-7bae5b5bdab3
Musicbrainz_trackid: 30a23275-11ef-4f07-bdc8-0192ae34e67d
```

```
Done.
extras/soundfiles/legal/legal1
extras/soundfiles/legal/legal2
extras/soundfiles/promo/promo1
extras/soundfiles/promo/promo2
```

That command-line call played the Ogg file (again, from my favorite band King Crimson) using a system call with ogg123, the appropriate value within PLAYERS for the .ogg extension, and then it "played" the other files with ls, the appropriate PLAYERS value for files with no extension at all.

Now let's filter, with fake playback.

```
$ ruby -w radio_player2.rb play legal

extras/soundfiles/legal/legal1
extras/soundfiles/legal/legal2
```

And again, without fake playback.

```
$ ruby -w radio_player2.rb dont legal

I'm not playing extras/soundfiles/legal/legal1. So there.
I'm not playing extras/soundfiles/legal/legal2. So there.
```

Notice that playback merely lists the dummy files, while non-playback executes the full dont_play_file_proc, including the immature So there. suffix.

Hacking the Script

The value of LOG_FILE is Unix-specific. Windows users (or anyone else) can certainly change that filename to something more appropriate for their operating system. Also, if you prefer a more robust system for the dummy files, you could give them their own extension, like dummy, and change PLAYERS so that the key for 'ls' is that new extension.

#39 Numbers by Name (to_lang.rb)

In previous scripts, notably "#16 Adding Commas to Numbers (commify.rb)" on page 75 and "#17 Roman Numerals (roman_numeral.rb)" on page 81, we talked about how numbers can be represented in a variety of ways. Both of those scripts showed meaningful ways of representing Integers as Strings, other than the handy but trivially different to_s method. This script, to_lang.rb, extends that discussion by representing Integers as Strings consisting of how those numbers are spoken in two real-world languages: English and Spanish.

The Code

This code is broken into three separate files, for reasons that I will make clear in "How It Works" on page 198.

representable_in_english.rb

```
=begin rdoc
This is intended for use with to_lang.rb
=end
```

❶ `module Representable_In_English`

```
=begin rdoc
Return a <b>Hash</b> whose keys are <b>Integer</b>s and whose values
are the words representing the same values.
=end
```

❷
```
  def create_english()
      need_ones_in_english.merge(dont_need_ones_in_english)

  end
```

❸
```
  def special_replacements_in_english(num_as_string)
      add_hyphens_to_tens(num_as_string).strip
  end
```

Syntactic Sugar ❹
```
  def to_english()
      to_lang('english')
  end
```

❺
```
  alias :to_en :to_english
```

❻
```
  private
```

❼
```
  def add_hyphens_to_tens(num_as_string)
      num_as_string.sub(/ty/, 'ty-').sub(/-?- ?/, '-')
  end
```

❽
```
  def need_ones_in_english()
      return {
        10 ** 9 => 'billion',
        10 ** 6 => 'million',
        10 ** 3 => 'thousand',
        100      => 'hundred',
      }
  end
```

❾
```
  def dont_need_ones_in_english()
      return {
        90 => 'ninety',
        80 => 'eighty',
        70 => 'seventy',
        60 => 'sixty',
        50 => 'fifty',
```

```
        40 => 'forty',
        30 => 'thirty',
        20 => 'twenty',
        19 => 'nineteen',
        18 => 'eighteen',
        17 => 'seventeen',
        16 => 'sixteen',
        15 => 'fifteen',
        14 => 'fourteen',
        13 => 'thirteen',
        12 => 'twelve',
        11 => 'eleven',
        10 => 'ten',
         9 => 'nine',
         8 => 'eight',
         7 => 'seven',
         6 => 'six',
         5 => 'five',
         4 => 'four',
         3 => 'three',
         2 => 'two',
         1 => 'one',
         0 => '',
    }
  end

end
```

Next will be a very similar file, also storing a module/mixin definition. The only meaningful differences pertain to the choice of language: this one details Spanish, rather than English.

representable_in_spanish.rb

```
=begin rdoc
This is intended for use with to_lang.rb
=end
```

❶ `module Representable_In_Spanish`

```
=begin rdoc
Return a <b>Hash</b> whose keys are <b>Integer</b>s and whose values
are the words representing the same values.
=end
```
❷
```
  def create_spanish()
    need_ones_in_spanish.merge(dont_need_ones_in_spanish)
  end
```

❸
```
  def special_replacements_in_spanish(num_as_string)
    add_hyphens_to_tens(num_as_string).strip
  end
```

Syntactic Sugar ❹   `def to_spanish()`

```ruby
    to_lang('spanish')
  end

  alias :to_es :to_spanish

  private

  def add_hyphens_to_tens(num_as_string)
    num_as_string.sub(/ta/, 'ta-').sub(/-?- ?/, '-')
  end

  def need_ones_in_spanish()
    return {
      10 ** 12 => 'billon',
      10 ** 9  => 'mil millones',
      10 ** 6  => 'millon',
      10 ** 3  => 'mil',
      100      => 'ciento',
    }
  end

  def dont_need_ones_in_spanish()
    return {
      90 => 'noventa',
      80 => 'ochenta',
      70 => 'setenta',
      60 => 'sesenta',
      50 => 'cincuenta',
      40 => 'cuarenta',
      30 => 'treinta',
      20 => 'veinte',
      19 => 'diecinueve',
      18 => 'dieciocho',
      17 => 'diecisiete',
      16 => 'dieciseis',
      15 => 'quince',
      14 => 'catorce',
      13 => 'trece',
      12 => 'doce',
      11 => 'once',
      10 => 'deiz',
       9 => 'nueve',
       8 => 'ocho',
       7 => 'siete',
       6 => 'seis',
       5 => 'cinco',
       4 => 'cuatro',
       3 => 'tres',
       2 => 'dos',
       1 => 'uno',
       0 => '', # 'cero'
    }
  end

end
```

Finally, we have the code that directly gives Integers the ability to represent themselves in spoken languages. It does so through the use of the modules above, as you'll see.

to_lang.rb

```ruby
#!/usr/bin/env ruby -w
# to_lang.rb

=begin rdoc
Implement representation of numbers in human languages:
1 => 'one',
2 => 'two',
etc.

This is an generalized extension of ideas shown for the
specific case of roman numerals in roman_numeral.rb

Note that similar work has already been done at
http://www.deveiate.org/projects/Linguistics/wiki/English
This version focuses only on converting numbers to multiple
language targets, and pedantically considers "and" to be
the pronunciation of the decimal point.
=end

class Integer
```

Requiring Our Own Mixins ❶
```ruby
  require 'representable_in_english'
  require 'representable_in_spanish'
```

❷
```ruby
  include Representable_In_English
  include Representable_In_Spanish
```

❸
```ruby
  EMPTY_STRING = ''
  SPACE        = ' '
```

❹
```ruby
  @@lang_of ||= Hash.new()
```

❺

The send Method
```ruby
  def need_ones?(lang)
    send("need_ones_in_#{lang}").keys.include?(self)
  end
```

❻
```ruby
  def to_lang(lang)
    return EMPTY_STRING if self.zero?

    @@lang_of[lang] ||= send("create_#{lang}")

    base      = get_base(lang)
    mult      = (self / base).to_i
    remaining = (self - (mult * base))

    raw_output = [
      mult_prefix(base, mult, lang),
      @@lang_of[lang][base],
```

```
          remaining.to_lang(lang)
        ].join(SPACE)

        return send(
         "special_replacements_in_#{lang}",
         raw_output)
      end

❼    private

❽    def get_base(lang)
        return self if @@lang_of[lang][self]
        @@lang_of[lang].keys.sort.reverse.detect do |k|
          k <= self
        end
      end

❾    def mult_prefix(base, mult, lang)
        return mult.to_lang(lang) if mult > 1
        return 1.to_lang(lang)     if base.need_ones?(lang)
        return EMPTY_STRING
      end

    end
```

How It Works

Let's examine each file in turn. Since representable_in_english.rb and
representable_in_spanish.rb are so similar, we can deal with them
simultaneously.

The Two Mixins

Both representable_in_english.rb and representable_in_spanish.rb are *mixins*,
the mechanism Ruby uses to give shared behavior to classes with different
ancestry, like giving both bats and birds the ability to fly. In our case, instead
of giving organisms the ability to fly, we're giving the object we mix our mixins
into the ability to represent itself in some human languages: English and
Spanish, in this case.

   We define the appropriate Module, in both representable_in_english.rb
and representable_in_spanish.rb, at ❶. I'll keep the numbered callouts in the
code in parallel across these two files throughout this example. At ❷, we
define our create_english or create_spanish methods. The purpose of either
method is to return a Hash whose keys are Integers and whose values are the
representation of those Integers in the module's language. The resulting
Hash's pairs will form our base cases, and we'll use them very similarly to
the ones we used in the roman_numeral.rb script in Chapter 5. Then at ❸,
we define a special replacements method, customized and named for the
language. Every language is likely to have some special treatment, even
beyond what we can do with the differences in the Hash returned by
create_english or create_spanish. So far, all we need to do is add hyphens

to numbers with tens components. To accomplish that task, we call the add_hyphens_to_tens method, which we define at ❼.

At ❹ and ❺, we add some of what programmers call *syntactic sugar*, or a simplification of a language's syntax. The term *syntactic sugar* can have a negative connotation, but it doesn't have to. It generally refers to a shortcut that a programmer uses to more easily accomplish a commonly needed technique, such as adding method aliases with alias. It's relatively easy to add syntactic sugar to Ruby, as our examples show. We can add methods like to_english or to_spanish by calling to_lang (soon to be defined in to_lang.rb) with the appropriate lang argument.[2] We can also use alias to make to_en refer to to_english, and to_es refer to to_spanish.

Some of our methods can be private, so we declare that at ❻. We've already discussed add_hyphens_to_tens ❼, so we can move on to need_ones_in_english and need_ones_in_spanish ❽. This method returns a Hash whose keys are Integers and whose values are the representation of those Integers in the module's language. This should sound familiar. What makes the pairs in this Hash notable is a characteristic they all share: They all need the prefix *one* (in the appropriate language) when there is in fact only one of those numbers. The number *100* is pronounced *one hundred* in English, for example.

"Of course!" you might think. However, contrast the Hashes returned by need_ones_in_english ❽ and dont_need_ones_in_english ❾. The Integer keys of the Hash created at ❾ do not need the *one* prefix. You don't say *one twenty* for *20*, for example, so we need a way to differentiate between numbers that need the prefix and those that don't. The different methods at ❽ and ❾ are our way to do so. When we want all of them together and when we don't care about the prefix issue we can simply merge the two Hashes together. This is exactly what we will do in the to_lang.rb file, which we're about to examine.

The Main Code

The first thing we do in to_lang.rb is open the Integer class, since we want to add new behavior to Integers. At ❶, we require the mixin files just discussed, and at ❷, we include them within the Integer class, giving all Integers the methods defined in the mixin files, including both aliases. We also want some Constants, mainly for convenient text manipulation, so we define those at ❸. We close off the pre-methods section by defining a class variable called @@lang_of at ❹. It's a Hash that will eventually store the merged result of the two Hashes from the mixins' markers at ❽ and ❾. Since we define it with ||=, it is only defined in the first Integer instantiated, and then it is shared among all of them.

At ❺, we define a predicate called need_ones?, which takes a lang argument and simply makes a call to either need_ones_in_english (defined in representable_in_english.rb) or need_ones_in_spanish (defined in representable_in_spanish.rb), as appropriate to the lang argument. It doesn't matter which of the files the called method is defined in, because they are both included at ❷ in to_lang.rb.

---

[2] Note that our definitions of to_english and to_spanish essentially curry to_lang, making new curried methods that are simpler to call (i.e., that take fewer arguments) by making assumptions, namely which language to convert into.

Our main workhorse method to_lang, appears at ❶; this method takes a single, mandatory lang argument. It returns early with the EMPTY_STRING if self is zero. This means that if we call 0.to_lang('english'), we get the empty string as the result, instead of the String 'zero'. (See "Hacking the Script" on page 202 for a way to change that.) Assuming the case should proceed beyond that, to_lang then sets the value of @@lang_of[lang]. The @@lang_of class variable had already been declared as a Hash when the first Integer was instantiated, but only as a Hash with no keys or values. The value put into @@lang_of[lang] is the result of calling a method called *send* with the argument "create_#{lang}", which you should recognize as an interpolating String.

The send method takes any number of arguments, the first of which must be an expression that evaluates to the name of a method. It then calls that method with the rest of the arguments. This allows you to do exactly what we're doing here, which is dynamically calling a method whose name you don't yet know. You could work around this by having a test on the lang argument, and there are many ways to do so. Instead of a traditional method like create_english or create_spanish, you could use Procs as Hash values, as we've done many times since Chapter 6. You could also do something like this:

```
@@lang_of = if (lang == 'english')
  create_english()
else
  create_spanish()
end
```

Note that we take advantage of the fact that all statements in Ruby return the last expression evaluated, including the if statement. You have many different options for calling a method whose name you don't know, but the point is that it doesn't need to be that difficult. Ruby provides us with the send method, which is incredibly useful and appropriate.

At this point, @@lang_of[lang] will contain the Hash that is the merged result of both need_ones_in_english and dont_need_ones_in_english (for English) or need_ones_in_spanish and dont_need_ones_in_spanish (for Spanish.) Let's take a cue from send and express those as "need_ones_in#{lang}" and "dont_need_ones_in#{lang}". We then want to create some local variables called base, mult, and remaining.

The base variable is the highest Integer key within @@lang_of[lang] that is equal to or less than self. We get it from the get_base method, defined at ❽, which finds the first key in a reverse-sorted version of @@lang_of[lang] that is equal to or less than self. It does this via the detect method (which I like to think of as "find first"). It also has a return guard, where it returns self if self is actually one of the keys of @@lang_of[lang].

The mult variable is simply how many times base can go into self, rounded down to the nearest Integer. The remaining variable is whatever's left. We then want to create raw_output, a String that holds the eventual output, before we make any of the special replacements already mentioned in "The Two Mixins" on page 198. The raw_output String will consist of something representing (base * mult), a space, and then the result of making a recursive call to to_lang on whatever is left (remaining.to_lang(lang)).

We accomplish that by constructing an Array. The first element is the output of a method called mult_prefix, defined at ❾; it takes the arguments base, mult, and lang. If mult is greater than one, we know we need to have a prefix: the number *200* is pronounced *two hundred*, so we need the *two*. If base needs a one (as described already, pertaining to the need_ones? predicate), we know that we need to have *one* as a prefix, such as for *one hundred* or *one thousand*. Finally, in all other cases, we return a prefix that is the EMPTY_STRING, so the number *20* is pronounced *twenty* rather than *one twenty*, and *5* is *five* rather than *one five*. That's the multiple prefix and the first part of our eventual output.[3]

Next, we need whatever base is, as pronounced in lang. We get that via @@lang_of[lang][base]. Finally, we need the rest of the number, which we get via remaining.to_lang(lang). This keeps happening recursively, with a smaller Integer calling to_lang and appending its results, until base is 0. Then to_lang returns the EMPTY_STRING due to its return guard, and the entire output is concatenated together within the first calling to remaining.to_lang.

That's the Array. You'll notice that to_lang joins that Array on a SPACE, so that the words in raw_output are separated by spaces, which is normal. Before we're done, we want to call our special replacements method (whichever one is appropriate for lang) on raw_output, and return the result of doing that. Since we again have a method name that depends on lang, we'll use send.

The Results

Let's take it out for a spin. I've written a simple test script called test_lang.rb that I stored inside the tests directory. It uses Test::Unit::TestCase again, in a manner similar to the way we tested the temperature converter in Chapter 7. Here's its code:

```ruby
#!/usr/bin/env ruby
# test_lang.rb

require 'to_lang'
require 'test/unit'

class Tester < Test::Unit::TestCase

  def test_langs()

    tests = {
      'en' => {
        1      => 'one',
        5      => 'five',
        9      => 'nine',
        11     => 'eleven',
        51     => 'fifty one',
        100    => 'one hundred',
        101    => 'one hundred one',
        257    => 'two hundred fifty seven',
        1000   => 'one thousand',
```

---

[3] All of these specific examples assume English, of course. Substitute the Spanish terms when lang is 'spanish'.

```
      1001  => 'one thousand one',
     90125 => 'ninety thousand one hundred twenty five',
    },
    'es' => {
      1     => 'uno',
      5     => 'cinco',
      9     => 'nueve',
      11    => 'once',
      51    => 'cincuenta-uno',
      100   => 'uno ciento',
      101   => 'uno ciento uno',
      257   => 'dos ciento cincuenta-siete',
      1000  => 'uno mil',
      1001  => 'uno mil uno',
      90125 => 'noventa-mil uno ciento veinte cinco',
    }
  }
  %w[ en es ].each do |lang|
    general_tester( tests, lang )
  end
end

private

def general_tester(tests, lang)
  tests[lang].each_key do |num|
    assert_equal( num.send("to_#{lang}"), tests[lang][num] )
  end
end

end
```

And here's its output:

```
Loaded suite tests/test_lang
Started
.
Finished in 0.004543 seconds.

1 tests, 22 assertions, 0 failures, 0 errors
```

Hacking the Script

We could modify to_lang to allow the pronunciation of zero, instead of returning the EMPTY_STRING Constant. In order to do that and still work with the recursion, we'll need to send another optional argument into to_lang that keeps track of the recursion depth (how many levels of recursion we have performed). We only care about distinguishing between the first call to to_lang and the rest of the calls. We could then return the EMPTY_STRING if self is zero and it's the first call to to_lang; we can skip the return guard in all other cases. We'd also need to change the value for 0 in both dont_need_ones_in_english and dont_need_ones_in_spanish.

#40 Elegant Maps and Injects (symbol.rb)

I'll close this chapter with a tiny script that I didn't even write. I certainly wish I had, because it's remarkably useful, especially for making your use of map, inject, and similar methods much more elegant. It's an example of the best kind of syntactic sugar, and it comes directly from the Ruby Extensions Project at http://extensions.rubyforge.org. This script and all other scripts at that site are licensed under the same terms as Ruby itself, which is what allows me to use it in this chapter.[4] The code is extremely simple.

The Code

Symbol.to_proc

```ruby
#!/usr/bin/env ruby
class Symbol
  def to_proc()
    Proc.new { |obj, *args| obj.send(self, *args) }
  end
end
```

What's the point of this? It lets you use uc_words = lc_words.map(&:upcase) to accomplish the same thing as uc_words = lc_words.map { |word| word.upcase }. In both cases, the uc_words variable now contains uppercase versions of all the words in lc_words. As I said, it's basically just syntactic sugar, but it's very, very nice and clever.

How It Works

First of all, this script creates a Proc using Proc.new that takes an object called obj and a variable number of args. Remember from to_lang.rb that obj.send(methodname) is the same as obj.methodname, so these are equivalent, with an Array a:

```ruby
a.send(push, some_item)
a.push(some_item)
```

The remaining arguments (represented by *args) are also passed along to obj, which is using each or map or some other iterating method.

Secondly, you may remember previous discussion about how to convert between Procs and blocks using the ampersand (&), but we can also use the ampersand to cast more than blocks into Procs. Doing so calls a method called to_proc, which you can see we've overridden. We end up using a double character prefix of &:, because a colon is already the prefix for a Symbol. When we use the expression &:some_name, what we mean is *the expression returned by the to_proc method of the Symbol named* some_name.

---

[4] Those terms are made explicit at http://www.ruby-lang.org/en/about/license.txt

The Results

Let's see it in action in irb.

```
irb -r symbol.rb
irb(main):001:0> digits = (0..9).to_a
=> [0, 1, 2, 3, 4, 5, 6, 7, 8, 9]
irb(main):002:0> digits.inject(&:+)
=> 45
irb(main):003:0> digits.map(&:inspect)
=> ["0", "1", "2", "3", "4", "5", "6", "7", "8", "9"]
irb(main):004:0> require 'to_lang'
=> true
irb(main):005:0> digits.map(&:to_en)
=> ["", "one", "two", "three", "four", "five", "six", "seven", "eight",
"nine"]
```

Hacking the Script

This script is already a very elegant hack. Note that you need to use `Proc.new` rather than `lambda`, because you want it to be able to handle a variable number of `args`.

Chapter Recap

What was new in this chapter?

- Callbacks
- CVS
- Mixins in action
- Calling methods with variable names via `send`
- Syntactic sugar
- `Symbol.to_proc`

That's it for this chapter. It tended to focus less on completely new concepts and more on new applications for familiar things, but it still managed to introduce more than a few novel ideas. The next chapter focuses on web programming, a venue in which Ruby has become quite popular.

11

CGI AND THE WEB

Ruby has gotten a lot of attention as a language particularly well suited for web programming, especially in the context of the Rails development framework. Some people even go so far as to categorize Ruby as a web language, suggesting that it is not a full-fledged general-purpose programming language. I hope that the previous chapters have played at least a modest role in convincing readers that this assertion is false.

That said, Ruby is very useful for web work, and it does have some characteristics that make it better suited for web programming than (for example) video game programming. Ruby operates at a very high level of abstraction, giving programmers a large toolset to work with, and it executes code at a slower speed than some other languages. These characteristics make Ruby well suited for web work, since development speed is often critical, but program execution speed is often less critical than in other types of programs, such as real-time action video games.

The Rails development framework has been instrumental in bringing Ruby to the attention of an ever-larger audience. Some say it's Ruby's "killer app," analogous to Perl's CPAN or the GNU project's gcc. This is a general

Ruby book, not a Rails book, but Rails is important enough that it gets its own chapter. (Since we'll be using RubyGems, Ruby's package-management system, to install Rails, this book also has a chapter devoted to RubyGems.)

You'll have to wait two chapters for Rails. Aside from knowing how to install it with RubyGems, by then you should also know something about web programs in general—that's what this chapter is for. If you're a web app veteran, feel free to skip this chapter, although you may find some of the specific scripts novel and interesting, even if you already know how they work.

Common Gateway Interface

The most common approach to web programming is the Common Gateway Interface (CGI). *CGI* is not a programming language; it's a set of rules for programs to follow when they run on the Web, regardless of the particular language in which each program might be written. CGI enables friendly cooperation among multiple files that could even be written in distinct programming languages but all exist together within a larger web application.

Using more than one language for a single web application is fairly common. I mentioned that Ruby's high level of abstraction makes it suitable for web programming. However, sometimes you might really want to use a library someone has already written in another language—like Python, for instance—in a web program. If you use CGI, you could write part of your web application in Python in order to use that library. You might also have a section of your web application that is highly speed critical, so you could write that part in C for execution speed, and the rest in Ruby for development speed. This is exactly the reason that Paul Graham and his colleagues chose to use a combination of Lisp and C for their company Viaweb, which eventually became Yahoo! Stores. They were able to do so because the CGI specification holds across multiple languages.

Preparation and Installation

Before we get going with Ruby and CGI, we've got to do a little work to get our webserver ready. For the purposes of this chapter, I'll be focusing on getting CGI working for the Apache webserver running on a Unix-like environment. Apache is the most popular webserver, and Unix-like operating systems are the most common (and most stable) server operating systems.

You can get a copy of the Apache webserver at http://httpd.apache.org, or you can use a package manager to install it. (Mac OS X comes with Apache pre-installed.) I used apt-get on my Ubuntu system, as follows:

```
apt-get install apache2 apache2-doc
Reading package lists... Done
Building dependency tree... Done
The following extra packages will be installed:
  apache2-common apache2-mpm-worker apache2-utils libapr0 libpcre3 ssl-cert
```

```
Suggested packages:
 lynx www-browser
The following NEW packages will be installed:
 apache2 apache2-common apache2-doc apache2-mpm-worker apache2-utils libapr0
 libpcre3 ssl-cert
0 upgraded, 8 newly installed, 0 to remove and 5 not upgraded.
Need to get 3555kB of archives.
After unpacking 16.4MB of additional disk space will be used.
Do you want to continue [Y/n]? Y
```

I answered Y. You can see that I chose the apache2 version of the Apache web-server. After installing Apache, you'll also want to install packages for mod_ruby, which allows Ruby programs to be run within the webserver. I'll explain the benefits of this when we get to the script that shows mod_ruby being used. You can install mod_ruby by typing apt-get install libapache2-mod-ruby liberuby on a Debian-based system. Now that the installation is done, let's start with our first simple CGI script.

#41 A Simple CGI Script (simple_cgi.rb)

This script is fairly quick and dirty, but it shows the basics of how to use Ruby for CGI and introduces Ruby's aptly named cgi library. You'll need to put this script in your system's cgi-bin directory. It's /usr/lib/cgi-bin/ on my system, although your system's location may be different. You can then browse to http://localhost/cgi-bin/simple_cgi.rb, because your webserver will provide access to the contents of your cgi-bin directory via http://localhost/cgi-bin/.

NOTE   *You'll also need to give* simple_cgi.rb *755 permissions, meaning that its owner can do anything with it and everyone else can read and execute it, but not write (change) it. For more information, see* man chmod.

Before we even get started with the script, you should also browse to http://localhost/. If you see either a page telling you that Apache is installed correctly or a listing of files in a directory, your webserver is probably working. If you don't see either of these things, consult the Apache documentation (available at http://httpd.apache.org/docs) to diagnose the problem. If your webserver is working, you can proceed to the script.

The Code

Requiring
CGI.rb

```ruby
#!/usr/bin/env ruby
# simple_cgi.rb

❶ require 'cgi'

❷ class Simple_CGI

❸   EMPTY_STRING = ''
    TITLE = 'A simple CGI script'
```

```
     def display()
❹     cgi = CGI.new('html4')
❺     output = cgi.html do
         cgi.head do
           cgi.title { TITLE }
         end +
         cgi.body do
           cgi.h1 { TITLE } +
❻         show_def_list(cgi)
         end
       end
❼     cgi.out { output.gsub('><', ">\n<") }
     end

     private

❽    def get_items_hash()
       {
         'script'   => ENV['SCRIPT_NAME'],
❾        'server'   => ENV['SERVER_NAME'] || %x{hostname} || EMPTY_STRING,
         'software' => ENV['SERVER_SOFTWARE'],
         'time'     => Time.now,
       }
     end

❿    def show_def_list(cgi)
       cgi.dl do
         items = get_items_hash.merge(cgi.params)
         items.keys.sort.map do |term|
           definition = items[term]
           "<dt>#{term}</dt><dd>#{definition}</dd>\n"
         end.join( EMPTY_STRING )
       end
     end

   end

   Simple_CGI.new.display()
```

How It Works

The first thing we do in the script is require the cgi library at ❶. Then we
define a class called Simple_CGI at ❷ and the Constants EMPTY_STRING and TITLE
at ❸. Next, within the display method (at ❹), we create an instance of CGI called
cgi, defining it in terms of html4, which is one of the versions of HTML that
CGI is aware of. We'll use cgi to create an HTML document that simple_cgi.rb
will output.

   Instances of CGI have several methods that take blocks, whose names are
the same as the tags they will create. Every HTML document needs an <html>
tag, so we include that at ❺. For reasons I'll explain shortly, I want to store
the contents of the <html> tag in a temporary local variable called output.

We can go through the HTML document we want to create, opening new tags with the appropriate method of cgi (like head, title, h1, etc.). Hierarchical nesting is accomplished using blocks, as you can see, and tags that are at the same level (*siblings*) are concatenated with the + method.

You'll notice that within cgi.body, which creates the <body> tag within our resulting output, I have used a method at ❻ called show_def_list (defined at ❿). This is mainly to avoid multiple levels of block nesting for the methods of cgi, but it also performs other tasks. Let's examine it at ❿. It outputs a definition list as you'd expect using cgi.dl with a block. To do so, it pulls both terms and their definitions from a Hash called items, wrapping them in <dt> and <dd> tags, respectively.

The items Hash is defined by the output of get_items_hash (❽) merged with cgi.params. The cgi.params Hash represents the query string, so if you browse to http://localhost/cgi-bin/simple_cgi.rb?key1=value1&key2=value2, cgi.params would be { 'key1' => 'value1', 'key2', 'value2' }. The get_items_hash method returns a Hash representing some values that I thought might be worth demonstrating, such as the script name, the server, and so on. In general, the script simply reads from the machine's environment, using values of the ENV Hash. At ❾, the value for 'server' in the Hash is slightly more complex than the others. It tries to read from ENV like the others, falling back to a system execution of the hostname command, and finally falling back to the EMPTY_STRING, if necessary. This resulting Hash is then returned implicitly, because it's the last evaluated expression in the method.

Back at ❼, we call cgi.out, giving it a block with a slight massaging of the output variable using gsub. I'll be the first to admit that this is a little unusual. Normally, you call cgi.out with a block that includes cgi.html and all the other methods I used to fill the output variable. Why did I do it this way? There are two related reasons.

The first reason is that cgi.out is not purely functional: It doesn't return a value to be printed using puts. Instead, it does the outputting by itself. The second reason is that cgi's methods don't introduce line breaks between tags. This is good for speed optimization, in that each new character, even just a line break, is slightly more content to transfer. However, it doesn't make the resulting HTML source very readable. I like readable HTML source, so I use gsub at ❼ to introduce line breaks between adjacent tags. If you don't mind your HTML all strung together in a single line, by all means, put your cgi.html and similar calls within the block for cgi.out.

Everything we have discussed so far has been within the display method. We call it on the last line of the script, directly on an anonymous new instance of Simple_CGI. There's no real need to instantiate it into a variable, like so:

```
scgi = Simple_CGI.new
scgi.display()
```

However, if you're more comfortable doing that, there's also no reason not to. Let's see how it works.

The Results

On your system, browse to http://localhost/cgi-bin/simple_cgi.rb and see what you get. It should be something more or less like Figure 11-1.

Note that the software value will probably differ, unless you're also using a fairly stock Ubuntu system, and the time will obviously differ a great deal. You can see that the tab shows the page title, which is *A simple CGI script* (the same as the large bold header). Values that should not differ are the script and server, unless you've intentionally changed the filename from `simple_cgi.rb` to something else or browsed to a hostname other than `localhost`. Astute readers will also see that I had another tab open to the Apache website.

Figure 11-1: The output of `simple_cgi.rb`

Now let's try changing the query string a bit, with http://localhost/cgi-bin/simple_cgi.rb?lang=Ruby. I won't bother showing a new screenshot, but you should now see five entries in the definition list instead of four. The new one is the key `lang`, which has a value of `Ruby`. This appears because `cgi.params` is a part of the items Hash within `show_def_list` at ❿, and when we use the query string `lang=Ruby`, `cgi.params` is `{ 'lang' => 'Ruby' }`, which is then one of the pairs in `items`.

Now let's try giving an explicit value within the query string to one of the keys that already appears in items, with the URL http://localhost/cgi-bin/simple_cgi.rb?lang=Ruby&server=some_other_server_name. You should still see the key `lang` with a value `Ruby`, but in addition, the value for `server` is no longer `localhost`, but is instead `some_other_server_name`. The reason this happens is that `cgi.params` is the argument to `merge`, and it overrides any conflicting pair already in the Hash on which `merge` is called. Therefore, anything in `cgi.params` takes precedence.

Hacking the Script

This is just a simple script showing the basics of CGI. You could modify and extend it in countless ways. One suggestion would be to incorporate part of `currency_converter2.rb`. For example, you could display the time, just as this script already does, and take arguments for the currencies to convert from and to as well as the amount of money to convert. Many people also use CGI to execute system calls on a machine and display the results, showing the processes running on the machine, how much disk space is used, and other information of interest to system administrators.

#42 Mod Ruby (mod_ruby_demo.rhtml and mod_ruby_demo.conf)

CGI is great for many applications. However, sometimes you may want to have files that are mainly HTML, with only subsections that need to be executed by your programming language, Ruby or otherwise. Wouldn't it be great if you had an HTML tag that meant *Start Ruby code now*, after which you could add some Ruby code, and then use another tag that meant *Done with Ruby code, go back to plain old HTML*?

There is such a system, for many languages. It's the default behavior for the PHP language, and similar systems are available for Perl and Python, among others. One of the systems that does this for Ruby is eRuby, which will be embedded directly within the webserver via the mod_ruby software.

One of the problems with CGI is speed. When someone makes a web request that needs dynamic CGI execution, that request spawns a new Ruby interpreter;[1] that interpreter then evaluates the CGI program, returns its value to the webserver process, and closes down. For the next CGI request, the whole process start all over again. All of this takes time. What mod_ruby and similar systems do is have a Ruby interpreter always running in the background, ready to evaluate scripts and return their results to the webserver, but without the overhead of spawning and shutting down a distinct ruby process for each script. This makes the webserver start up a bit slower, because it needs to do more, but it saves a lot of machine overhead after just a few requests.

In the code, you'll see <% and %>, the opening and closing tags that mean *Interpret my contents in Ruby, not as HTML*. But first we need to set up Apache so that it knows how to handle mod_ruby. We've already installed the mod_ruby packages, but we need a configuration file. That's mod_ruby_demo.conf below.

The Code

mod_ruby_demo.conf

An Apache Config File

```
<IfModule mod_ruby.c>
  # for Apache::RubyRun
  RubyRequire apache/ruby-run

  # for Apache::ERubyRun
  RubyRequire apache/eruby-run

  # handle *.rcss as eruby files.
❶ <Files *.rcss>
    AddType text/css .rcss
    AddType application/x-httpd-ruby *.rb
    SetHandler ruby-object
    RubyHandler Apache::ERubyRun.instance
  </Files>
```

---

[1] Or an interpreter for whichever language the CGI program uses.

```
      # handle *.rhtml as eruby files.
❷  <Files *.rhtml>
     AddType text/html .rhtml
     AddType application/x-httpd-ruby *.rb
     SetHandler ruby-object
     RubyHandler Apache::ERubyRun.instance
   </Files>

   RubyRequire auto-reload

</IfModule>
```

This file isn't Ruby code—it uses Apache's configuration file format. Put this file in /etc/apache2/mods-available/, with a symlink in /etc/apache2/mod-enabled/.[2] If you're using Apache version 1.*X* (such as 1.3, which is still popular), you'll add the contents of this file within your /etc/apache/httpd.conf file. As I noted for the cgi-bin directory, these specific file and directory locations are accurate for my system, but yours might be different.

mod_ruby_demo.rhtml

This file should be more recognizable as a weird hybrid of HTML and Ruby code.

```
<!DOCTYPE html
     PUBLIC "-//W3C//DTD XHTML 1.0 Strict//EN"
    "http://www.w3.org/TR/xhtml1/DTD/xhtml1-strict.dtd">
<html xmlns="http://www.w3.org/1999/xhtml" xml:lang="en" lang="en">

<head>
<title>Mod Ruby</title>
<style>
code {
 background-color: #ddf;
 color: #f00;
 padding: 0.3em;
}
</style>
</head>

<body>
<h1>Mod Ruby</h1>

<p>
The eRuby command below should print <q>Hello, world!</q>
</p>

<p>
```
% tags   ❸ `<q><% print "Hello, world!" %></q>`
```
</p>
```

---

[2] You can create a symlink with the command ln -s in a Unix shell.

```
    <p>
❹ Welcome to <em><%= ENV['SERVER_NAME'] %></em>. If you see a server name,
❺ <%= 'e' + 'Ruby' %> is probably working.
    </p>

    <p>
❻ The current time is <%= Time.now %>.
    </p>

    <p>
    <%
❼ def function_within_mod_ruby(input)
      "#{input} was passed through a function.\n"
    end

    print function_within_mod_ruby("Some sample input")
    print '<br />'
    print function_within_mod_ruby("Some other sample input")
    %>
    </p>

    </body>
    </html>
```

Put this file somewhere browsable via the Web. I'll assume it's in http://localhost/mod_ruby/, making it accessible as http://localhost/mod_ruby/mod_ruby_demo.rhtml.

How It Works

Hopefully, `mod_ruby_demo.conf` will be completely opaque. I'm kidding, of course, but it's not critical at this point if you don't understand everything about this file. It's great to know about Apache configuration files, and you can certainly learn a great deal from the Apache website (http://www.apache.org) or the various Apache-related books out there, but what's important for our purposes are points ❶ and ❷. At ❶, we declare that files having the .rcss extension are to be interpreted as Ruby files. At ❷, we make the same declaration about files having the .rhtml extension.

NOTE *Why these extensions? It's a fairly common practice to define filename extensions for dynamically interpreted files with the normal extension and an additional preceding letter representing the programming language used. For example, .rhtml is used for Ruby files that generate HTML output, .rcss is used for Ruby files that generate CSS stylesheets, and so on. You may also sometimes see .phtml files that integrate Perl or PHP, or even .mhtml files that use the software Mason, written in Perl.*

That's it for `mod_ruby_demo.conf`. In `mod_ruby_demo.rhtml`, we have some additional points of interest. It should look like standard HTML until ❸. At that point, we see this line: `<q><% print "Hello, world!" %></q>`. The `<%` and `%>` are the *Interpret my contents as Ruby* tags I mentioned earlier, so anything within those tags will be interpreted as Ruby code. In this case, we're asking Ruby to print 'Hello, world!', which it does, incorporating the printed output within the eventual HTML.

You'll probably expect that we often want to print output that will be incorporated into the HTML. It would be tedious to keep using print statements, so there's a shortcut, which you can see at ❹. If you use an initial code tag of <%=, Ruby assumes that you want the evaluated expression to be printed. At ❹, we incorporate the value of ENV['SERVER_NAME'] within an <em> tag. Just to show that what falls between <%= and %> can be any expression, at ❺, we concatenate two Strings, only caring about the result.

The printed output doesn't have to be a simple literal expression, either. At ❻, I show the value of a method call, which in this case results in the current local time. Finally, at ❼, we define a completely new method within our .rhtml file called function_within_mod_ruby, which is then available anytime afterward for use, as you can see in the code.

The Results

When I call this script via my own webserver, I get the results shown in Figure 11-2.

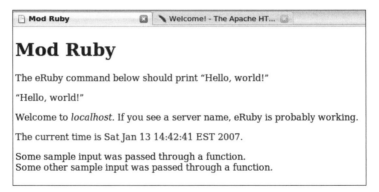

Figure 11-2: The output from mod_ruby

The time will obviously be different in your result, but that should be the only difference, unless you specifically browse to your machine by a name other than localhost, or you placed mod_ruby_demo.rhtml under a different directory or gave it a different name.

Hacking the Script

This script is a modification playground. You can put any Ruby expressions you want within those <% or <%= tags. Try using require, either with files that you know are part of the standard library (like cgi) or your own files. This technique lets you define all your real "things" as classes in .rb library files, reserving your .rhtml files for display.

#43 CSS Stylesheets, Part I (stylesheet.rcss)

Having .rhtml files is great—they allow you to dynamically generate whatever visible HTML you want. But you can use mod_ruby for more than that. A major portion of any well-designed modern website will be its stylesheets. One of the frustrations that web designers have to deal with is incomplete or incompatible CSS support among the various browsers. There are lots of potential solutions for those frustrations, which you can find at sites like http://www.richinstyle.com or http://alistapart.com. One obvious solution for programmers is to determine exactly which browser someone is using (via ENV['USER_AGENT']) and serve that user a stylesheet customized for his or her specific browser.

That's a great solution, put into practice countless times all over the Web. There is another solution, however. Why not make the stylesheet itself a dynamic .rcss file? With this approach, the stylesheet becomes polymorphic, to use a term from object-oriented programming. Every browser would refer to the same stylesheet by name and would then receive specific content that works just right for that browser. Here's an example.

The Code

```
/*
This file outputs CSS data customized by user_agent via eruby.
There is a blog entry about some similar ideas at
http://blog.airbladesoftware.com/2006/12/11/cssdryer-dry-up-your-css
*/
<%
# define functions
❶ def alpha_width(user_agent)
    width =
      if (user_agent =~ /Windows/)
        11.8 if (user_agent =~ /Opera/)
        11.8 if (user_agent =~ /MSIE 6/)
        14   if (user_agent =~ /MSIE/)
        11.8
      elsif (user_agent =~ /Palm/)
        5
      else
        11.8
      end
❷   return %Q[\twidth:#{width}em;]
  end

❸ def beta_width(user_agent)
    width =
      if (user_agent =~ /Windows/)
        15.8 if (user_agent =~ /Opera/)
        15.8 if (user_agent =~ /MSIE 6/)
        18   if (user_agent =~ /MSIE/)
        15.8
      elsif (user_agent =~ /Palm/)
        7
```

```
              else
                 15.8
              end
❹      return %Q[\twidth:#{width}em;]
      end

❺  def margin_left(user_agent)
      margin =
         if (user_agent =~ /Mac/)
            3   if (user_agent =~ /Opera/)
            1   if (user_agent =~ /MSIE/)
            2.5 if (user_agent =~ /Safari/)
            2   if (user_agent =~ /Gecko/)
            2.7
         elsif (user_agent =~ /Windows/)
            1.5
         else
            2   if (user_agent =~ /Opera/)
            2   if (user_agent =~ /onqueror/)
            1.8 if (user_agent =~ /Galeon/)
            2.5
         end
❻      return %Q[margin-left:-#{margin}em;]
      end
      %>

❼  li { <%= margin_left(ENV['HTTP_USER_AGENT']) %> }

      #navAlpha {
         position:absolute;
❽       <%= alpha_width(ENV['HTTP_USER_AGENT']) %>
         top:2em;
         left:2em;
         border:0.5em double #333;
         background-color:#ada;
         padding:1em;
         z-index:2;
      }

      #navBeta {
         position:absolute;
❾       <%= beta_width(ENV['HTTP_USER_AGENT']) %>
         top:2em;
         right:2em;
         border:0.5em double #333;
         background-color:#ada;
         padding:1em;
         z-index:1;
      }
```

How It Works

Much like mod_ruby_demo.rhtml, this is mainly a file with some other format
(in this case a CSS stylesheet) that happens to have a little Ruby interspersed

within it. We define a new function called `alpha_width` at ❶ that determines the value of a local variable called `width`, finally returning it within a bit of text that follows CSS formatting at ❷. Note that this function takes advantage of the fact that even `if` statements in Ruby return a value, in this case, assigning that value into `width`. We do something similar with `beta_width` at ❸, which returns its own CSS-formatted output at ❹. Finally, we define `margin_left` at ❺, which returns CSS at ❻.

NOTE *Why those particular functions? I found that the CSS support variations that frustrated me the most were the differences involving margins and padding and left margins for list items, so those are the functions I made. People who know more about CSS than I do have probably found more elegant solutions, but sometimes a pretty good solution now is better than a perfect solution when it's too late. The point of this script is also to demonstrate that the polymorphic stylesheet technique* can *be done, but this isn't precisely how* it should be done. *If you care a great deal about CSS, you can use this technique to accomplish much bigger things.*

Then we use the output of `margin_left` within a CSS declaration for a list element at ❼. The stylesheet also defines two IDs called `#navAlpha` and `#navBeta`, which are just identifiers for column divs. Within `#navAlpha` at ❽, we use the output of `alpha_width` for the width of `#navAlpha`, and at ❾, we do something analogous for `#navBeta`.

The Results

Here's the output of `stylesheet.rcss` when I browse to it using Mozilla Firefox on an Ubuntu system:

```
/*
This file outputs CSS data customized by user_agent via eruby.
There is a blog entry about some similar ideas at
http://blog.airbladesoftware.com/2006/12/11/cssdryer-dry-up-your-css
*/


li { margin-left:-2.5em; }

#navAlpha {
  position:absolute;
        width:11.8em;
  top:2em;
  left:2em;
  border:0.5em double #333;
  background-color:#ada;
  padding:1em;
  z-index:2;
}

#navBeta {
  position:absolute;
        width:15.8em;
```

```
top:2em;
right:2em;
border:0.5em double #333;
background-color:#ada;
padding:1em;
z-index:1;
}
```

You'll notice that the appropriate values are interpolated within the li
and width CSS declarations. Your results may differ, since the whole point of
this file is to provide different output for different browsers.

Hacking the Script

There are many hacking options for this script. One is our next script,
stylesheet2.rcss.

#44 CSS Stylesheets, Part II (stylesheet2.rcss)

In many ways, this script is just a glorified hack of stylesheet.rcss. I separated
it mainly to allow for comparison. The major difference between the two files
is that stylesheet2.rcss generalizes the width values into a single function.

The Code

```
/*
This file outputs CSS data customized by user_agent using eruby.
*/
<%
# define functions
❶ def width(type, user_agent)
❷   small = {
      'alpha' => 11.8,
      'beta'  => 15.8,
    }
❸   large = {
      'alpha' => 14,
      'beta'  => 18,
    }
❹   palm = {
      'alpha' => 5,
      'beta'  => 7,
    }
❺   width =
      if (user_agent =~ /Windows/)
        small[type] if (user_agent =~ /Opera/)
        small[type] if (user_agent =~ /MSIE 6/)
        large[type] if (user_agent =~ /MSIE/)
        small[type]
```

```ruby
      elsif (user_agent =~ /Palm/)
        palm[type]
      else
        small[type]
      end
    return %Q[\twidth:#{width}em;]
  end

  def margin_left(user_agent)
    margin =
      if (user_agent =~ /Mac/)
        3   if (user_agent =~ /Opera/)
        1   if (user_agent =~ /MSIE/)
        2.5 if (user_agent -~ /Safari/)
        2   if (user_agent =~ /Gecko/)
        2.7
      elsif (user_agent =~ /Windows/)
        1.5
      else
        2   if (user_agent =~ /Opera/)
        2   if (user_agent =~ /onqueror/)
        1.8 if (user_agent =~ /Galeon/)
        2.5
      end
    return %Q[margin-left:-#{margin}em;]
  end
%>

li { <%= margin_left(ENV['HTTP_USER_AGENT']) %> }

#navAlpha {
  position:absolute;
  <%= width('alpha', ENV['HTTP_USER_AGENT']) %>
  top:2em;
  left:2em;
  border:0.5em double #333;
  background-color:#ada;
  padding:1em;
  z-index:2;
}

#navBeta {
  position:absolute;
  <%= width('beta', ENV['HTTP_USER_AGENT']) %>
  top:2em;
  right:2em;
  border:0.5em double #333;
  background-color:#ada;
  padding:1em;
  z-index:1;
}
```

How It Works

At ❶, we define the general `width` function, which you'll see now takes two arguments: the user agent as before, but also the type of column we're generating `width` for. We then have separate Hashes for `small` (❷), `large` (❸), and `palm` (❹). Palm devices always use their own Hash, while other browsers use either the `small` or `large` Hash, depending on the specific user agent. Then at ❺, we determine the `width`.[3] The type is simply the key for whichever Hash has already been decided on. Everything else is identical to `stylesheet.rcss`, except that calls to either `alpha_width` or `beta_width` are now calls to `width`, as described already.

The Results

As before, here's the output with my setup.

```
/*
This file outputs CSS data customized by user_agent using eruby.
*/


li { margin-left:-2.5em; }

#navAlpha {
   position:absolute;
        width:11.8em;
   top:2em;
   left:2em;
   border:0.5em double #333;
   background-color:#ada;
   padding:1em;
   z-index:2;
}

#navBeta {
   position:absolute;
        width:15.8em;
   top:2em;
   right:2em;
   border:0.5em double #333;
   background-color:#ada;
   padding:1em;
   z-index:1;
}
```

This output is basically the same as that for `stylesheet.rcss`, except for the preliminary comments.

---

[3] Don't be confused by the fact that there is both a function called `width` and a local variable inside it also called `width`. Anything outside the function can't get at the variable, and the function knows to check whether or not there's a variable by that name before automatically making a recursive call to itself.

Hacking the Script

As I already noted, someone with a better grasp of CSS could really customize this script to do some marvelous things. There are undoubtedly better ways to accomplish what this script does, but its point was to show the technique in broad strokes. I hope you found it useful.

Chapter Recap

What was new in this chapter?

- Using Ruby for CGI scripts
- The cgi library
- `cgi.params`
- `mod_ruby`
- .rhtml and .rcss files
- Apache configuration files

This chapter scratches the surface of CGI programming, with Ruby or other languages. Its purpose was to get you comfortable with using Ruby to interact with a webserver and browser. Most web-based coding in Ruby makes use of the Rails framework, which we'll get to soon. But first, we'll be installing Rails with the RubyGems system, so that is the subject of our next chapter.

12

RUBYGEMS AND RAILS PREPARATION

In this chapter, we'll discuss Ruby's package-management system, RubyGems, as well as Ruby's most prominent web development framework, Rails. These somewhat disparate subjects are lumped together because the "canonical" way to install Rails is with the RubyGems software. By the end of this chapter, you will be able to install Rails via RubyGems and understand the basic structure and purpose of the files that make up a Rails application.

RubyGems

Good operating systems have good package-management systems—software that can keep track of the other software needed or provided by that operating system and make sure everything stays up to date. Mac OS X has Software Update, Windows has Windows Update, and the various flavors of GNU/Linux have programs like RPM, YUM, and my favorite, APT. Good programming languages have similar programs that give programmers and other users access to vast libraries of software written in that language. Perl has the Comprehensive Perl Archive Network (http://cpan.org), Python has the Cheese Shop (http://cheeseshop.python.org/pypi), and Ruby has RubyGems (http://rubygems.org).

NOTE *The most up-to-date RubyGems information is available at http://docs.rubygems.org. This chapter is intended to give you a basic introduction and help you get Rails up and running. If you find your curiosity piqued about RubyGems (as I hope you will), I highly recommend making http://docs.rubygems.org one of your regular stops on the Web.*

RubyGems has already become the de facto method of creating stand-alone Ruby software (especially libraries and programmer utilities) for use by others in the Ruby community. With this system, you can easily use other programmers' software to make your job easier, and you can also share your own work, likely making some other programmer's job easier. Each bundle of software that is packaged together as a single unit via RubyGems is called a *gem*, and users are able to manipulate such gems with the appropriately named gem command.

Installing RubyGems

You will want to browse to http://rubyforge.org/frs/?group_id=126 to download the most recent version of RubyGems. Files are provided in both TGZ and Zip formats, as well as gem files (for updating after you already have RubyGems installed) and patch files. For this example, I've downloaded `rubygems-0.9.2.tgz`. Uncompress the downloaded file, and use the command `ruby setup.rb` to run the `setup.rb` program found inside the newly created directory. You'll probably have to do this as the root user (if applicable to your operating system). You can type `gem -v` to see which version of RubyGems you now have installed on your system.

Using RubyGems

If you run gem with no arguments, it should return something similar to this:

```
RubyGems is a sophisticated package manager for Ruby.  This is
a basic help message containing pointers to more information.

  Usage:
    gem -h/--help
    gem -v/--version
    gem command [arguments...] [options...]

  Examples:
    gem install rake
    gem list --local
    gem build package.gemspec
    gem help install
```

```
Further help:
    gem help commands           list all 'gem' commands
    gem help examples           show some examples of usage
    gem help <COMMAND>          show help on COMMAND
                                    (e.g. 'gem help install')
Further information:
    http://rubygems.rubyforge.org
```

Listing Installed and Installable Gems

By executing gem list --local, you can see which gems are already installed on your system. Here is the result of running gem list --local immediately after installing RubyGems on my machine:

```
*** LOCAL GEMS ***

sources (0.0.1)
    This package provides download sources for remote gem installation
```

The sources gem makes it possible for you to install other gems by maintaining retrieval information about them. We can query that information via gem query --remote, which outputs a very long list of available gems, shown here in highly truncated form:

```
*** REMOTE GEMS ***

abstract (1.0.0)
    a library which enable you to define abstract method in Ruby

ackbar (0.1.1, 0.1.0)
    ActiveRecord KirbyBase Adapter

action_profiler (1.0.0)
    A profiler for Rails controllers
```

Installing Gems

Each individual gem is installable via the command gem install --remote *some_gem_name*. As an example, let's install the rails gem with gem install --remote rails.

```
Install required dependency rake? [Yn]
Install required dependency activesupport? [Yn]
Install required dependency activerecord? [Yn]
Install required dependency actionpack? [Yn]
Install required dependency actionmailer? [Yn]
Install required dependency actionwebservice? [Yn]
Successfully installed rails-1.2.2
Successfully installed rake-0.7.1
Successfully installed activesupport-1.4.1
Successfully installed activerecord-1.15.2
Successfully installed actionpack-1.13.2
```

```
Successfully installed actionmailer-1.3.2
Successfully installed actionwebservice-1.2.2
Installing ri documentation for rake-0.7.1...
Installing ri documentation for activesupport-1.4.1...
Installing ri documentation for activerecord-1.15.2...
Installing ri documentation for actionpack-1.13.2...
Installing ri documentation for actionmailer-1.3.2...
Installing ri documentation for actionwebservice-1.2.2...
Installing RDoc documentation for rake-0.7.1...
Installing RDoc documentation for activesupport-1.4.1...
Installing RDoc documentation for activerecord-1.15.2...
Installing RDoc documentation for actionpack-1.13.2...
Installing RDoc documentation for actionmailer-1.3.2...
Installing RDoc documentation for actionwebservice-1.2.2...
```

I answered Y to all requests for confirmation. You can see that the RubyGems system is intelligent enough to know which gems are required by other gems, and it will install your requested gem's dependencies automatically. We now have a functioning Rails system, which we'll explore in the next chapter.

NOTE *At the time of my installation, there were some minor warnings related to actionpack's ri and RDoc documentation. They had no impact on the functioning of the code and may be out of date by the time you read this book, so I have omitted them from the output examples in this chapter.*

Updating Gems

You can update gems already present on your system with the gem update command. A good precursor is to query whether any gems need updating with gem outdated. I ran this command on one of my systems that had some out-of-date gems and I got the following results:

```
Bulk updating Gem source index for: http://gems.rubyforge.org
activerecord (1.15.1 < 1.15.2)
rails (1.2.1 < 1.2.2)
actionwebservice (1.2.1 < 1.2.2)
rubygems-update (0.9.1 < 0.9.2)
actionpack (1.13.1 < 1.13.2)
actionmailer (1.3.1 < 1.3.2)
activesupport (1.4.0 < 1.4.1)
```

Updating the gems with gem update rails (as root) produced this output:

```
Updating installed gems...
Bulk updating Gem source index for: http://gems.rubyforge.org
Attempting remote update of rails
Install required dependency activesupport? [Yn]
Install required dependency activerecord? [Yn]
Install required dependency actionpack? [Yn]
Install required dependency actionmailer? [Yn]
Install required dependency actionwebservice? [Yn]
```

```
Successfully installed rails-1.2.2
Successfully installed activesupport-1.4.1
Successfully installed activerecord-1.15.2
Successfully installed actionpack-1.13.2
Successfully installed actionmailer-1.3.2
Successfully installed actionwebservice-1.2.2
Installing ri documentation for activesupport-1.4.1...
Installing ri documentation for activerecord-1.15.2...
Installing ri documentation for actionpack-1.13.2...
Installing ri documentation for actionmailer-1.3.2...
Installing ri documentation for actionwebservice-1.2.2...
Installing RDoc documentation for activesupport-1.4.1...
Installing RDoc documentation for activerecord-1.15.2...
Installing RDoc documentation for actionpack-1.13.2...
Installing RDoc documentation for actionmailer-1.3.2...
Installing RDoc documentation for actionwebservice-1.2.2...
Gems: [rails] updated
```

I specifically chose rails as the gem to be updated because it is a gem with many dependencies, as we learned when installing it for the first time. Therefore, updating it shows how dependencies are automatically updated along with the requested gem. Rails depends on Active Record (a software package that provides sophisticated database access tools), so updating the rails gem also automatically updates the activerecord gem, as you can see in the update session results above. All other rails dependencies are updated in a similar manner.

NOTE   *After updating your gems, you probably want to execute rake rails:update within each of your Rails application directories. This ensures that any application files you have already generated will be updated to account for the change in gems, as well.*

Learning More About RubyGems

You can always learn more about the gem command as it exists on your own machine with gem help and gem help *some_specific_command*. This information will always be up to date and specific to your system.

Rails Preparation

You should now know enough about RubyGems to have used it to install Rails. The rest of this chapter will familiarize you enough with Rails that you can start creating a Rails application in the next chapter. This book introduces Rails (with a focus on general design philosophy, rather than an exhaustive list of the API), but it would be silly to think that a few chapters could give Rails the attention it deserves. The definitive text on Rails is *Agile Web Development with Rails*, now in its second edition, by Dave Thomas, David Heinemeier Hansson (creator of Rails), and others (Pragmatic Bookshelf, 2006). Other members of the Rails community also give high praise to *Ruby for Rails* by David Alan Black (Manning Publications, 2006).

What Is Rails?

According to its website (http://rubyonrails.org), Rails is "an open-source web framework that's optimized for programmer happiness and sustainable productivity. It lets you write beautiful code by favoring convention over config- uration." The site describes it as "Web development that doesn't hurt." What does that mean?

Since it optimizes for programmer happiness and focuses on the ability to write beautiful code, Rails is well within the design philosophy of Ruby itself. Rails picks sensible defaults for its behavior, and as long as you are willing to follow those conventions, your job as the programmer becomes relatively easy. Rails provides shortcuts and tools for you to generate a skeleton of a web application very quickly; it allows you to place each piece of code in a reasonable location within the directory structure that is appropriate to the job that code is expected to perform. This provides clean, well-ordered, reusable code that helps you develop an application quickly, efficiently, and painlessly.

Other Options for Installing Rails

Using RubyGems isn't the only way to install Rails. There are several other options that you may want to use, for example, if you haven't been following along with the text, or if you simply wish to install Rails via some other method. It should be noted, however, that installation as a gem is the recommended way to install Rails.

Via Operating System Package Manager

Some operating systems' package managers, such as APT, provide Rails as an installable package. For example, on my Ubuntu system, the command `apt-cache search rails` shows (among other packages) this result:

```
rails - MVC ruby based framework geared for web application development
```

If you want to use Rails, but you don't need the most recent bleeding-edge version, and you want to avoid installing RubyGems (for whatever reason), this option may work well for you.

From Source

As with any free or open source software, there is always the option to install from source. You can browse to http://rubyonrails.org/down for the most recent recommended source tarball.

Pre-Packaged

There are also some pre-packaged versions of Rails available. For Windows, there is Instant Rails (http://instantrails.rubyforge.org), and for Mac OS X, there's Locomotive (http://locomotive.sourceforge.net). Either of these pieces of software can get you up and running with Rails. Note that there may be subtle differences in configuration between these packages and the default Rails setup. Consulting the website for your chosen pre-packaged application is probably your best bet when encountering such a situation.

Databases

Rails needs to have access to a database program to function properly. Generally, that database is MySQL (http://mysql.com), although other options are possible. If you're installing via gems or through your operating system's package manager, you should install MySQL. This is probably easiest to do through your operating system's package manager. The pre-packaged Rails installers like Instant Rails and Locomotive generally come with their own pre-configured databases; however, for all subsequent examples, I'll assume you installed Rails as a gem and you're using MySQL.

The Structure of a Rails Application

Rails operates under a design philosophy (or *pattern*) for software called Model-View-Controller (MVC), developed by Norwegian computer scientist Trygve Reenskaug[1] while he was working at Xerox PARC in the late 1970s. It was originally developed in relation to traditional graphical user interfaces (GUIs), but MVC has recently become very popular in web development. The basics of this pattern are as follows. The *Model* represents the data and is an object of some sort. The *View* is a way of presenting data, whether directly to a user or to some other computer, or as any other type of output. The *Controller* is the traffic cop or manager that keeps track of any requested actions, queries or manipulates the Model to get or update data, and gives the View whatever information it needs to format the data as necessary.

Let's consider an example to help explain this pattern. Back in our second currency conversion script ("#19 Currency Conversion, Advanced (currency_converter2.rb)" on page 90), we used data retrieved from an RSS feed. In MVC terms, that data is the Model. That same data could have been presented (or Viewed) on a traditional HTML web page, as a plaintext file for download, or as a YAML file. In all of these different examples, the Model would stay the same and would be something like ExchangeRate or CurrencyUnit, depending on how the application was designed. The Controller would also be the same, and it would be responsible for retrieving the data from a server. We'd probably call it the Download Controller, since it would be used to download data from a server.

For the sake of argument, let's say that we also wanted to present our Model in some completely different way, perhaps written down on paper. The written piece of paper would use a different Controller, one that deals with paper instead of servers. Perhaps we'd call it the Pencil Controller. The View would also be different in each of these examples: RSS, HTML, ASCII, WrittenOnAPieceOfPaper, and so on. These are all simply different ways of presenting the same data, which is the Model. For example, our Rails application in the next chapter has Views for both HTML and RSS display of photographs and related information.

---

[1] Dr. Reenskaug is online at http://heim.ifi.uio.no/~trygver.

Generating a Rails Application

You create a Rails application with the command rails *application_name*. If you execute rails rails_sample_app in a suitable workspace directory, you should see a very long output similar to the following truncated version:

```
$ rails rails_sample_app
      create
      create  app/controllers
      create  app/helpers
      create  app/models
      create  app/views/layouts
      (several lines deleted)
      create  public/javascripts/application.js
      create  doc/README_FOR_APP
      create  log/server.log
      create  log/production.log
      create  log/development.log
      create  log/test.log
```

A large number of directories and files are automatically created for you. We'll briefly touch on the app, doc, lib, log, public, script, and test directories. The app directory contains the code you'll write for your application: Models, Views, Controllers, and so on. The doc directory contains documentation. Nothing is initially created in the lib directory, but you'll put generic library files (such as extensions that add new methods to existing classes) here. The log directory contains the application log files, which are split up for production, development, and testing. The public directory contains non-Ruby files that are viewed or used in a web browser, such as static HTML files, images, JavaScript files, CSS stylesheets, and the like. The script directory contains useful small programs meant to be run by the developer or administrator of the application. The test directory contains files that allow you to easily automate testing of the application.

We'll discuss what each of these files and directories does shortly, but first, let's test our application to make sure it's running properly.

Viewing Your Rails Application

Execute cd rails_sample_app to navigate to the newly created directory rails_sample_app, and execute the command ruby script/server. This starts Rails' built-in webserver that it uses for development purposes. You should see output similar to the following:

Starting
WEBrick

```
$ ruby script/server
=> Booting WEBrick...
=> Rails application started on http://0.0.0.0:3000
=> Ctrl-C to shutdown server; call with --help for options
[2007-02-10 12:43:54] INFO  WEBrick 1.3.1
```

```
[2007-02-10 12:43:54] INFO  ruby 1.8.4 (2005-12-24) [i486-linux]
[2007-02-10 12:43:54] INFO  WEBrick::HTTPServer#start: pid=27162 port=3000
```

Your specifics may be different. The pid value will almost certainly be different, and your Ruby version may be a later one. Your webserver may also be something else, such as Mongrel, which is a newer webserver for Rails. (WEBrick is the older webserver that serves as a default fallback.) What is unlikely to be different is the port: 3000. You can test your application by browsing to that port on your local machine (just point your favorite web browser to http://localhost:3000). Figure 12-1 shows what that URL looked like when I viewed it on my Ubuntu machine with the Epiphany web browser.

Figure 12-1: Viewing your application in a web browser with the URL http://localhost:3000

As you can see, this page provides useful information about how to set up your application as well as links to Rails-related information on the Web. Two points of particular interest are that the database connection is described in the YAML file config/database.yml and that script/generate is available to help you generate Models and Controllers.

Basics for Generating Applications

Within the directory `rails_sample_app`, execute the command `ruby script/generate model ExchangeRate`, following our MVC example earlier. We're telling Rails that we want to *generate* something, the thing we want to make is a *Model*, and the name of the Model is *ExchangeRate*. Here are the results:

Making a Model

```
ruby script/generate model ExchangeRate
      exists  app/models/
      exists  test/unit/
      exists  test/fixtures/
      create  app/models/exchange_rate.rb
      create  test/unit/exchange_rate_test.rb
      create  test/fixtures/exchange_rates.yml
      create  db/migrate
      create  db/migrate/001_create_exchange_rates.rb
```

As well as some useful testing- and database-related files, this command created a Ruby file called app/models/exchange_rate.rb, the contents of which are the following:

```
class ExchangeRate < ActiveRecord::Base
end
```

There doesn't seem to be a lot there, but appearances can be deceiving. The Model follows the Rails naming convention of using CamelCase for class names and multi_word_separated_lowercase for filenames. You'll also notice that `ExchangeRate` is a child of something called `ActiveRecord::Base`. Active Record is the software that gives Rails its intuitive database interaction. It defines Models (which are classes) such that each instance represents a record in a database table. Not only that, but the name of the table is always the plural of the class. Therefore, the file exchange_rate.rb defines a class called `ExchangeRate`, each instance of which is stored in a database table called `exchanges_rates`. This all takes place under the hood—Rails does it for you automatically, and it is even smart enough to know that the plural of `person` is `people`, the plural of baby is babies, and so on.

NOTE *Active Record provides what's called object-relational mapping (ORM). ORM enables a specific instance of a class to represent a record in a database table. For those who are curious, each field in the table also represents an instance variable in the appropriate class. We'll talk about this topic more in the next chapter.*

Our Model doesn't do anything yet. We won't start adding to Models until the next chapter, so let's make a Controller with the command `ruby script/generate controller server_access rss html ascii yaml`, telling Rails that this time we want to generate a Controller and that it should have the Views `rss`, `html`, `ascii`, and `yaml`. Here are the results:

Making a Controller

```
ruby script/generate controller server_access rss html ascii yaml
      exists  app/controllers/
      exists  app/helpers/
```

```
create    app/views/server_access
exists    test/functional/
create    app/controllers/server_access_controller.rb
create    test/functional/server_access_controller_test.rb
create    app/helpers/server_access_helper.rb
create    app/views/server_access/rss.rhtml
create    app/views/server_access/html.rhtml
create    app/views/server_access/ascii.rhtml
create    app/views/server_access/yaml.rhtml
```

This output is slightly more complicated. We see that we now have a Controller called server_access_controller.rb in app/controllers/, and we now have the files rss.rhtml, html.rhtml, ascii.rhtml, and yaml.rhtml inside app/views/server_access/. Let's take a look at app/controllers/server_access_controller.rb.

```
class ServerAccessController < ApplicationController

  def rss
  end

  def html
  end

  def ascii
  end

  def yaml
  end
end
```

We now see another class definition, this time descended from ApplicationController, and several empty methods whose names match the names of our requested Views. Now point your browser at http://localhost:3000/server_access and see what's there (Figure 12-2).

Figure 12-2: Unknown action

What happened? We browsed to the same top-level URL for our Rails application, this time adding the name of our new server_access Controller, and our application complained. Let's try the URL http://localhost:3000/server_access/rss instead. My result is shown in Figure 12-3.

Then try using http://localhost:3000/server_access/ascii as the URL (Figure 12-4).

Figure 12-3: The RSS View's default result   Figure 12-4: The ASCII View's default result

In the latter two cases, Rails told us which file provides content for the URL requested. We browse to the top-level Rails application and provide the Controller name as the first directory and the View name as the next element in the URL. This means that in our first example (http://localhost:3000/server_access), we provided no View. How will Rails interpret that?

Similar to how the default HTML file in a directory is index.html, the default View used when none is explicitly provided is index. However, ServerAccessController does not have a method called index, so it complained. Don't worry—we'll create an index View in our sample application in the next chapter.

However, the URL http://localhost:3000/server_access/ascii used a View that we know we have, ascii, and its results told us to look inside app/views/server_access/ascii.rhtml. Let's do so.

```
<h1>ServerAccess#ascii</h1>
<p>Find me in app/views/server_access/ascii.rhtml</p>
```

There's just enough HTML content there to provide the visible information. The file informs us that the Controller name is the class, and the View name is the method, using the # sign to indicate that it's an instance method (the # sign is often used in the Ruby community to distinguish an instance method from a class method). To write a real Rails application, we'll start filling these empty classes, methods, and HTML stub files with real content, and we'll also connect to a database to retrieve our information.

Since our View files are .rhtml files, not just static .html files, we can use techniques similar to those we've already seen in the context of mod_ruby to put Ruby code directly into our .rhtml files.[2] This will be crucial in the next chapter.

Chapter Recap

What was new in this chapter?

- Package management
- Installing RubyGems
- Installing, updating, and querying specific gem package files
- Rails basics
- Installing Rails
- The MVC pattern
- ORM basics
- Viewing your first Rails application
- Generating Models and Controllers
- The index View used as the default View
- Distinguishing instance methods from class methods with #
- HTML stub files for Views

With just that information, you could create some interesting applications that do a variety of dynamic tasks. However, the real power of Rails stems from its ability to access a database and manipulate content. That will be the focus of our next and final chapter.

---

[2] Technically, mod_ruby uses eRuby, while Rails uses erb; these are two different ways to embed Ruby code within markup, but they are very similar in practice.

13

A SIMPLE RAILS PROJECT

In the previous chapter, you installed Rails and became acquainted with the basics of the internal structure of a Rails application. In this chapter, we'll be creating a Rails app that is a bit more complex—it retrieves multiple instances of a given data type from a database and iterates over those instances for presentation. We'll also look into some more sophisticated ways of organizing code within Rails.

Creating the Application

For our purposes, any simple application will suffice. I've chosen to create a photo album that will display a few photos from my wedding. It will be able to display all of the photos in a list as thumbnail images with accompanying descriptive text, as well as display each individual image in greater detail. It will also provide navigation tools to allow the user to jump around within the list. All of this will be accomplished via HTML, the default presentation format for the Web. In addition, the application will provide an RSS feed (the XML format we used as a data source in currency_converter2.rb) that will describe all the images.

Initial Creation

We'll create our application (called photo_album) within an appropriate directory with the command rails photo_album. Then type cd photo_album and ruby script/server to start the app. We can verify that Rails is running by browsing to http://localhost:3000, as we did in "Viewing Your Rails Application" on page 230.

Preparing the Database

For this application, I'll be using the MySQL database. I'll assume that you can get MySQL running on your machine and are able to do simple queries. If that's not the case, you may want to brush up on MySQL with a book specifically on that topic, such as *Managing and Using MySQL*, by George Reese, Randy Jay Yarger, and Tim King (O'Reilly, 2002). If you are using a database other than MySQL, I'll assume you are able to work out the subtle differences in the resulting Rails app on your own, with the help of the documentation available from your database vendor and at http://rubyonrails.org.

One thing you may need to do is alter the config/database.yml file, especially if you're using a database program other than MySQL. I had to edit the value for socket: to be /var/run/mysqld/mysqld.sock. If you get the error No such file or directory - /tmp/mysql.sock, a mismatch in the socket description is the most likely cause. Rails is looking for the MySQL socket file at /tmp/mysql.sock, and you need to set it to the right file location. You can find the location of the socket file with this command (preferably as root) on a Unix-like operating system: find / mysqld.sock | grep mysqld.sock.

Adding Data

The photo album app differs from the simple structural example in Chapter 12 in that it has real data in a database, which we will now assume is handling that data. One of the most convenient ways to manage data for Rails (especially for simple test data like ours), is by using a migration. A *migration* in Rails is a description of data in Ruby that is created and deleted as needed. Let's take a look at our migration file at db/migrate/001_create_photos.rb:

Migrations

```
class CreatePhotos < ActiveRecord::Migration
```

❶　　COLUMN_NAMES = [:description, :image_path, :title, :photographer]

❷　　SAMPLE_PHOTOS = [

```
      {
        :title        => 'Tonawanda Creek',
        :description  => 'A waterway in Tonawanda, NY.',
        :image_path   => '001_creek.jpg',
        :photographer => 'Vince',
      },
      {
        :title        => 'Travis',
        :description  => %q[My friend Travis. His wife Laura's head is partly in
view as well.],
        :image_path   => '002_travis.jpg',
        :photographer => 'Vince',
      },
      {
        :title        => 'Liam & Ducks',
        :description  => 'My nephew Liam with some ducks.',
        :image_path   => '003_liam.jpg',
        :photographer => 'Vince',
      },
    ]
```

❸ ```
  def self.up
```

❹ ```
    create_table :photos do |t|
      COLUMN_NAMES.each { |c| t.column c, :text }
    end
```

❺ ```
    SAMPLE_PHOTOS.each do |sp|
      p = Photo.create(sp)
      p.save!
    end

  end
```

❻ ```
  def self.down
    drop_table :photos
  end
end
```

At ❶ and ❷, we define Constants for both the COLUMN_NAMES and
SAMPLE_PHOTOS, which we use for data insertion. COLUMN_NAMES should be obvious,
and each element of SAMPLE_PHOTOS is a Hash representing a database record, in
which each key is the Symbol representation of a column name and the value is
whatever data will be in that database field. At ❸, we define the self.up method,
which contains all the code that will run when we perform our migration.

One of the most important tasks within self.up is the creation of the
table, which is done at ❹. The create_table method takes a Symbol argument
for the table name and a block describing what should be done to that table.
In our case, create_table loops through the COLUMN_NAMES, creating a column
for table t, named with the current value of c, of type text.

NOTE *All our database table fields are of type text. If we had more complex data with different types, we would probably replace the Array* COLUMN_NAMES *with a Hash called* COLUMNS, *in which each key would be the column's name and each key's value would be the column's data type.*

At ❺, we create a new Photo instance called p; it is based on each member of SAMPLE_PHOTOS, which we call sp in turn. We then save! each version of p, which stores its data into the database table. At ❻, we show that when we're done with this migration, the :photos table will be dropped. We execute the migration with the command rake db:migrate. Let's examine the results.

NOTE *Note that* save! *is named with a bang, because it is destructive (since it saves to the database). Also, running* rake db:migrate *runs whichever of your defined migrations is needed to make your migrations current. We only have one, so that's the only one that runs.*

```
== CreatePhotos: migrating
=====================================================
-- create_table(:photos)
   -> 0.1226s
== CreatePhotos: migrated (0.3359s)
=====================================================
```

The migration was successful. We can double check that by querying MySQL (or whichever database you're using).

NOTE *At the prompt, I entered the password I have already set up for my specific MySQL installation. Yours is whatever you have already chosen, or it may be unset. This will depend on the specific way you installed MySQL on your machine.*

```
echo 'select * from photo_album_development.photos' | mysql -uroot -p
Enter password:
id      description      image_path      title      photographer
1       A waterway in Tonawanda, NY.    001_creek.jpg   Tonawanda Creek Vince
2       My friend Travis. His wife Laura's head is partly in view as well.
002_travis.jpg  Travis  Vince
3       My nephew Liam with some ducks. 003_liam.jpg    Liam & Ducks    Vince
```

We can now see that we have data in the database for use in our Rails app. Let's move on to creating the other portions of the app.

Creating the Model and Controllers

As you've already seen in the previous chapter, Rails makes it very easy to create Models, Controllers, and Views. For the photo album application, we'll be creating a Model called *Photo* and Controllers called *Album* and *Feed*.

Creating the Photo Model

Within the photo_album directory, execute ruby script/generate model photo, which creates the Model file app/models/photo.rb.

Creating the Album and Feed Controllers

Next, within photo_album, execute ruby script/generate controller album index show and ruby script/generate controller feed images. These create the Album Controller with the index and show Views and the Feed Controller with the images View, implemented by multiple files within the app/controllers and app/views subdirectories.

Dissecting the Application

Now that we have created the basic skeleton of our application, let's examine how it works. Think of this section as similar to the sections "The Code" or "How It Works" in previous chapters.

Dissecting the Photo Model

Our photo album app has one basic piece of data, represented in a Model called Photo. Let's add some code to what's already there and explore what it does. Edit app/models/photo.rb to match the following:

```
class Photo < ActiveRecord::Base

=begin explain
Closely follows Object-Relational Model, each instance is
also a record in the table called 'photos'.
=end
❶   def next_id()
       return Photo.minimum(:id) if last_id?
       next_id = @attributes['id'].to_i.succ
       next_id.succ! until Photo.find(next_id)
       next_id.to_s
    end

❷   def prev_id()
       return Photo.maximum(:id) if first_id?
       prev_id = (@attributes['id'].to_i - 1)
       prev_id = (prev_id - 1) until Photo.find(prev_id)
       prev_id.to_s
    end

    private

❸   def last_id?()
       @attributes['id'] == Photo.maximum(:id).to_s
    end

❹   def first_id?()
       @attributes['id'] == Photo.minimum(:id).to_s
    end


end
```

At ❶ and ❷, we have the next_id and prev_id methods, respectively. Within them, we make free use of built-in Rails methods. One of these is minimum, which is available to all Models; it takes a Symbol argument that establishes which attribute of that Model the minimum status will be based on. Another method is the find method, which is a wrapper for SELECT statements in SQL that takes specific arguments for filtering. Also available in Rails is the @attributes instance variable, which is a Hash whose keys are the field names from the database table and whose values are that column's content for that particular instance of the Model. The Photo instance representing the database record with the ID 2 would have an @attributes['id'] equal to 2, for example.

At ❸ and ❹, we also have two private predicates that inform us if our Photo instance is the one with the last_id? and first_id?, respectively. We accomplish this by performing some simple equality testing with the known maximum and minimum id values. Note that the returned id values from maximum and minimum are Integers, while the values stored in @attributes are Strings. The photo.rb Model therefore makes liberal use of the to_i and to_s methods as needed.

Dissecting the Controllers

Now that we understand our Photo Model, we need to interact with it in some way. That's the job of one or more Controllers. Our photo album app has two Controllers, Album and Feed, each of which have their own Views.

Dissecting the Album Controller

Similar to what we did with the Photo Model, let's add code to the Album Controller and explore what it does. Edit app/controllers/album_controller.rb to match the following:

```
class AlbumController < ApplicationController

=begin explain
This metaprogramming directive allows us to define a specific
helper called FooterHelper in app/helpers/footer_helper.rb
that can be shared among multiple Controllers.
=end
❶   helper :footer

=begin explain
As with HTML files, this is the default implicit behavior.
all_photos is found in app/controllers/application.rb
=end
❷   def index()
       @photos = all_photos()
    end

=begin explain
Set up any instance variables to be used in the View
or Helper, such as @photo here.
=end
```

```
❸   def show()
      @photo = Photo.find(params[:id])
    end

  end
```

As is customary in an MVC application, `album_controller.rb` will be responsible for manipulating and processing data in ways that pertain to our photo album. In this particular case, `album_controller.rb`'s methods generally redirect to something defined in another file or simply provide a useful shortcut.

For this demonstration Rails app, I wanted to have an HTML footer that would remain consistent across multiple pages within the Album Controller. The question is then how to implement that feature and where to place its code. One answer would be to duplicate the necessary code in every View that has the footer, but that would be bad design. A better option would be to place the footer creation code in the appropriate Controller and simply call that code in every View where it's needed.

However, there are situations in which you'd want the code outside of the base Controller. What if you want to implement a common feature across multiple Controllers? Each Controller in a Rails app is a child of the next file we'll look at (`app/controllers/application.rb`), so putting the code in that file is an option. Another option is to use what Rails calls Helpers. *Helpers* are add-ons to the MVC framework and are similar to the mixin concept we used in to_lang.rb in Chapter 10. At ❶ in `album_controller.rb`, we see from the RDoc that our footer-related code is in a distinct file called `app/helpers/footer_helper.rb`, and we can make use of that code within `album_controller.rb` by simply including the line `helper :footer`. If we had a Helper at `app/helpers/credit_card_authorization_helper.rb`, we could make use of its code in a Controller with the line `helper :credit_card_authorization`, and so on. In true object-oriented fashion, this allows us to organize code according to problem domain or topic in separate files, make use of them where needed, and not have to worry about the specific implementations. Of course, we'll discuss the implementation of the footer code when we get to `app/helpers/footer_helper.rb`, but it's very convenient that `album_controller.rb` needn't concern itself with that level of detail.

NOTE   *Helpers are even defined as Modules, just as traditional mixins are. This application has a lot of code in Helper files, which I'll describe shortly, after I talk about the Controllers.*

Along with the Helper inclusion at ❶, we also have definitions of methods corresponding to the `index` and `show` Views at ❷ and ❸. The `show` method at ❸ is merely a shortcut for the built-in Rails method `find`. In this case, it takes an argument of the `id` parameter passed into the web application, which is available to us as `params[:id]`. This is how we show the specific requested photo. The `index` method at ❷ is (as we know from Chapter 12) the default method called when none is explicitly provided. It merely establishes an instance variable within the Controller called `@photos`. To do so, it calls a method named `all_photos`, which is defined in our next file, `app/controllers/application.rb`.

NOTE *The params Hash in a Rails app is equivalent to* cgi.params, *which we saw in the* simple_cgi.rb *script in Chapter 11.*

Dissecting the Application Controller

The application.rb file in any Rails application describes the superclass of all Controllers. If there is any behavior or characteristic that you want to be truly universal across all Controllers, this is the place to put it.

NOTE *Note that you can modularize your code (i.e., break it down by topic into Helpers) and still make it universal. Just organize your code into Helpers, and then include all of those Helpers with* helper *lines in* app/controllers/application.rb. *Easy.*

Edit app/controllers/application.rb to match the following:

```
# Filters added to this Controller apply to all Controllers in the
application.
# Likewise, all the methods added will be available for all Controllers.

class ApplicationController < ActionController::Base
  # Pick a unique cookie name to distinguish our session data from others'
  session :session_key => '_photo_album_session_id'

=begin explain
Now all_photos() can be used in any other Controller.
=end
❶   def all_photos()
      Photo.find(:all)
    end

end
```

All we've done in this file is define the all_photos method at ❶. This is arguably silly, in that it only provides a slightly shorter way to call Photo.find(:all). However, this is primarily a demonstration app, and it does show that all_photos is now available to any Controller, anywhere in the application.

NOTE *The session information is automatic, and it helps Rails disambiguate among multiple users that are using the app at the same time. For example, I can browse the entire list of photos with the Album's index View, while you simultaneously look in greater detail at the second photo with Album's* show *View.*

Dissecting the Feed Controller

The Album Controller is not our only Controller. I also want to provide an RSS feed of information about these images, and the Feed Controller is our way of doing so. Just like album_controller.rb, it descends from app/controllers/application.rb, so it has the all_photos method available to it.

Edit app/controllers/feed_controller.rb to match the following:

```
class FeedController < ApplicationController

❶   CONTENT_TYPE = 'application/rss+xml'

    =begin explain
    all_photos() found in app/controllers/application.rb
    =end
❷   def images()
      @photos = all_photos()
      @headers['Content-Type'] = CONTENT_TYPE
    end

end
```

At ❶, we define a constant for the CONTENT_TYPE, declaring something appropriate for an RSS feed. Then at ❷, we declare our only method, images. It establishes the @photos instance variable just as album_controller.rb does, and also sets @headers['Content-Type']. The @headers variable is, as you might expect, the variable used to define the HTTP headers of the application's output. Before moving on to the Views, let's see what's going on in our Helper files.

Dissecting the Helpers

Models, Controllers, and Views are not the only types of files in a Rails app. I touched on the concept of Helpers in our discussion of the Photo Model, but now we'll explore them in depth.

Dissecting the Album Helper

Edit app/helpers/album_helper.rb to match the following:

```
module AlbumHelper

❶   CONFIRM_MESSAGE = %q[Are you sure you want to see the full list?]

    NUMBER_OF_ROW_TYPES_FOR_DISPLAY = 3

    LISTING_HEADER_COLUMNS =<<END_OF_HERE_DOC
    <tr>
      <th>Image</th>
      <th>Description</th>
    </tr>
    END_OF_HERE_DOC

❷   IMAGE_STYLE = {
      :base  => 'margin-bottom: 0.5em; padding: 0.5em;',
      :thumb => 'height:48px; width:64px;'
    }
```

```
=begin explain
Outputs a CSS classname used for prettification.
=end
❸  def row_class_from_index(i)
      'row' + ((i % NUMBER_OF_ROW_TYPES_FOR_DISPLAY) + 1).to_s
    end

❹  def show_listing_header_columns()
      LISTING_HEADER_COLUMNS
    end

❺  def show_photo(photo)
      image_tag(
        photo.image_path,
        :alt => "Photo of #{photo.title}"
      )
    end

❻  def show_thumbnail_for_list(photo)
      image_tag(
        photo.image_path,
        :alt   => "Photo of #{photo.title}",
        :style => IMAGE_STYLE[:thumb]
      )
    end

❼  def page_title()
      @photo ? @photo.title : controller.action_name
    end

❽  def title_with_thumbnail(photo)
      [h(photo.title), show_thumbnail_for_list(photo)].join(
          ApplicationHelper::HTML_BREAK
        )
    end

end
```

At ❶, we start defining some useful Constants, including one of our old friends, a Hash with Symbol keys, at ❷. At ❸, we define a method called row_class_from_index, whose RDoc explains that it merely outputs text representing the appropriate CSS class. This allows us to change the CSS style of a row easily, and the modulus makes it repeat. At ❹, we have a method called show_listing_header_columns that simply returns the corresponding Constant. The show_photo method at ❺ uses the built-in Rails method image_tag, which takes the location of the image (the src attribute of the img tag, in other words) as the first argument. The second argument is a Hash whose keys will be any additional img attributes and whose values will be used as the values for the corresponding img attributes. The location (i.e., img src) is the photo's image_path, and since all img tags should have an alt attribute, we provide that, with an appropriate identifying String based on the photo's title. At ❻, we define `show_thumbnail_for_list`, which is a Helper method for presentation that is very similar to `show_photo`. It only differs by including a style attribute for the resulting img tag, whose value is `IMAGE_STYLE[:thumb]`.

NOTE *One easy way to refactor this code (meaning to change its internal structure without changing its overall behavior) would be to combine `show_photo` and `show_thumbnail_for_list` into a single `show_photo` method that takes an optional third argument, which declares whether or not the photo is a thumbnail. You can read more about the process of refactoring in Martin Fowler's book* Refactoring *(Addison-Wesley Professional, 1999).*

Next, at ❼, we define `page_title`. If there is a `@photo` present, `page_title` will return that `@photo`'s title. If there is no `@photo`, it will fall back to the `action_name` of the controller. What does that mean? The `@photo.title` should be straightforward. The `action_name` is essentially the name of the View. This means that when we browse using the `index` View (or `action_name`) and have not yet selected a specific photo to view in greater detail with the `show` View, the `page_title` will simply be `index`.

Finally, at ❽, we define `title_with_thumbnail`. It uses several other methods and Constants. Rails has a built-in method called `h`, which formats its input for HTML presentation. For example, `h(&)` returns `&amp;`. This is useful in our app because we have a photo whose title is *Liam & Ducks*, but we don't want that ampersand to break the HTML validity of the output. The `title_with_thumbnail` method uses our home-brewed `show_thumbnail_for_list` and joins it with `page_title`, using whatever we've defined `HTML_BREAK` to be within the `ApplicationHelper`.

WHERE TO PUT CODE: CONTROLLER OR HELPER (OR ELSEWHERE)?

As you can see, the Album Helper is noticeably bigger than the Controller it aids. When should you put code in the Controller, and when should you put it in a Helper? That's a good question. When there isn't a clear division by topic, such as for the `footer_helper.rb` below, it becomes more difficult to answer. When something is truly fundamental to the data, such as the Photo methods that directly pertain to ids, it probably belongs in the Model. When something is completely presentation-specific, it can probably go in the appropriate View. However, it's considered bad style to have too much dynamic content in a View file. Anything more complicated than looping over a set of items should probably be abstracted into a method, rather than being in the View itself.

That leaves either the Controller or a Helper. As you can see, I like to have a fairly sparse, minimalist Controller—critics might say that makes my Helpers too busy. Other coders might put many methods directly in the Controller, making little use of Helpers at all. Still others might have broken anything related to thumbnail images into yet another Helper called `thumbnail_helper.rb`.

There are many options. As long as you don't put presentation-related methods in your Model, and you keep your Views relatively free of code that actually *does stuff* (instead including mostly code that *presents stuff*), you're probably doing fine.

Dissecting the ApplicationHelper

We've already seen that album_helper.rb expects a definition for HTML_BREAK within ApplicationHelper. Let's see how it does it.

Edit app/helpers/application.rb to match the following:

```
# Methods added to this helper will be available to all templates in the
application.
module ApplicationHelper

  HTML_BREAK = '<br />'

end
```

There isn't much there—it's basically just the Constant definition we expected. Why is it defined here, and not in AlbumHelper? Because we'll also need it in FooterHelper. Note that while Controllers automatically descend from ApplicationController, Helpers don't automatically descend from ApplicationHelper.

Dissecting the FeedHelper

Edit app/helpers/feed_helper.rb to match the following:

```
module FeedHelper

❶  AUTHOR      = 'Kevin C. Baird'

   DESCRIPTION = %q{Photos from Jenn and Kevin's Wedding}

   ICON       = {
     :url     => 'rails.png',
     :width   => 77,
     :height  => 69,
   }

   LANGUAGE    = 'en-us'

❷  LINK_OPTIONS_DEFAULTS = {
       :only_path  => false,
       :controller => 'album',
   }

❸  LINK_OPTIONS = {
     :index => LINK_OPTIONS_DEFAULTS.merge( { :action => 'index' } ),
     :show  => LINK_OPTIONS_DEFAULTS.merge( { :action => 'show'  } ),
   }

   RSS_OPTIONS = {
     'version'  => '2.0',
     'xmlns:dc' => 'http://purl.org/dc/elements/1.1/'
   }
```

```
        TITLE       = 'Baird/Cornish Wedding Photos'

❹   def feed_description()
        h( DESCRIPTION )
      end

❺   def rss_url_for_image(image)
        return url_for( FeedHelper::LINK_OPTIONS[:index] ) unless image
        url_for( FeedHelper::LINK_OPTIONS[:show].merge( { :id => image } ) )
      end

end
```

At ❶, we start with our usual Constant declarations. These include a declaration at ❷ for LINK_OPTIONS_DEFAULTS, which stores information common across multiple types of links, and one for LINK_OPTIONS at ❸, which uses these defaults and also adds a pair whose key is :action and whose value is either :index or :show, depending on how it's called. These :index and :show values represent Views within the Album Controller, of course, as the value for :controller in LINK_OPTIONS_DEFAULTS indicates. FeedHelper also defines several other Constants with values useful for an RSS feed.

At ❹ we have a method called feed_description, which simply passes the value of the DESCRIPTION Constant through the Rails built-in method h, which we've already seen and which formats for HTML presentation. Finally, rss_url_for_image at ❺ is a wrapper we've built around the Rails method url_for, which behaves as its name suggests. (It is described in greater detail at http://api.rubyonrails.org/classes/ActionView/Helpers/UrlHelper.html#M000484.) If an image is not passed in, rss_url_for_image returns the url_for the LINK_OPTIONS appropriate for an :index View. If there is an image, rss_url_for_image returns the url_for the LINK_OPTIONS appropriate for a :show View and includes the :id of the image to be shown.

NOTE   *The behavior of rss_url_for_image, which differs depending on whether or not there is an image, is similar to the potential melding of AlbumHelper.show_photo and AlbumHelper.show_thumbnail_for_list proposed earlier.*

Dissecting the FooterHelper

Edit app/helpers/footer_helper.rb to match the following:

```
module FooterHelper
❶   BAR_SEPARATOR = %q[ | ]

    RSS = {

      :icons => %w[feed-icon16x16.png xmlicon.png],

      :link_options => {
        :action    => %q[images],
```

```
                          :controller -> %q[feed],
            }

        }

❷    def show_footer()
        '<p id="rails_img_wrapper">' +
        [rails_link_to_top, rss_icon_links].join(
          ApplicationHelper::HTML_BREAK
        ) + '</p>'
      end

      private

❸    def rails_link_to_top()
        link_to(
          image_tag(
            'rails.png',
            :alt    => 'Home',
            :border => 0,
            :id     => 'rails_img',
            :style  => AlbumHelper::IMAGE_STYLE[:base]
          ), :controller => 'album'
        )
      end

❹    def rss_icon_links()
        RSS[:icons].map do |icon|
          link_to(
            image_tag(
              icon,
              :alt   => 'RSS Feed',
              :class => 'xmlicon'
            ), RSS[:link_options]
          )
        end.join(BAR_SEPARATOR)
      end

    end
```

The link_to and image_tag Methods

At ❶, we define two Constants, BAR_SEPARATOR and RSS. The BAR_SEPARATOR Constant is a simple delimiter for presentation, while RSS is another Hash with Symbol keys that details information pertinent to :icons and :link_options, respectively. In these definitions, I've used %q[] instead of single quotes to define BAR_SEPARATOR, just as a reminder that the option is available.[1]

At ❷, our main public method, show_footer, just returns the outputs of the private methods rails_link_to_top and rss_icon_links, joined on the HTML_BREAK Constant that we've already seen, and all wrapped in an HTML paragraph tag with the id rails_img_wrapper. We create our paragraph tag the old-fashioned way—by outputting plaintext. You can still do that in Rails, although the availability of methods like url_for and image_tag make the practice uncommon.

---

[1] For example, you might want to use %q[] instead of quotation marks if the String to be defined included quotation marks; some programmers might simply prefer using %q[].

So what do the private methods do? The `rails_link_to_top` method at ❸ just creates a link with the Rails built-in `link_to`, which takes the link argument and a Hash describing the `:controller` to be used: `'album'`, in this case. The Hash can also describe the `:action`, if needed. The `rss_icon_links` method at ❹ maps an operation onto each member of `RSS[:icons]`. That operation is also a call to `link_to`, where the linked image is the current element within `RSS[:icons]` (called `icon`) and the Hash describing the `:controller` and `:action` is always `RSS[:link_options]`. The Array resulting from the map is then joined on the `BAR_SEPARATOR`.

Dissecting the Album Controller's Views

Now, let's move on to the Views. Since we've already defined so much of the application in methods within either the Model, Controller, or various Helpers, our Views should be fairly sparse. View files differ from the files we've seen so far in that they are .rhtml files (similar to mod_ruby_demo.rhtml), not pure Ruby .rb files. That's one of the reasons (apart from good application design principles) that having too much dynamic Ruby content in your View files is discouraged. It's relatively easy to debug Ruby within Ruby, but it isn't so easy when you have to keep shifting back and forth between Ruby and HTML.

Dissecting the index View

Edit app/views/album/index.rhtml to match the following:

❶
```
<!--
row_class_from_index()
show_listing_header_columns()
show_thumbnail_for_list()
all in app/helpers/album_helper.rb

@photos derived from AlbumController's index method

-->

<h1>Listing photos</h1>

<table>
```
❷
```
  <%= show_listing_header_columns() %>
```
❸
```
  <% @photos.each_with_index do |photo,i| -%>
  <tr>
```
❹
❺
```
      <td class="<%= row_class_from_index(i) %>">
      <%=
            link_to(
                title_with_thumbnail(photo),
                :action => 'show',
                :id => photo.id
            )
      %>
      </td>
```

```
⓺        <td class="<%= row_class_from_index(i) %>">
⓻          <%= photo.description %>
         </td>

         </tr>
⓼      <% end %>

     </table>

     <hr />

⓽  <%= show_footer %>
```

At ❶, we have HTML comments explaining where to find the methods that we put to use within this file. The file then continues with ordinary, unsurprising HTML. You may wonder why there are no <html>, <head>, or <body> tags. For that answer, you'll have to wait until we introduce the concept of layouts and describe the file app/views/layouts/album.rhtml later in this chapter.

The first appearance of Ruby at ❷ is a call to show_listing_header_columns, which we know (and which our HTML comments remind us) was defined in app/helpers/album_helper.rb. This allows the View to call a method whose name says what it does, without worrying about the implementation. Next, at ❸, we will loop through each photo within @photos, along with its index, which we'll call i. You'll notice that the each_with_index line ends its Ruby escape with -%>, not just %>. This tells Rails that there should not be an automatic carriage return in the interpreted output. It's not critical here, but you can imagine this could be very useful within a <pre> tag, for example.

What do we do with each photo? We'll present it within a table, applying the CSS class of row_class_from_index(i) to each <td> element at ❹. The content within that <td> element will be the result of a multi-line Ruby call that begins at ❺. Its value is the result of a link_to call on the title_with_thumbnail that points to the 'show' :action and displays the photo identified by photo.id.

In addition to the thumbnail <td> cell, we also want another <td> cell that contains the photo's description. That begins at ❻, with another call to row_class_from_index. Its <td> cell contains simply photo.description at ❼. We then close the each_with_index call from ❸ with end at ❽. Finally, at ❾ we call show_footer, which we've already discussed in footer_helper.rb.

Dissecting the show View

Now let's look at the show View, which displays a particular photo in greater detail. Edit app/views/album/show.rhtml to match the following:

```
<!--
image_tag is built in to Rails
prev_id and next_id are in app/models/photo.rb
show_photo is in app/helpers/album_helper.rb
-->
```

```
      <table id="dark_bg">
        <tr>
          <td>
            <div class="photo">
❶             <%= show_photo( @photo ) %>
            </div>
          </td>

          <td class="desc_wrapper">
            <div class="description">
❷             <h1><%= h(@photo.title) %></h1>
❸             <p class="description"><%= @photo.description %></p>
            </div>
          </td>
        </tr>
      </table>

      <hr style="clear:both;" />

      <ul class="navlinks">
❹     <li><%=
            link_to 'First',
                :action => 'show',
                :id     => Photo.minimum(:id)
        %></li>

❺     <li><%=
            link_to 'Previous',
                :action => 'show',
                :id     => @photo.prev_id %></li>

❻     <li><%=
            link_to 'Next',
                :action => 'show',
                :id     => @photo.next_id     %></li>

❼     <li><%=
            link_to 'Last',
                :action => 'show',
                :id     => Photo.maximum(:id) %></li>

      <!-- You have the option of some GUI helpers in the optional parameters
    hash -->

      <!-- like :confirm for a JS confirm box -->
❽     <li><%= link_to(
            'Full List',
            { :action  => 'index' },
            { :confirm => AlbumHelper::CONFIRM_MESSAGE }
        ) %></li>
```

```
<!--
    See RSS[:link_options] in app/helpers/footer_helper.rb
    for how to link across multiple Controllers
-->

</ul>

❾ <%= show_footer %>
```

We start off again with some HTML reminder comments. The first real Ruby appears at ❶—it is a call to show_photo from AlbumHelper, passing in @photo, which is the particular photo instance that matches the id parameter used to call the show View. Then at ❷, we pass @photo's title through the h formatter method, and at ❸, we wrap the @photo's description within an appropriately classed paragraph tag.

Under a horizontal rule, we have an unordered list, each item of which is a call to the link_to method. At ❹, we provide a link called 'First' that shows the photo with the minimum :id. At ❺, the link destination shows the photo with the previous id via the text 'Previous', and at ❻, the destination shows the Photo with the next_id via the text 'Next'. At ❼, it shows the 'Last' photo, defined as the one with the maximum :id.

The links so far have all been formatted in the simple <a href> style, but there are other options available. For instance, Rails provides many built-in methods to perform some common JavaScript operations. One of these is the confirm box, which interrupts your browsing with a box asking you to confirm some question. I'm sure you've seen them while browsing, but Figure 13-1 shows one in the Epiphany browser on Ubuntu.

The code at ❽ creates this box for us. Choosing Cancel makes it do nothing, while choosing OK causes it to proceed as if it were a standard link, this time to the 'index' :action. The code to describe this also adds a second Hash to link_to, with the key :confirm and with a value taken from the AlbumHelper::CONFIRM_MESSAGE

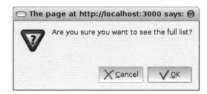

Figure 13-1: A confirm box automatically generated by Rails

Constant. Notice that this link provides the otherwise-optional curly brace delimiters for the Hashes, to show which pairs go with which Hash. The text for the confirm box link is 'Full List', since it brings us back to the index View. After some more HTML comments, we see a call to show_footer at ❾.

Dissecting the Feed Controller's images View

In general, everything I've said about the Album Controller's Views will also apply to the Feed Controller's View. The same basic design principles apply. However, there are a few slight differences. The Feed Controller is more lightweight and has fewer responsibilities. It also only has one View, which we're about to explore.

As already noted, Album is not our only Controller. We also want to use Feed to display our images within an RSS Feed. Let's see how that's done. Edit app/views/feed/images.rxml to match the following. Note that the file extension is .rxml instead of .rhtml, since we're creating XML for an RSS Feed instead of regular HTML.

```
=begin explain
The various FeedHelper:: Constants are in app/helpers/feed_helper.rb,
as are the feed_description() and rss_url_for_image() methods.
=end
```

Outputting XML ❶ `xml.instruct!`

❷ `xml.rss( FeedHelper::RSS_OPTIONS ) do`

❸
```
    xml.channel do
        xml.title       FeedHelper::TITLE
        xml.language    FeedHelper::LANGUAGE
        xml.link        rss_url_for_image( nil )
        xml.pubDate     Time.now
        xml.description feed_description()
```

❹
```
        xml.image do
          xml.title       FeedHelper::TITLE
          xml.link        rss_url_for_image( nil )
          xml.url         FeedHelper::ICON[:url]
          xml.width       FeedHelper::ICON[:width]
          xml.height      FeedHelper::ICON[:height]
          xml.description feed_description()
        end
```

❺
```
        @photos.each do |image|
          xml.item do
            xml.title       image.title
            xml.link        rss_url_for_image( image )
            xml.description h( image.description )
            xml.pubDate     Time.now
            xml.guid        rss_url_for_image( image )
            xml.author      FeedHelper::AUTHOR
            # image.photographer could also be the author
          end
        end

    end

end
```

This file uses a project called XML::Builder (http://rubyforge.org/projects/builder), an XML generation library that comes built in to Rails. At ❶, we call xml.instruct!, which starts the XML document. (XML::Builder's relationship to Rails ensures that the xml variable is available, and we don't have to do anything ahead of time.) Then at ❷, we set up our RSS Feed by calling xml.rss with FeedHelper::RSS_OPTIONS. Each RSS Feed has a channel, which we establish at ❸, and an associated image, which we define at ❹.

The content (or articles) within our RSS Feed are each a single photo with associated descriptive text. At ❺, we use @photos from the FeedController's images method, looping through each of them, calling them image in turn. Then we create an xml.item, passing in a block defining each of the appropriate characteristics. Notice how many of them are either expressible as a Constant (such as FeedHelper::TITLE) or as the result of a method call (such as rss_url_for_image, with or without an image argument).

Dissecting the Album Controller's Layout

Remember when I first talked about app/views/album/index.rhtml and mentioned that that file lacked certain expected HTML content, such as the <html> tag? Think about that for a minute. You might expect such content to appear in every View's .rhtml file, but that would produce a great deal of duplicated content. Duplication is precisely what programmers try to avoid, so we should find some other solution to that problem. One approach would be to define methods in the Controller or a Helper like doctype_tag, html_tag, head_tag, and so on, similar to the image_tag method that Rails already provides for us.

That would be a reasonable approach, except that invariably what is being created is content in a format that is tightly bound to a particular type of View, most commonly HTML. We already have .rhtml files for that express purpose. Shouldn't we find a way to have some sort of .rhtml template?

That's exactly what layouts are. They wrap View output within a template. Edit app/views/layouts/album.rhtml to match the following:

```
<!--
This (app/views/layouts/album.html)
is a "wrapper" that encloses all Views for the
Album Controller.
-->

<html lang="en-us">

<head>

<title>
Album: <%= page_title %>
</title>
```
CSS Link Tag
```
<%= stylesheet_link_tag('master') %>
<%= stylesheet_link_tag(controller.action_name) if controller %>

</head>

<body>

<!--
"yield :layout" outputs the View's results, whichever it is.
-->
```

❹ `<%= yield :layout %>`

`</body>`

`</html>`

At ❶, we use `page_title` from app/helpers/album_helper.rb for the `<title>`. At ❷ and ❸, we use Rails' built-in `stylesheet_link_tag` method to include stylesheets. We always want the `master.css` stylesheet, and if the Controller has an `action_name`, we want that associated stylesheet as well. Finally, at ❹, we see `yield :layout`. What does this do?

We already know that `yield` within a method that takes a `block_argument` functions the same way as `block_argument.call` does. This is similar, except that the output from the requested View takes the place of the block. It's the equivalent of saying *Always wrap whatever is requested inside me, and place whatever was requested at this point.*

NOTE   *If you already know Rails, you know that there are other options for solving this problem, such as using partials, which approach the problem from the bottom up, rather than from the top down. Read more at http://wiki.rubyonrails.org/rails/pages/Partials if you're interested.*

Using CSS

The `master.css` stylesheet is used throughout the application, and each action automatically includes a stylesheet with the same name (see ❷ and ❸ in app/views/layouts/album.rhtml in "Dissecting the Album Controller's Layout" on page 256). When we browse with the show View, we will make use of the `show.css` stylesheet, for example. If you're curious about CSS, you can learn more at websites like http://csszengarden.com. The stylesheets `master.css`, `public.css`, and `index.css` are available for download at this book's website.

Using the Application

At this point, we have a photo album application, as well as a decent understanding of how its component parts are organized and how they work, both individually and as part of the whole. Now let's take a look at this app in action, starting by opening it in a web browser.

Figure 13-2 shows how the default action of the Album Controller looks when I view it with the Epiphany web browser. Its appearance should differ only trivially in other graphical browsers, like Firefox or Internet Explorer. Figure 13-3 shows the appearance of the first image, as displayed by the show View of the Album Controller.

Figures 13-4 and 13-5 show the appearance of the images View of the Feed Controller. Figure 13-4 shows it (again) in Epiphany, while Figure 13-5 shows it in Akregator, which is a program designed specifically for viewing RSS feeds.

Figure 13-2: Browsing the Album Controller

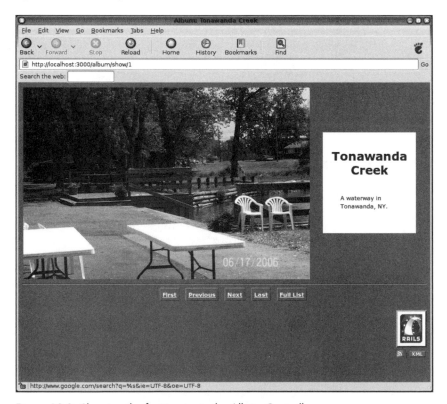

Figure 13-3: Showing the first image in the Album Controller

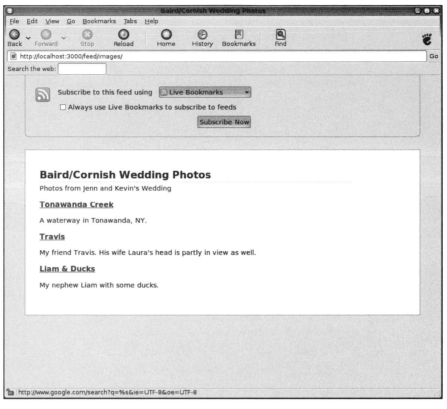

Figure 13-4: Browsing the RSS images in the Feed Controller with Epiphany

Figure 13-5: Browsing with the Akregator RSS reader

Learning More About Rails

This chapter has only scratched the surface of Rails. I've barely described some of the Helper methods (like image_tag and link_to), and I haven't even touched on topics like ActiveRecord's ability to create relationships between multiple Models, Unit Testing within Rails, forms within Rails, user creation and authentication, session handling, and much more. Even so, this is already the longest chapter in a Ruby book that tried very hard to be about Ruby, as distinct from Rails—and I even had to describe the basic anatomy of a Rails application in the chapter before this one. There's a lot to learn in Rails, and you can always read more at http://rubyonrails.org. Just don't forget that Ruby has a lot to offer apart from Rails, too, as I hope the other chapters in this book have shown.

Chapter Recap

What was new in this chapter?

- Using Rails with MySQL
- Adding data with migration files
- Creating a Model
- Creating multi-View Controllers
- Adding methods to Models and Controllers
- The ApplicationController superclass
- Using Helpers
- The ApplicationHelper module
- MVC as it relates to Controllers and Helpers
- Creating Views as .rhtml files
- Doing common JavaScript with Rails' built-in Helper methods
- Using layouts and incorporating the results of [view].rhtml within them
- Using stylesheets modularized by View type

I hope this book has given you some useful information about coding in Ruby. I've tried to play to what I see as the language's greatest strengths: readability, a high level of abstraction (and great ease in extending that abstraction even higher), internal consistency, and conceptual elegance. All of these characteristics of Ruby remain, whether or not you're working within Rails. If you do find yourself using Rails, don't forget that along with each, you can still use map and inject.

Thanks for reading.

HOW DOES RUBY COMPARE TO OTHER LANGUAGES?

One of the best ways to describe something is to talk about what it isn't. This appendix describes similarities and differences between Ruby and some other popular languages.

C

Even though it isn't the oldest language around, *C* is the granddaddy of languages in many programmers' minds. For the purposes of this discussion, we'll be focusing more on the differences between Ruby and C than the similarities. C is *procedural*, meaning that its programs are intended to be thought of as sets of instructions that proceed stepwise through time: *Do this, then do this, then do that.* C is neither object oriented nor functional, although the closely related languages C++ and Objective C are object oriented. C undeniably has *functions*, bits of reusable code that accept various inputs and return various outputs, but they are generally not *purely functional* functions. C functions often depend on information other than the strict inputs to the function, and they have side effects that mean the second call to a given function will not necessarily produce the same result as the first call. C functions often return values indicating their success, relying on side effects to accomplish their main purpose.

C's advantages over Ruby include execution speed, greater familiarity to more people, more widespread deployment, and the additional benefits that come from its code being compiled, rather than interpreted. (Note that compiled versus interpreted is its own holy war.) When a C program compiles, you know it has passed at least one specific benchmark of reliability.

Ruby's advantages over C include a faster development cycle, flexibility, conceptual elegance, and configurability. If you are interested in combining the strengths of both Ruby and C, you can start by exploring the RubyInline project, available as the `rubyinline` gem or at http://www.zenspider.com/ZSS/Products/RubyInline.[1]

C also has what is called *strong, static typing*. This means that variables in C are defined to be a certain type of data (the integer 42, for example), and they will always remain that type of data. That's the static part. If you wanted to express the integer 42 as a floating-point number, such as 42.0, you would need to pass it through a casting conversion function. Ruby is also strongly typed (requiring programmers to convert integers to floating-point numbers before using them that way), although it is *dynamic*, meaning that variables can change type. C also lacks anything similar to Ruby's irb.

Haskell

The fact that Haskell is included in this listing of languages indicates how important the functional paradigm is to this book. *Haskell* is a purely functional language designed by committee and released in 1998. It has several fascinating features, most notably *lazy evaluation*, whereby the value of a given piece of data does not need to be known (or even meaningful) until it needs to be used. This allows a programmer to define things in terms of infinite series, such as the set of all integers.

Haskell is the language used for *Pugs*, an implementation of the new Perl 6 language, which some people think is drawing more attention to Haskell than to Perl itself. Haskell has an interactive environment similar to Ruby's irb, but it doesn't allow function definitions except in external files that are imported, whereas irb allows full definitions for classes, methods, and functions. Like C, Haskell has both strong and static typing. Haskell is an excellent language that's very suitable for teaching purely functional techniques, as well as general-purpose programming. You can read more about it at http://haskell.org.

Java

For the purposes of this discussion, Sun Microsystems' *Java* is a moderately complex, object-oriented language similar to C. Java has both strong and static typing. In one way, Java is more object oriented than Ruby is: A programmer coding in Java must use an object-oriented paradigm for his own

---

[1] I was lucky enough to see a demonstration of RubyInline by its author, Ryan Davis, at the 2005 RubyConf. It's a very impressive piece of code, and I highly recommend it to anyone interested in combining Ruby and C.

programs. On the other hand, Java is less object oriented than Ruby is in the way that it implements its own built-in features. For example, to get the absolute value of the integer 100 in Java, you would do this:

```
Math.abs(100)
```

This means that the programmer wants to use a method called abs, which is associated with Math, to perform that method's action on the integer 100. The equivalent operation in Ruby would be performed as follows:

```
100.abs
```

Using Ruby's methodology, the programmer simply asks the number 100 to report its own absolute value. This approach is common in Ruby, and it assumes that every piece of data knows the best way to deal with operations on itself. An advantage of this is that the same symbol can be used for different (but conceptually related) operations. The + sign signifies simple addition for numbers, for example, while signifying concatenation for strings, as discussed in Chapter 1.

Java is also compiled, rather than interpreted, generally using a special type of compilation called *bytecode*, which is the same method that projects like Parrot, Python, and Ruby 2.0 use.[2] There is also an interesting project called JRuby (http://jruby.codehaus.org), which is an implementation of Ruby written in Java. Java is described in greater detail at http://java.sun.com. The Java specification was written by Guy Steele, although he didn't create the language itself (fellow Lisper James Gosling did). When he wrote the Java specification, Steele already had the distinction of being the co-creator of Scheme, arguably the most conceptually pure version of Lisp.

Lisp

As one of Ruby's most prominent ancestors, *Lisp* deserves some space in this section. Lisp has been called "the most intelligent way to misuse a computer."[3] It is properly understood as a family of languages or a language specification, rather than a single language. It is also diverse enough to resist many classification attempts, but for our purposes, the Lisps can be thought of mainly as functional languages with weak, dynamic typing. Renowned Lisper Paul Graham describes "What Made Lisp Different" at http://paulgraham.com/diff.html, and it's interesting to note that Ruby shares all of these features except for Lisp's peculiar syntax.

Lisp's syntax (or lack thereof) is probably its most noteworthy feature, at first glance. Lisp code consists of bits of data bound by opening and closing parentheses. These bits are called *lists*, and they give Lisp its name (which

---

[2] You can read more about Parrot at http://www.parrotcode.org; I'll cover Python later in this appendix.

[3] Dutch computer science Edsger Dijkstra said this; you can find this and other interesting quotes compiled by Paul Graham at http://www.paulgraham.com/quo.html.

comes from *LISt Processing*).[4] Having a syntax that is representable as a data structure within the language itself is Lisp's most defining characteristic. Arguably, another language that implemented this same feature would not be a distinct language per se, but rather another dialect of Lisp.[5] A good argument can be made that Ruby tries to take concepts from Lisp and present them within a more user-friendly framework that also takes advantage of good ideas from object orientation, as well as good text manipulation. Matz has said, "Some may say Ruby is a bad rip-off of Lisp or Smalltalk, and I admit that. But it is nicer to ordinary people."[6] Ruby owes much to Lisp, and along with many other languages, it owes much of its powerful text manipulation to this next language, Perl.

Perl

Perl is known by its mantra TMTOWTDI, and it is an extremely flexible and utilitarian language—one that has certainly had an impact on both Ruby and programming, in general. *TMTOWTDI* stands for *There's More Than One Way To Do It*, which is a design philosophy that Perl certainly exemplifies. Its role in stressing the importance of regular expressions is enough to earn it a place in history. Perl was invented in 1987 by Larry Wall, and it was primarily intended to perform a role similar to that of Unix-centric languages like shell, awk, and sed. Perl focuses on ease of use for tasks like Unix system administration, and it is heavily used for web applications, as well. Perl's initial design was procedural, but in recent years it has moved in an increasingly functional direction. It can also be used for object-oriented programming, a task for which it was never intended and for which it is not ideally suited—but the fact that this is even possible in Perl is a testament to its flexibility.

A new version of Perl is in the works (see the discussion of Pugs under Haskell), and it reminds me a great deal of Ruby. Coming from me, that is a compliment. Perl has weak dynamic typing, and like Ruby, it is interpreted. It has been called the *swiss army chainsaw* and the *Jeep* of programming languages, and it can be found at http://perl.com.

PHP

PHP is another interpreted language using weak dynamic typing that is very popular for web applications. In fact, some people erroneously believe that PHP is only usable for web applications. It is technically a complete, general-purpose programming language, although it has several features that make it

---

[4] Critics contend that this feature makes Lisp a more appropriate acronym for *Lots of Irritating Superfluous Parentheses*. Larry Wall, the creator of Perl, suggested that Lisp code has all the aesthetic appeal of "oatmeal with toenail clippings." Clearly, Lisp has some public relations problems.

[5] Relatedly, Philip Greenspun's tenth Rule of Programming at http://philip.greenspun.com/research is "Any sufficiently complicated C or Fortran program contains an ad-hoc, informally-specified bug-ridden slow implementation of half of Common Lisp."

[6] This quote also comes from Paul Graham's website, http://www.paulgraham.com/quotes.html.

more popular for web work. Many of the languages discussed here can be used in embedded code within web pages, provided that the code is marked off from the rest of the page with the appropriate tags. PHP is unusual in that it must always be demarcated with such tags, even when it is used for command-line tasks that will never come near a webserver. It has weak, dynamic typing and is interpreted.

PHP and Ruby share the characteristic of having a relatively large number of built-in functions. Despite PHP's general applicability, its primary focus is undoubtedly on making it easy for relatively inexperienced programmers to generate dynamic web content quickly. PHP's web integration is such an important part of its most frequent use (if not its design) that it is often best compared to other programming languages when combined with their own web integration systems, such Perl and Mason, or Ruby and eRuby or Rails. PHP's creator Rasmus Lerdorf began work on the project that would eventually become PHP in 1995. You can find out more about it at http://php.net.

Python

Python is a language very similar to Ruby. Its creator, the "Benevolent Dictator For Life" Guido van Rossum, named it after the British comedy troupe Monty Python when he invented it in the early 1990s. It has strong, dynamic typing very similar to Ruby's and a similarly clean syntax, which is aided by its use of semantically significant whitespace. In Python, neither functions, blocks of code, nor statements need to have an explicit end-of-line mark (often a semicolon). Ruby's use of ending markers is also quite minimal, although not to the same degree as Python's is.

One area where Python and Ruby differ significantly is in flexibility. Python explicitly embraces the idea of *There should be one—and preferably only one—obvious way to do it*, reporting this along with other ideas at Python's interactive prompt when given the command import this.

Python and Ruby have an interesting relationship. Python has added several new features recently that borrow heavily from Ruby and Lisp, and at the time of this writing book sales for Ruby-related books also generally surpass those of Python-related books. Obviously, I hope those trends continue in relation to *this* book. Python and Ruby seem like contentious siblings who will hopefully continue to challenge and inspire each other to excel. The Pythonistas live at http://python.org.

Smalltalk

Smalltalk is a fully object-oriented programming language invented at Xerox PARC by a team led by Alan Kay. While Simula is generally recognized as the first object-oriented language, Smalltalk was instrumental in popularizing object orientation. Ruby borrows very extensively from Smalltalk in two major areas: the notion that everything is an object, and the concept of methods as messages that are passed to objects.

What does it mean to say that everything is an object? We've touched on this briefly in the Java discussion. In many languages, real "object" status is reserved for larger or more complicated things, while basic parts of the language are not considered objects. That's why coders must invoke the abs method from within the Math namespace to get the absolute value of the integer 100 in Java. The *Everything is an object* idea that Ruby inherited from Smalltalk is what allows the more consistent approach of asking the integer 100 to report its own absolute value. We explored the benefits of methods being implemented as messages also in the to_lang.rb script in Chapter 10.

Check out Smalltalk at http://smalltalk.org and http://squeak.org.

Summary of Ruby vs. Other Languages

To sum up, Ruby is interpreted, not compiled, making it fast to develop in and slow to run. It is object oriented and functional, not procedural. It has strong, dynamic typing, instead of either weak or static typing, and it only automatically casts type for Boolean tests. It has built-in regular expression support and a clean, readable syntax. It is a general-purpose programming language both in theory and in practice. It has a very large collection of built-in methods, and it allows you to add to, alter, and extend those methods easily. Like its ancestor Lisp, Ruby has a real, usable nil value, and it treats all values except for nil and false as true. Ruby is also very fun to program in, and it stays out of your way.

INDEX

S

Electronic Frontier Foundation
Defending Freedom in the Digital World

Free Speech. Privacy. Innovation. Fair Use. Reverse Engineering. If you care about these rights in the digital world, then you should join the Electronic Frontier Foundation (EFF). EFF was founded in 1990 to protect the rights of users and developers of technology. EFF is the first to identify threats to basic rights online and to advocate on behalf of free expression in the digital age.

The Electronic Frontier Foundation Defends Your Rights!
Become a Member Today!
http://www.eff.org/support/

Current EFF projects include:

Protecting your fundamental right to vote. Widely publicized security flaws in computerized voting machines show that, though filled with potential, this technology is far from perfect. EFF is defending the open discussion of e-voting problems and is coordinating a national litigation strategy addressing issues arising from use of poorly developed and tested computerized voting machines.

Ensuring that you are not traceable through your things. Libraries, schools, the government and private sector businesses are adopting radio frequency identification tags, or RFIDs – a technology capable of pinpointing the physical location of whatever item the tags are embedded in. While this may seem like a convenient way to track items, it's also a convenient way to do something less benign: track people and their activities through their belongings. EFF is working to ensure that embrace of this technology does not erode your right to privacy.

Stopping the FBI from creating surveillance backdoors on the Internet. EFF is part of a coalition opposing the FBI's expansion of the Communications Assistance for Law Enforcement Act (CALEA), which would require that the wiretap capabilities built into the phone system be extended to the Internet, forcing ISPs to build backdoors for law enforcement.

Providing you with a means by which you can contact key decision-makers on cyber-liberties issues. EFF maintains an action center that provides alerts on technology, civil liberties issues and pending legislation to more than 50,000 subscribers. EFF also generates a weekly online newsletter, EFFector, and a blog that provides up-to-the minute information and commentary.

Defending your right to listen to and copy digital music and movies. The entertainment industry has been overzealous in trying to protect its copyrights, often decimating fair use rights in the process. EFF is standing up to the movie and music industries on several fronts.

Check out all of the things we're working on at http://www.eff.org and join today or make a donation to support the fight to defend freedom online.

ELECTRONIC FRONTIER FOUNDATION · 454 SHOTWELL STREET · SAN FRANCISCO, CA 94110 · 415.436.9333

CODE CRAFT
The Practice of Writing Excellent Code

by PETE GOODLIFFE

Code Craft shows how to move beyond writing correct code to writing excellent code. The book covers code writing concerns, including code presentation style, variable naming, error handling, and security, as well as the wider issues of programming in the real world, such as good teamwork, development processes, and documentation. *Code Craft* presents language-agnostic advice that is relevant to all developers, from an author with extensive practical experience.

DECEMBER 2006, 624 PP., $44.95 ($55.95 CDN)
ISBN 978-1-59327-119-0

WRITE GREAT CODE, VOLUME 1
Understanding the Machine

by RANDALL HYDE

Write Great Code, Volume 1 explains the fundamental concepts of low-level computation in a friendly, language-independent fashion. Covering topics like binary arithmetic, bit operations, I/O, memory access and more, author and professor Randall Hyde illustrates machine organization without requiring a mastery of assembly language. Readers can also expect to learn about floating-point, numeric, and character representation; constants and types; Boolean logic; CPU and instruction set architecture; and how compilers work. This is the perfect book for high-level programmers ready to move from *good* to *great.*

NOVEMBER 2004, 464 PP., $39.95 ($55.95 CDN)
ISBN 978-1-59327-003-2

WRITE GREAT CODE, VOLUME 2
Thinking Low-Level, Writing High-Level

by RANDALL HYDE

Write Great Code, Volume 2 shows software engineers what too many college and university courses don't: how compilers translate high-level language statements and data structures into machine code. Armed with this knowledge, readers will be better informed about choosing the high-level structures that will help the compiler produce superior machine code, all without having to give up the productivity and portability benefits of using a high-level language.

MARCH 2006, 640 PP., $44.95 ($58.95 CDN)
ISBN 978-1-59327-065-0

THE BOOK OF JAVASCRIPT, 2ND EDITION
A Practical Guide to Interactive Web Pages

by THAU!

This book teaches readers how to add interactivity, animation, and other tricks to their websites with JavaScript. Rather than provide a series of cut-and-paste scripts, thau! takes the reader through real-world JavaScript code examples with an emphasis on understanding. Each chapter focuses on a few important JavaScript features, shows how professional websites incorporate them, and shows readers how they might add those features to their own websites. This thoroughly updated and completely reworked second edition includes coverage of Ajax, revised appendices, and new examples throughout.

DECEMBER 2006, 528PP., $39.95 ($49.95 CDN)
ISBN 978-1-59327-106-0

HACKING, 2ND EDITION
The Art of Exploitation

by JON ERICKSON

While many security books merely show how to run existing exploits, *Hacking: The Art of Exploitation* was the first book to explain how exploits actually work—and how readers can develop and implement their own. In this all new second edition, author Jon Erickson uses practical examples to illustrate the fundamentals of serious hacking. You'll learn about key concepts underlying common exploits, such as programming errors, assembly language, networking, shellcode, cryptography, and more. And the bundled Linux liveCD provides an easy-to-use, hands-on learning environment. This edition has been extensively updated and expanded, including a new introduction to the complex, low-level workings of computers.

AUGUST 2007, 480 PP. W/CD, $39.95 ($49.95 CDN)
ISBN 978-1-59327-144-2

PHONE:
800.420.7240 OR
415.863.9900
MONDAY THROUGH FRIDAY,
9 A.M. TO 5 P.M. (PST)

FAX:
415.863.9950
24 HOURS A DAY,
7 DAYS A WEEK

EMAIL:
SALES@NOSTARCH.COM

WEB:
WWW.NOSTARCH.COM

MAIL:
NO STARCH PRESS
555 DE HARO ST, SUITE 250
SAN FRANCISCO, CA 94107
USA

COLOPHON

Ruby by Example was laid out in Adobe FrameMaker. The font families used are New Baskerville for body text, Futura for headings and tables, and Dogma for titles.

The book was printed and bound at Malloy Incorporated in Ann Arbor, Michigan. The paper is Glatfelter Thor 60# Antique, which is made from 15 percent postconsumer content. The book uses a RepKover binding, which allows it to lay flat when open.

UPDATES

Visit **http://www.nostarch.com/ruby.htm** for updates, errata, and other information.